EASTERN EUROPE:

POLITICS,
REVOLUTION,
& DIPLOMACY

Henry L. Roberts

Eastern Europe:

POLITICS,

REVOLUTION,

& DIPLOMACY

ALFRED A. KNOPF · NEW YORK · 1970

THIS IS A BORZOI BOOK
PUBLISHED BY ALFRED A. KNOPF, INC.

FIRST EDITION

ACKNOWLEDGMENTS

I AM PARTICULARLY BEHOLDEN TO MY FRIEND, FELLOW historian, and summer neighbor, Fritz Stern, for the appearance of this book. His was the suggestion that I bring together a selection of my essays; he was instrumental in winnowing and arranging the pieces, and he amiably prepared the way for publication. My intellectual debts over the last two decades are extensive, but I am especially cognizant of four sets of associations: with the staff and scholars at the Council on Foreign Relations, where, during the years 1953–5, I worked with a study group on Soviet-American relations; with my former colleagues in the Russian Institute and the Institute on East Central Europe, Columbia University; with my editorial associates on the *Slavic Review* (1965–7) ; and, most recently, with colleagues in the History Department and the seminar on Revolution at Dartmouth College.

These essays are not the fruit of delvings in the archives; they are, for the most part, occasional pieces. Still, time for reflection and writing was indispensable; for that I am grateful for grants from the Russian and East Central European Institutes, Columbia University, and the Institute on Social Change, Dartmouth College, and for a fellowship from the John Simon Guggenheim Memorial Foundation.

Most of the essays have been published previously. I should like to acknowledge the permissions for them to appear here:

"Eastern Europe and the Historian" and "Russia and the West: A Comparison and Contrast," *Slavic Review* (October 1961 and March 1964 respectively), © The American Association for the Advancement of Slavic Studies; "Russia and America," from *Russian Foreign Policy: Essays in Historical Perspective,* edited by Ivo J. Lederer, © 1962 Yale University; "International Relations Between the Wars," from *Challenge in Eastern Europe,* edited by C. E. Black, copyright 1954 Trustees of Rutgers College in New Jersey; "Maxim Litvinov" and "The Diplomacy of Colonel Beck," from *The Diplomats 1919– 1939,* edited by Gordon A. Craig and Felix Gilbert, copyright 1953 Princeton University Press; "Politics in a Small State: The Balkan Example," from *The Balkans in Transition: Essays on the Development of Balkan Life and Politics since the Eighteenth Century,* edited by Charles and Barbara Jelavich, © 1963 The Regents of the University of California; "Eastern Europe and the Balance of Power," from *Resources and Planning in Eastern Europe,* edited by Norman J. G. Pounds and Nicolas Spulber, Slavic and East European Series, Volume 4, © 1957 Indiana University; "Lenin and Power," reprinted from *The Responsibility of Power: Historical Essays in Honor of Hajo Holborn,* edited by Leonard Krieger and Fritz Stern, copyright © by Doubleday & Company, Inc., 1967; "The Crisis in the Soviet Empire," *Foreign Affairs,* January 1957, © Council on Foreign Relations; "The Succession to Khrushchev in Perspective," reprinted with permission from the *Proceedings of The Academy of Political Science,* Vol. XXVIII,

April 1965, pp. 2–12, © 1965 The Academy of Political Science; "Soviet-American Relations: Problems of Choice and Decision," *The Texas Quarterly,* Vol. I, No. 3, Summer-Autumn 1958, © 1958 The University of Texas Press.

The quoted passage from W. B. Yeats, "Who Goes with Fergus," is reprinted with permission of The Macmillan Company from *Collected Poems* by W. B. Yeats. Copyright © The Macmillan Company, renewed 1934 by William B. Yeats.

INTRODUCTION

ALTHOUGH THE ESSAYS THAT FOLLOW WERE WRITTEN AT various times and for various occasions or purposes in the years since 1951, they all deal with three related themes: Eastern Europe, revolutionary and Soviet Russia, and recent international relations concerning these areas. Taken as a whole this cluster of topics represents what started out as a wholly unplanned and unexpected side excursion but came to be the main track of my professional interests for over two decades.

As a beginning historian concentrating on German *Geistesgeschichte*, I found myself, in the spring of 1942, in the African Section of the Office of Strategic Services. Having become an instant specialist on the railway and electric power networks of French North Africa, I was led by a series of natural steps to Sicily, southern Italy, and thence, on what proved to be an extremely long weekend, to Rumania. It was in Bucharest that I acquired the Balkan virus, which I have nourished ever since. But the Balkans in 1944–5 necessarily brought one face to face with the Soviet Union and, as it turned out, with the opening rounds of the Cold War. These latter experiences largely determined the pattern of my concerns upon my return to academic life after the war. I have always felt embarrassed when asked by students to advise them in charting their career.

In retrospect I find both advantages and disadvantages in having pursued these lines of inquiry as a result of such stimuli. I am not particularly pleased with a number of my answers, but I cannot complain of any absence of absorbing and fascinating questions. Moreover, the sense of urgency—"relevance" is now the term—undoubtedly gave an impetus to one's study and writing. Though most of the present pieces were written under the pressure of a deadline and are certainly not products of the contemplative life, I had, and have, the feeling that the work was worth the doing.

The disadvantages are simply the reverse side of the coin. As a historian I felt uneasy, despite my conditioning in government service, to be commenting so frequently about what was still headline news. A historian should be cautious about writing in the future tense (or the imperative mood). Over the years I have become increasingly reluctant to play the Sovietologist (I never aspired to Kremlinology) or to be an international ambulance chaser. This is partly a matter of temperament, but in my work as a bibliographer I have been struck by the disconcerting transcience of most such endeavors. One need not write for the ages; current and pressing issues do require serious commentary and analysis, but the necessary price is the early obsolescence of much that one has said.

More serious is the fact that, given the way in which I became involved in Soviet, East European, and international affairs, my relation to my subject has been critical and diagnostic rather than affectionate or appreciative. Such a relation is not necessarily discreditable and may at times be indispensable, but I really do not think that it is good, for a historian at any rate, to spend too many years dealing with a subject for which he has little empathy. (Here I must except the Balkans, which, for all their perversity, have remained a continuing pleasure to study.) I would suggest that this is more than a personal problem. A couple of years ago I had occasion to remark:

> Finally, I must admit to the sheer pleasure of inquiring into something that is behaving well, functioning properly, demonstrating vitality and creativity, as against assuming the rather bleak, if dutiful, stance of the clinician. Both are necessary for a balanced view of our world and its inhabitants. But I do wish, after my years of exposure to Slavic and East European studies, that we would engage ourselves more in the positive and creative features (more Bela Bartok and less Bela Kun). They exist, and ours would be a gayer field if more effort were made to bring them to light.

Undoubtedly, this distortion, like so much else, can be blamed on the Cold War. In teaching the present generation of college students I am acutely aware that the greater part of my career has been intimately tied in one way or another to the problems and premises of that epoch of recent history. One should resist these days the temptation to self-flagellation, but it is undeniable that my whole cast of mind has been profoundly influenced by an effort to grapple with what seemed to me to be some salient pathological features of our world.

These essays, apart from a few stylistic and editorial revisions, appear as originally prepared. Whenever I have read such a statement prefacing another writer's essays, I have dismissed it as a sign of laziness—the fellow wanted to get as much mileage as possible with as little effort as possible. I must confess to this "laziness," but I have also found, in reviewing these pieces, that I simply could not tinker with them seriously. My present intellectual stance is not identical with the one I had five, ten, or twenty years ago. If I am not to start anew, they must appear as conceived, warts and all. In the present selection I find some statements with which I now disagree, others which strike me as remarkably inapposite; several of my inquiries have subsequently been carried much farther by other writers.

The essays have been arranged topically rather than chronologically. While a number of my views have changed and developed over the years, their evolution is likely to be of more interest to me than to the reader. The pieces fell, with no prior intent, rather nicely into three major rubrics. The first, Eastern Europe and the Historian, in part reflects my continuing effort to master the historiographical questions one encounters in dealing with that area. Politics and Diplomacy in Eastern Europe is largely devoted to interwar diplomacy, with some reference to problems of balance of power. Power and Stability in Soviet Russia concerns the Russian Revolution and its aftermath, but includes some "Cold War" themes on the matter of stabilizing East-West relations.

Apart from formal acknowledgments, indicated elsewhere, I should like here to express my debt and gratitude to two scholars who have been very important to me: Hajo Holborn, whose profound sense of the historian's function has been a continuing if unrealized ideal for me ever since I first studied with him in the late 1930's, and Geroid T. Robinson, whose austere sense of the need for historical integrity in meeting the most controversial and contemporary of issues has played a signal part in Russian studies in the United States. Word of Hajo Holborn's death reached me while I was writing this introduction. To him, to GTR, and to my wife, Deborah, I should like to dedicate these essays.

Rochester, Vermont
June 22, 1969

CONTENTS

PART ONE

Eastern Europe
and the
Historian

I ❧ Eastern Europe and the Historian

[1961]

IT IS NOT MY INTENTION TO DISCUSS THOSE TWO ISSUES THAT always seem to be debated whenever Eastern Europe is mentioned: the argument over the importance or utility of the study of its history, and the game of defining its precise geographic limits or its internal unity. These issues may not have been exhausted—though they are pretty limp by now—but I think it may be more profitable to turn our attention to some of the substantive and methodological problems that confront the working historian, once he has accepted this area as a field of proper concern and once he has arrived at his own definition of its scope and limits.

More specifically, I should like to consider some of the problems connected with the intimate but ambiguous relationship of Eastern Europe—including Russia—to Western Europe, both as an *object* of historical study and as an *influence* on historical research and writing. It is important to emphasize that, whatever the differences, Eastern Europe is part of Europe in a double sense: first, and most obviously, the history of Eastern Europe is intelligible only in this larger setting, and conversely an understanding of general European history involves an understanding of its eastern marches; second, and perhaps less obviously, as a part of Europe, Eastern Europe shares in considerable measure the historical mode of thinking about itself—its self-perception is, in part at least, provided by its historical awareness and a tradition of historiography, that is, the past as organized and interpreted by the historian. This latter point is of some significance, for there have been many societies, and not simply "static" tribal communities, in which the historical component of self-identification is not at all prominent, its place being taken either by a set mythology or by all-embracing religious or legal norms. I might suggest that for such societies it is much more difficult to write history, or to develop a historiographical tradition—even from the outside—precisely because the historical dimension is not used consciously to inform the society, its norms, and its goals. Fortunately, this problem, which I rather expect will be troublesome with the current extension of historical studies to all regions of the globe, is not a major one for Eastern Europe.

Nevertheless, this double relationship between Eastern and Western Europe of history as past and as reconstruction of the past, a relationship that is not an identity, has been productive of many of the problems and quandaries that confront the historian dealing with Eastern Europe. To illustrate, I should like to touch on three subjects that seem to have been almost obsessive preoccupations in Eastern European historiography: the question of origins, of continuity, and of Eastern Europe's connection with Western Europe.

For the moment, I should like to reserve comment on my use of the term "obsessive," but there can be little doubt that these themes have loomed large in the historiography of the Eastern European nations. For example, an article on nineteenth-century Russian historiography observes:

The Russian historians of the nineteenth century again and again became engaged with five problems, and, depending on their answers, there was produced their conception of the development of Russian history, whether entirely autonomous or determined by foreign influences. These problems are:

1) The origins of the Slavs-Russians, or, the question of the Indo-Germans
2) The beginnings of Russian state history, or, the Varangian question
3) The religious and cultural influence of Byzantium
4) The Mongols
5) Peter the Great.[1]

Interestingly, an American study on Soviet interpretations of Russia's past reveals that Soviet historians deal very substantially with these same themes with equal intensity if less finesse than their nineteenth-century predecessors.[2] Professor Gasiorowski's illuminating article on the controversy among Polish historians over the origins of the Polish state portrays a similar concern,[3] as does the very title of the late Professor Iorga's long essay, *La Place des Roumains dans l'histoire universelle.*[4]

Before trying to decide whether these concerns represent anything exceptional we should perhaps look more closely at these three themes to determine in what measure they are a product of Eastern European history, as past, or of its historiography, as a reading of the past.

The search for origins would seem to be a natural con-

1 Klaus-Detlev Grothusen: "Die russische Geschichtswissenchaft des 19. Jahrhunderts als Forschungsaufgabe," *Jahrbücher für Geschichte Osteuropas* (Munich; 1960), VIII, No. 1, 53-4.
2 *Rewriting Russian History,* ed. Cyril E. Black (New York; 1956).
3 Zygmunt Gasiorowski: "The Conquest Theory of the Genesis of the Polish State," *Speculum* (October 1955), pp. 55-60.
4 Nicolae Iorga: *La Place des Roumains dans l'histoire universelle* (Bucharest; 1935).

cern of every national historiography, and certainly we can find parallels to the debates among Eastern European historians in Western European arguments over the Normans, the Germanic tribes, the influence of Rome, the theory of kingship, and so on. And yet these problems somehow seem more vexing in Eastern Europe. Why? The usual explanations are inclined to find the difficulty in the past itself, either in the confusion and murkiness of the *Völkerwanderung,* or in the paucity of reliable sources. And yet one may wonder whether this is—though doubtless correct so far as it goes—a sufficient explanation. Although I can speak with no professional authority, it is my impression that, when one gets down to it, the student of Western European or British origins also runs into difficulties sufficiently serious to suggest that the difference is not completely to be explained by the ancient past itself or the surviving records thereof. Consequently, one is led to ask whether the answer may not, in part at least, lie in the historian himself, in the questions he asks, in what he is trying to prove by this search for origins. From this perspective one has the impression that Eastern European historiography has, in fact, attached rather greater importance to this question of origins, to the extent perhaps of trying to have history and historical evidence carry a burden of meaning which is intrinsically beyond them— and hence the exasperating but constantly recurring sense of the inadequacies of the evidence. In other words, without elaborating on this point, we may suggest that in their effort to create through history a self-image of their nation and its place, historians of Eastern Europe have been inclined to put very heavy stress on this question of origins, a stress that, for all the parallels with similar problems in Western Europe, does have a different flavor.

As an aside—though we certainly must regard Communist historiography as being a very special case—it is interesting to note in an issue of *Voprosy istorii* the passion with which Soviet historians are still attacking the "Norman" problem.[5]

If we turn now to the second theme of particular concern—that of continuity—we find a similar problem. In reviewing the histories of the various Eastern European nations one is struck by the great importance that has been attributed in nearly every case to discontinuity—to an abrupt and deep interruption of the normal progress of the society: in Russia and the Ukraine, the Mongols; among the South Slavs, the Ottoman conquest; in Rumania, the century of Phanariot rule; in Poland, the partitions; in the Czech lands, the Battle of the White Mountain; in Hungary, Mohács. Now obviously these traumatic disasters were historical realities and had important consequences. And yet the question suggests itself: Do these events actually account for the feeling of discontinuity which the historians have, and for which they are trying to find explanation? An indication that these events, as historical occurrences, may not be able to carry such a weight of significance can be seen in the fact that nearly every one of them has produced a "revisionist" school: those who question the shattering impact of the Mongol incursion, who find creative contributions in the Phanariot hospodars, who attribute the Polish partition to internal rather than external factors, who find the Ottomans inheritors rather than destroyers of the Byzantine tradition in the Balkans. Without going into the merits of these various disputes, one can surmise the existence of a common pattern: a *felt* sense of historical discontinuity which,

---

[5] V. P. Shusharin: "O sushchnosti i formakh sovremennogo normanizma," *Voprosy istorii,* No. 8 (August 1960), 65–93.

in seeking for an identifiable historical explanation, presses too hard on one particular event as the occasion and leads in turn to a contradiction or the need for modification. I rather suspect that we historians have a professional tendency to be "revisionists," in that we feel impelled to counter or modify all preceding historical generalizations, but in this case the "revisionists" may have a substantial point: it is doubtful that the *sense* of interruption, of discontinuity, in Eastern Europe (and I do not question its existence as a subjective reality) is fully to be explained by these catastrophic events, important though they may have been.

When we move to our third example—relations with Western Europe—we encounter the same problem, but posed even more intricately and subtly. For not only has there been a constant preoccupation with Eastern Europe's role in European history, but Western European history and culture have come to serve as a basis for comparison, as a kind of measuring rod, whether the comparison be regarded as favorable or unfavorable. More than that, the very categories of Western historical thought have, along with other influences, been absorbed into Eastern European historiography and historical methodology. It is difficult indeed to sort out the subjective and objective components of this relationship, but again it seems clear, as with our first two examples, that the concept of the relationship, whether it be seen in terms of essential identity or essential contrast, owes as much to the historian as to the historical reality. A recent article on Russian historiography observes that the question of Russian relations to Europe has been given three formulations: Russia *and* Europe, Russia *in* Europe, and Russia *against* Europe.[6]

---

[6] Grothusen: op. cit., p. 53.

Among Polish historians there has been much stress upon a Western identification, with correspondingly heavy emphasis upon those cultural features, such as Roman Catholicism, which would highlight that identity. Among Rumanian historians one finds both an impulse toward identification—Latinity as against a Slavic East—and, through the populist heritage, an emphasis upon Rumanian uniqueness as against the capitalist-industrial West.[7] Among the Hungarians there is a similar tension between Hungary as Western Christendom's outermost bastion and Hungary as the homeland of the isolated Magyars.

There are, however, several remarkable features about this whole act of comparison, whether the search is for identity or differentiation. They all give a unity, a singleness, to Western Europe that seems artificial and unreal when one actually considers the profound variety of Western European history. Is there, or has there ever been, that "Europe" which Eastern European historiography so often has sought to identify itself with or distinguish itself from? It seems doubtful. Wladimir Weidlé has acutely observed that the Russian "Westernizers" failed to note that France's participation in "European unity was not only in virtue of what it had in common with Italy or England but also in virtue of what distinguished it from them."[8] In other words, the whole problem has been complicated, and probably rendered insoluble, by this projection of unity, within which or against which self-identification is to be achieved.

Moreover, it is worth noting that precisely those categories of historical analysis that have been used to argue

[7] Henry L. Roberts: *Rumania: Political Problems of an Agrarian State* (New Haven; 1951), pp. 339–40.
[8] Wladimir Weidlé: *Zadacha Rossii* (New York; 1956), p. 13.

for identity or difference are themselves largely of Western European origin, taken over and translated by Eastern European historiography. This has been well illustrated in the familiar case of the Slavophiles: precisely the ideas that were developed to establish an antithesis between the Slavic and the Germanic cultures had an obvious German source in Herder and subsequent German idealists and romantics. This process by which an idea, in being taken over from one nation to another, suffers a sea change into something rich and strange is of course not unique with Eastern Europe. One has only to recall the impact, say, of Hobbes, or Hume, or Darwin upon the Continent to find the same process in operation. Indeed, much of the diversity and relatedness that make up the rich complexity of European culture as a whole derives from these borrowings and transmutations over a thousand years or more. And in nothing does Eastern Europe show its connection with Western Europe more than in its ability to participate in this process, even if the result, as in the case of the Slavophiles, appears to be a sharply expressed antithesis.

Nevertheless, in East European historiography this adaptation and application of categories developed initially in Western European history has created a number of special problems in the field of history writing itself. I would suggest that a good deal of the confusion that has surrounded such debated terms and classifications in Eastern European history as "feudalism," "serfdom," the ingredients of "nationalism," the definition of social "classes," and "stages of economic development," results from this process: a word or concept, which in the course of time and more or less scholarly usage came to describe or identify (with more or less precision and adequacy) a French or German or Italian phenomenon, would be taken as the most readily available label or category and applied, with probably less accuracy and practical utility, to an Eastern European society. This lack of congruence would, in turn, produce debates as to whether Eastern Europe "really" had feudalism or whether there "really" were classes in Russia. To make matters more confusing these terms were also constantly subject to revision and redefinition in their place of origin, as succeeding generations of Western European scholars sought to clarify their own history (for example, in the recent British debate about the gentry and the Civil War in the seventeenth century). In consequence a time lag could develop to render still more difficult the process of intelligible communication between scholars.

The effect at times has been to reinforce the tendency (to which Western European and American scholars have also contributed) either to reduce Eastern European history to identity with Western Europe by forcing these categories upon it, or to abandon the categories entirely and go to the other extreme of finding Eastern Europe, its social and political institutions, and its historical periods, essentially different and only superficially comparable. I would submit that neither alternative is valid. The principal point to make here, however, is that a real and valid problem on the objective level—the comparison of Eastern and Western European history—has been paralleled, and probably made more difficult, by this historiographical or methodological complication.

From the examples we have taken—the problems of origins, of continuity, and of comparison with Western Europe—we seem to find, in the historiography of Eastern Europe from the eighteenth to the twentieth centuries, a special and rather intense preoccupation which places a stress on those factors of historical background that

appear to involve more than drawing inferences and conclusions from the past. It is, rather, a projecting or impos-
ing upon the past of some urgent concerns of the historian,
and presumably of the society for which he is writing—
concerns which, if they are explicable by history, do not
seem to be so by these particular areas of preoccupation.

Conversely, one can discern in historical writing on
Eastern Europe the absence—only a relative one to be
sure—of certain themes, subjects, or types of work that
have been quite important in the historiographical tradition of, say, France or Britain. On the whole there has
been less interest in local history. I realize the danger of
generalization here: the picture varies from country to
country, and over time (I have the impression of a more
active tradition in the Polish and Czech cases). There
have, of course, been numerous regional histories; indeed,
these have played an important part in developing national and historical awareness. In areas of territorial dispute—Transylvania, Silesia, etc.—intensive historical research from several sides has been part of the effort to
establish a political claim. But are the motivation, purpose,
and function of such regional or territorial studies the
same as those that have produced, say, British local or
family histories? In general, I would say not, though I am
prepared to grant many exceptions. On the whole I have
found in Eastern European history *comparatively* little
of what one might call the "flower-in-the-crannied-wall"
approach to history: the sense that a single community, or
a particular episode, warrants affectionate recording—
especially as a living tradition—and also contains within
it much of universal value.

The reason, again, may be in the stresses and strains of
Eastern Europe's history, the relative weakness in many
areas of a flourishing municipal or urban culture, and the

destruction of local and family records. But in addition I would suggest that the attention of the historian was directed elsewhere, that the answers he sought—and all live history, consciously or unconsciously, is looking for answers—seemed not to reside in this particular plane of experience.

If this tendency to dwell on certain themes, perhaps at the expense of others, amounts to a real preoccupation, why should this have been so? While such an outlook need not make for poor history—indeed, a passionate concern, even an obsession, may provide the necessary motor to drive one to the exhausting rigors of serious historical research—it does make for a rather distinctive type of history, with the virtues of acuity rather than empathy.

Perhaps a clue to this preoccupation is the word one finds so poignantly in Russian writing of the nineteenth century—*samobytnost'*—the declared search for self-identity and self-knowledge. This preoccupation, at the level of social life, would naturally attach itself to such questions as those of origin, continuity, foreign influences, and comparison with Western Europe. And yet, as suggested above, it may be doubted whether uncertainty as to origins, the occurrence of national catastrophes, or the incursions of exernal influences really produced this need or can fully explain it.

It may be that the answer is a simple one, lying in history but not in the direction sought. Eastern Europe, as a part of Europe, is part of a congeries of diverse but related cultures. But also through a variety of internal and external developments—some abrupt, some proceeding over many decades—this area was somewhat belated in absorbing, through the interchanges of European cultures, that complex of ideas and perspectives comprising modern secular thought, including the modern discipline of history itself. This combination of relatedness and belated-ness—something quite different in quality from the impact of the West upon, say, Japan or India—may have contributed substantially to these tendencies in East European historiography which in natural consequence have entered into our own picture of Eastern European history itself—something seen in the first instance, in most cases, through the eyes of the native historian.

I have been speaking very generally and with no particular reference to periods of time. In concluding, I should like to add that in historical studies in East Central Europe in the interwar years and in Russia in the decades just before 1914 the picture was changing rapidly. I have mentioned the various "revisionist" schools that were reconsidering and reappraising the national past. There was an effort to rise above the national clichés and polemics, to find common ground with historians of other lands. In other words, these characteristics which I have tried to delineate were in the process of major change, brought about, as it should be, by continuing research, thought, and criticism on the part of the historians themselves.

And herein lies a special tragedy of our time. It is not necessary to dwell here on the general impact of Communist rule in Eastern Europe or even on the stultifying influence of Marxist-Leninist orthodoxy upon historiography.[9] But in addition to these broader cultural and intellectual effects, Marxism-Leninism has had, as a doctrine, both a preoccupation with, and a dogmatic approach to, the question of identity and alienation. The superimposition of this mode of thought, with its predilection

[9] For two depressing examples, see E. Ambartsumov: "Historians in Congress in Stockholm," *World Marxist Review* (November 1960), 9, and "Sovetskaia istoricheskaia nauka na novom etape razvitiia," *Voprosy istorii*, No. 8 (August 1960), 3–18.

for rigid categories of periodization and social analysis, upon Eastern European historiography has produced a curious and unattractive retrogression, blighting the promise of the preceding period. Much contemporary Communist historiography, as suggested above, seems to have reverted to the controversies of the nineteenth century, fighting the issues in somewhat different terms to be sure, but in a discouragingly similar arena. Where this will lead in time it is impossible to say. But the present state of historical scholarship under Communist auspices only makes it the more important that we who are interested professionally in Eastern Europe and its history maintain our efforts to sharpen and deepen our understanding of that region in its complex European setting.

II ❦ Russia and America

[1961]

IN RECENT YEARS THE PROBLEMS ASSOCIATED WITH SOVIET-American relations have become so universal, so pervasive, and so intrusive that it is difficult to define or delimit them. There is scarcely a domestic or diplomatic issue anywhere in the world that does not, in one way or another, become involved in the mutual concerns of these two great powers. Indeed, such tangential, peripheral, or "third-nation" disputes, rather than direct conflicts of interest, seem often to form the substance of their relationship.

This being so, it is not easy to place the relations between the two states in any simple "historical perspective." In his preface to *America Faces Russia: Russian-American Relations from Early Times to Our Day*, Thomas A. Bailey remarks: "It is to be hoped that a clearer comprehension of our relationships with the Russians in the past will enable us to deal more intelligently with them in the future."[1] But is this not a vain hope? Could it not be argued that an attempt to derive the present phase of Soviet–United States relations from their diplomatic re-

[1] Thomas A. Bailey: *America Faces Russia: Russian-American Relations from Early Times to Our Day* (Ithaca; 1950), p. v.

lations in the nineteenth century would be exceedingly misleading, that this earlier period of diplomatic history, while of proper interest for its own sake, really tells us very little about recent, current, or future developments?

Nor can we fall back upon that popular, and by now rather overworked, theme of "continuity and change"[2] as a means of defending the relevance of the historical approach. A comparison of "constants" and "variables" can hardly give us that sense of process which is at the core of historical understanding.

This essay, then, will be chiefly concerned with exploring the question: *How* are we to see Russian-American relations in a useful historical perspective? To illustrate the nature of the question I will first consider certain theses that have strongly emphasized either the "essential" continuity or the discontinuity of this relationship.

It is probably obligatory for anyone discussing Russian-American relations to cite Alexis de Tocqueville's famous observation in *Democracy in America,* which appeared in 1835. It provides quite startling evidence in support of "continuity" and has been seized upon happily by authors wishing to demonstrate that the virtue of the American case has deep historical roots. The passage is worth repeating, for, whatever one wishes to make of it, it does have an uncanny quality:[3]

[2] No criticism is here implied of the excellent essays appearing in the work edited by Ernest J. Simmons: *Continuity and Change in Russian and Soviet Thought* (Cambridge, Mass.; 1955). The author has the impression, however, that the phrase "continuity and change" has subsequently gained popularity as a neat formula for avoiding serious thought about a most difficult historical problem. The difficulties become apparent if we think of writing an essay on Continuity and Change in English History.

[3] Alexis de Tocqueville: *Democracy in America,* trans. Henry Reeve (New York; 1899), I, 441–2.

There are, at the present time, two great nations in the world which seem to tend towards the same end, although they started from different points: I allude to the Russians and the Americans. Both of them have grown up unnoticed; and whilst the attention of mankind was directed elsewhere, they have suddenly assumed a most prominent place amongst the nations; and the world learned of their existence and their greatness at almost the same time.

All other nations seem to have nearly reached their natural limits, and only to be charged with the maintenance of their power; but these are still in the act of growth; all the others are stopped, or continue to advance with extreme difficulty; these are proceeding with ease and with celerity along a path to which the human eye can assign no term. The American struggles against the natural obstacles which oppose him; the adversaries of the Russian are men; the former combats the wilderness and savage life; the latter, civilization with all its weapons and its arts: the conquests of the one are therefore gained by the ploughshare; those of the other by the sword. The Anglo-American relies upon personal interest to accomplish his ends, and gives free scope to the unguided exertions and common-sense of the citizens; the Russian centers all the authority of society in a single arm: the principal instrument of the former is freedom; of the latter servitude. Their starting-point is different, and their courses are not the same; yet each of them seems to be marked out by the will of Heaven to sway the destinies of half the globe.

This is all very gratifying to the American ear: to have a French observer assigning to us both power and freedom. But what is the historian to do with this sort of prediction? Between De Tocqueville's day and our own some major historical possibilities—victory of the South in our Civil War, the death of Lenin as a young boy, or the victory of Germany in either of the two world wars—could have altered completely the destiny of either Russia or the United States.

Moreover, while we may feel, from our present perspective, that this continuity of a basic antithesis between the two societies has the ring of truth to it, it is perfectly possible to cull other quotations from the past to suggest a quite different continuity. For example, in 1886 the historian Michael Pogodin had the following to say at a banquet celebrating Gustavus Vasa Fox's naval mission to Russia:[4]

> I will add that this sympathy [for the United States] is increased by the resemblance of our institutions, by our connections with Europe, and history generally. I do not speak of the likeness as regards the extent of our territory, our power and means; nor of the abundance of our natural productions. As regards institutions, the United States is a republic, and Russia an absolute monarchy; but here, as well as on the map, extremes meet. In the Russian absolute monarchy there is a democratic stream that flows uninterruptedly throughout its history. . . .
>
> I have but to speak, in conclusion, of the resemblance between Russia and the United States in reference to the Old World. It is impossible not to agree that Europe looks on the New World with some apprehension, some suspicion, some jealousy. I believe I make no mistake in asserting that the principal European governments, influenced severally by their own views and particularities . . . did not look at the American conflict so impartially . . . as we did. . . . They regard with the same eyes the other New World—I mean Russia. For fifty years . . . Russia was the chief supporter of peace in Europe; but, as soon as there was an op-

[4] Quoted in Max M. Laserson: *The American Impact on Russia—Diplomatic and Ideological—1784–1917* (New York; 1950), pp. 192–3. Laserson points out that Pogodin did not use the word *demokraticheskaia* but *zemskaia*.

portunity, all this was forgotten, and Europe . . . leagued with Turkey against us. . . . Where are we to look for the cause of such a disposition? Perhaps in the jealousy of her old age, in the general and involuntary conviction that America and Russia will have as much in their future as she has had in her past.

Emphasis upon parallels in the Russian and American experience was not infrequent in the mid-nineteenth century, especially in conjunction with such coincidences as the liberation of the serfs and the Emancipation Proclamation, the suppression of the Polish revolt of 1863 and the Union's victory over the Confederacy, or both nations' tariff protection of infant industries.

This theme of similarity does not appear persuasive today, and yet, if one looks back to the years of the wartime alliance, 1941–5, one can certainly find expressions of it: the Soviet Union and the United States were the two nations with a revolutionary past unmarred by a subsequent "restoration" of the old order; the frank and even crude behavior of their citizens and soldiers (bourbon and vodka *vs.* wine and small beer) was set in contrast to that of the West Europeans; as vast continental powers neither had got deeply involved in overseas colonialism. Today President Roosevelt's note to Secretary of State Hull in January 1944 makes rather poignant reading, but it does recall this brief sense of parallel interests, contrasting with those of Western Europe, that vanished with the defeat of Germany:[5]

I saw Halifax last week and told him quite frankly that it was perfectly true that I had, for over a year, expressed the opinion that Indo-China should not go back to France

[5] *The Memoirs of Cordell Hull* (New York; 1948), II, 1597.

but that it should be administered by an international trusteeship. France has had the country—thirty million inhabitants—for nearly one hundred years, and the people are worse off than they were at the beginning. . . . As a matter of interest, I am wholeheartedly supported in this view by Generalissimo Chiang Kai-shek and by Marshal Stalin. I see no reason to play in with the British Foreign Office in this matter. The only reason they seem to oppose it is that they fear the effect it would have on their own possessions and those of the Dutch.

In such a mood one could easily praise Pogodin for his remarkable insight eighty years earlier. But the inadequacy of attempts to set American-Russian relations in such patterns of continuity, whether of similarity or of antithesis, is apparent. Like efforts to use the Marquis de Custine as a Baedeker to the Soviet Union or to present Stalin as an atavistic throwback to Ivan the Terrible, they involve a highly arbitrary selection of facts and a disregard of the infinitely tangled and problematic nature of historical causality.

Against such cases for continuity in Russian-American relations it can be argued that their chief and most striking feature is discontinuity: that Soviet–United States relations today have really nothing to do with Russian-American relations in the nineteenth century, which may for all intents and purposes be disregarded in our quest for an understanding of present discontents and future prospects. This argument could be made in terms of ideology, or of power, or a combination of both.

Thus, some would urge that Soviet-American relations today are essentially a product of the aims, expectations, and methods of Communism or Marxism-Leninism, that the advent of the Bolsheviks to power marked a break in the continuity of Russian foreign policy, and hence that for an understanding of Soviet–United States relations it would be far more profitable to investigate the realm of ideology than to look back into prerevolutionary diplomatic history. While diplomatic studies dealing with regional issues may point to concrete facts of geography as providing threads of continuity throughout changes in regime (defense of Russia's western approaches, interest in the Persian Gulf or the Straits), these constants seem to be largely lacking in American-Russian relations, and we are struck by the enormous role of the ideological conflict, whether it is seen as deriving from the ideas of Marx or from the impulses comprising twentieth-century totalitarianism.

The argument that Soviet-American relations reflect the necessities of "power politics" is often brought forward in opposition to, or as a corrective of, this picture of ideological conflict. Yet, in the present context this argument, too, has the effect of stressing discontinuity rather than continuity in Russian-American relations. For in this view, it is the enormous industrial and military potential of the two states in the twentieth century—their arrival at the status of "superpowers"—that provides the key to their relationship. Separated geographically, with relatively few local issues to divide them, it was only when they became major, and then decisive, factors in the world's balance of power that their relationship took on its present importance. In other words, recent and contemporary Russian-American relations can be understood only as the pivot point of the general equilibrium, or disequilibrium, of international power relations, which have been radically altered by two world wars and the advent of a type of technology that seems to require a continental base.

There is undoubtedly much to this argument. When we look back at Russian-American diplomatic relations in the nineteenth century they do seem to be, for the most part, marginal to the interests of each nation and having their principal importance in connection with some third power—often Great Britain—which was the central preoccupation of both Russian and American foreign policy. Friendship usually meant being the enemy of an enemy. The warmth of American-Russian and of American-British relations was usually in inverse ratio. From the Russian perspective the United States was useful either as a counterpoise to the Western European powers or as a means of detaching England from its Crimean War ally, France.

Thus, in 1863 we find M. N. Katkov writing:[6]

Our rapprochement with the United States is useful for all purposes. Russia at present enjoys there a distinct popularity, and the United States can ally herself only with Russia. *In the event of a European war, the Americans are our natural and genuine allies. . . .*

Our rapprochement with the United States would also be very useful for Russia in the sense that it would help her gain more independence and freedom in her European alliance. This alignment, expanding the circumference of her political action, will move England to become more flexible and yielding in her relations with Russia. The nature of our international relations is such that friendliness toward France means enmity toward England, while every step of our rapprochement with the United States will be accompanied by a step on the part of England nearer to us, provided that we manage our relations with America so that, should she be in need of help, she would be reasonably sure to get it from us. The more profitable our alliance is to the United States, the more desirable will it become for England to bolster her good relations with us.

[6] Laserson: *American Impact on Russia,* pp. 180–1.

Whatever one may think of the soundness of Katkov's calculations, it is evident that his eye was ultimately upon Britain and France, not the United States.

At the turn of the twentieth century, when the United States was moving into the Western Pacific, an area of real concern to Russia, Russian-American relations still seemed of indirect rather than direct importance. Thus, the Russian ambassador to Washington, Cassini, wrote to Lamsdorff, assistant minister of foreign affairs, on June 23, 1898:[7]

> If our old friend the United States found, after the war, that the Philippines were suitable as a point of departure in the Far East, we would have to limit ourselves to the mere affirmation of a new factor in the Far-Eastern situation, which in the last period has attracted so many self-interested sentiments. But the rapprochement which has taken place between the United States and England during the war, a rapprochement which might in spite of everything lead to a closer agreement between these two great naval powers, compels us to regard the occupation of the Philippines by the United States with considerably less well-wishing.

It is true, of course, that Russian interest in the United States as a potential opponent of other unfriendly powers carried on into the Soviet period. Lenin in 1920 saw the United States as the chief enemy of Japan and also an opponent of the Western European states. In 1933 a principal motive of the Soviets in establishing diplomatic relations with the United States was to find an ally against the expanding power of Japan.[8] The Grand Alliance of

[7] Quoted in Edward H. Zabriskie: *American-Russian Rivalry in the Far East, 1895–1914* (Philadelphia; 1946), p. 205.

[8] See Robert Paul Browder: *The Origins of Soviet-American Diplomacy* (Princeton; 1953).

1941–5 turned out to be, despite some hopes to the contrary, only an enemy's-enemy sort of friendship. (It is melancholy to reflect on the kind of enemy it took by then to induce even such a friendship.)

Nevertheless, the United States' involvement in the First World War and its leading role in the peacemaking marked a profound change despite its diplomatic withdrawal for the next several years. The rapid emergence of this country as a great power, if a reluctant one, had decisively affected the classical European *Staatensystem*, and by the mid-1920's the great Communist heresiarch, Trotsky, was writing: "The superiority which Britain in her heyday held vis-à-vis Europe is insignificant in comparison with the superiority which the U.S.A. has gained over the entire world, including Britain."[9]

Although fears were voiced on the eve of the First World War that Russia would come to overshadow Europe, their realization was delayed for a generation by the ensuing catastrophes that struck Russia. After 1945, however, the polarization of the world was an unmistakable though not necessarily enduring fact, and Soviet-American relations became a central and oppressive theme of international politics.

It is obvious that ideological differences alone could not have produced this encounter, which has dominated all others since the end of the Second World War. It is much less obvious that the economic and military strength of the Soviet Union and the United States can alone account for it. The stubborn failure of the United States and Great Britain to become antagonists in the earlier decades of this century, despite the hopes of Communists and other

[9] Isaac Deutscher, *The Prophet Unarmed—Trotsky: 1921–1929* (London; 1959), p. 213.

well-wishers, would suggest that something other than national income is involved in rivalry between nations. And if the United States was increasingly concerned about Soviet military strength after 1945 it was because this strength was seen as a reflection less of industrial dynamism than of political intent.

But however we may choose to relate "ideology" and "power" as determinants of Soviet-American relations—an engaging question that would carry us beyond the limits of this essay—there would appear to be a strong case for the conclusion that the complex of factors making up this relationship in the midtwentieth century is of comparatively recent origin and may not be usefully illuminated by efforts to gain a century's perspective on Russian-American relations. Could not an economist, a political scientist, and a military analyst between them—with perhaps a RAND computer thrown in—provide about all the insights we can hope to gain concerning Soviet-American relations?

The historian must protest vigorously against such a suggestion, of course. Even were we to admit that the period of relevant inquiry was limited to four decades, we are nonetheless concerned with understanding processes through time, the proper domain of the historian. Indeed, a principal shortcoming of much discussion about Soviet-American relations is precisely a lack of historical sensitivity. It would appear to be fairly self-evident that our relations with Khrushchev's Russia are not identical with those we had with Stalin's Russia and yet are not totally different: it is a continuing story, and it would seem that our task is to grasp as best we can the meaning and movement of that story, and not reduce it to a debate whether $A = B$ or $A \neq B$.

But the case for history has even better foundations,

foundations embedded in the more distant past. The arguments for discontinuity in Russian-American relations, as outlined above, left several important problems in mid-air. While it may have been the physical and military power of the United States and the Soviet Union that thrust them from opposite wings into direct confrontation at the center of the stage, this power did not appear *ex nihilo*; it had its own historical origins. Similarly, Communism is no divine or demonic afflatus; it is a body of doctrines and practices hammered out over time by Russian minds in a Russian setting. Whatever its German antecedents, it is part of Russian history.

To put it another way, while we may agree that *at the level of foreign policy* Russian-American relations have undergone a decisive change in character in the course of the last fifty years, a change that is not to be explained by their earlier experience *on this level*, we may also contend that the fact that the two states did then encounter each other in this fashion and at this particular time, and that they had the propensity to react to this encounter in the way they did, may well have deep roots in the whole domestic history of the two societies.

From this it would follow that our search for historical perspective would lead us along two distinct tracks—Russian history and American history—and for the most part these tracks in the past would not be on the plane of foreign policy. Viewed in this light the mutual relations of the two states in the nineteenth century, or comparisons of the two societies, are to be seen not as strands of a single narrative—attempts at such narrative have had little inner cohesion—but, rather, as signposts or symbols suggesting the possible configurations of the two societies or adumbrating possible confrontations. Such, if we can rid ourselves of the temptation to read prophecy in it, was the remarkable achievement of De Tocqueville's insight. But Pogodin saw truths too, though his eye was less discerning and history failed to bring about his expectations.

If, as we have just proposed, the search for a historical perspective on Russian-American relations leads us from the plane of their respective domestic histories to an abrupt confrontation on the plane of foreign relations, then we might expect that this point of translation, or eruption, would be of critical significance to our understanding of this historical process. And indeed, our expectations are not disappointed. The more one reflects on the focal years 1917–19 and on the personalities and roles of the two great figures emerging at this time from the turmoil of international conflict and upheaval—Wilson and Lenin—the more one comes to feel that Soviet-American relations as we have known them in our lifetime were born in that confrontation, which in turn is intelligible only through the histories that brought these two figures to the fore, and almost immediately made them symbols. It is not surprising that George Kennan, an experienced diplomat and perceptive historian, should have singled out these years for study and contemplation.[1]

It is obvious, of course, that we cannot make everything hinge on these two or three critical years. From the beginning of the century we find emerging—in the United States' move into the Pacific and its role during and after the Russo-Japanese War, in the growing criticism of Russian autocracy's ineptitudes and domestic practices (most sharply in connection with its anti-Semitism), in the somewhat uninformed enthusiasm that greeted the March revolution—several of the components of later relations. Moreover, there have been many important changes in

[1] George F. Kennan, *Soviet-American Relations, 1917–1920*, 2 vols. (Princeton; 1956–8).

Russia and the United States, and in their mutual relations, in the four decades following the revolution. Still, it is astonishing the extent to which the terms of their relationship and the various modes of viewing and dealing with it appeared almost simultaneously with the initial confrontation of Wilsonian America and Leninist Russia. As historians we often speak of the advantages of hindsight and distance in sizing up the meaning of events; contemporaries presumably cannot see the forest for the trees. But perhaps the most striking impression one receives from a reading of contemporary sources in this period—whether from Versailles or from Moscow—is of their close family resemblance to views and concepts current today, whether in the United States or in the Soviet Union. With the Bolshevik régime only a little over a year old the statesmen at the peace conference were already wrestling with the various—and not very satisfactory—ways that seemed open for dealing with this new force: destruction, roll-back, *cordon sanitaire*, or accommodation.[2] By the time the Bolsheviks had swallowed the bitter pill of Brest-Litovsk they were well on their way to envisaging the various ways open to them—also not altogether satisfactory—for dealing with the external world of "imperialism" to which they felt related as Zeus to Chronos.

Despite the ensuing "Red Scare" in the United States and despite Trotsky's prediction in the mid-1920's—"We are entering an epoch of the aggressive unfolding of American militarism"[3]—it would be pressing the familiarity much too far to read back into these earlier years the great antagonism of the post-1945 decade. There was nothing like the equivalence of power relations that obtained in the

[2] See, for example, John M. Thompson: *Russia, Bolshevism, and the Versailles Peace* (Princeton; 1966) .

[3] Deutscher: *Prophet Unarmed,* p. 214.

later period. Russia in 1917–19 was a shambles, bled white by war and convulsed by civil strife. Nevertheless, in the realm of ideas, or rather of *idées-forces*, the encounter had a certain absolute quality right from the beginning. The Wilsonian and Leninist universes met amidst the moral as well as the physical wreckage of the old European order. Indeed, the fact that Russian-American relations moved to a new level at this time is probably to be attributed more to the spiritual vacuum created by the collapse of Europe than by the fact that the two states had been physical participants in the great cataclysm.

Certainly both Wilson and Lenin felt that the traditional system of European diplomacy had been "forever discredited." Certainly both had a vision of a world order that would prevent a recurrence of the fateful disaster of 1914. And while the timing and formulation of certain of their statements show signs of conscious competition, much more than propaganda or public relations was involved. Some people in both countries nourished the hope of finding common interests in these two visions that swept across the world in the wake of the war, but the similarities were superficial and the occasional verbal correspondences misleading. The Wilsonian and Leninist outlooks were profoundly different in content and style, rooted as they were in the national cultures of their two creators.

This is not to say that either man was the epitome of his country. Politically Wilson and Lenin were spokesmen of only one of a multitude of currents and attitudes alive in their respective lands; personally neither of them was precisely a "representative man." Yet the goals and methods of each are comprehensible only through the interplay in earlier years of the person and his political and social environment.

Significantly, the intellectual formation of neither man was determined by activity in, or responsibility for, foreign affairs. In neither do we find that belief in the *Primat der Aussenpolitik,* characteristic of so much European thought, diplomatic and historical. In the case of both Wilson and Lenin we feel that their view of diplomacy and world politics was a projection of domestic considerations outward upon the international scene. The very universality of their prescriptions for a world order betrayed a parochial origin. Not that their internationalism was in any way a cloak for nationalism. Lenin's "proletarian internationalism" was a very real conviction. His goal of replacing "capitalist imperialism" with a new revolutionary world order was not just a device for defending Soviet Russia: it was a self-evident good in itself. Nevertheless, the whole bent of Marxist analysis was upon an internal mechanism— the class struggle—as against external mechanisms such as the balance of power. Lenin's long sojourns outside Russia and his growing interest in imperialism and the national question—issues that came to concern him after he was forty—may have extended his range, but one has the sense that his central goal, toward which he drove with cold determination, was always The Revolution and that the grounds for this lay deep inside Russia and inside Lenin himself.

It is worth noting that neither Wilson nor Lenin knew much about the other's country; in this at least they were fairly representative of their two nations. As George Kennan has observed with respect to the American President:[4]

Wilson was a man who had never had any particular interest in, or knowledge of, Russian affairs. He had never been in Russia. There is no indication that the dark and violent

[4] Kennan: *Soviet-American Relations,* I, 18.

history of that country had ever occupied his attention. Like many other Americans, he felt a distaste and antipathy for Tsarist autocracy as he knew it, and a sympathy for the revolutionary movement in Russia. Precisely for this reason, the rapid degeneration of the Russian Revolution into a new form of authoritarianism, animated by a violent preconceived hostility toward western liberalism, was a phenomenon for which he was as little prepared, intellectually, as a great many of his compatriots.

In a recent study Kennan goes on to suggest that Wilson's reaction to the Russian question, together with his image of himself as "the defender of the helpless, the simple, the innocent, against the economic and social mighty of this world," was of central importance in determining his attitude toward the peace.[5]

As for Lenin, in his earlier writings he displayed relatively little interest in, or information about, the United States.[6] American agriculture is mentioned favorably from time to time but as a weapon in his attack on the Russian agrarian system. Occasionally the United States is credited with displaying certain "progressive" features of the bourgeois order: in the salaries of its teachers, in its attractiveness to immigrants, in the presumed vigor of its working class. But in general Lenin was not well informed on these subjects and showed little inclination to exempt American capitalism from the general Marxist laws of historical development.

With the outbreak of the First World War Lenin's views toward the whole Western capitalist world became much

[5] George F. Kennan: *Russia and the West under Lenin and Stalin* (Boston; 1961), p. 122.

[6] For a survey of Lenin's attitude, see Charles H. Holbrow: "Lenin's View of the United States" (unpublished essay for the Certificate of the Russian Institute, Columbia University, 1957).

more hostile. The United States, he argued, entered the conflict for ulterior imperialistic purposes:

> And the actual aim of the entrance of America into the War is preparation for the future war with Japan. Inasmuch as the American people enjoy significant political freedom, it is difficult to believe that they will put up with compulsory military service or the creation of any army for some aggressive aim, for the struggle with Japan, for instance. . . . And thus it is necessary for the American capitalists to enter into this war in order to have a pretext, while hiding behind the high ideals of a struggle for the rights of little nationalities, for creating a strong permanent army.

In *State and Revolution* Lenin clearly stated that whatever "progressive" features the United States may have displayed in the past, it was no longer an exceptional case:

> Both England and America, the greatest and last representatives of Anglo-Saxon "liberty" in the sense of the absence of militarism and bureaucracy, have today plunged headlong into the all-European, filthy, bloody morass of bureaucratic military institutions. . . .

He had little use for Wilson's war aims; Wilson's note of December 22, 1916, was dismissed as "a downright lie and hypocrisy." From the time of the Revolution and intervention onward, the United States was simply an imperialist enemy, and the varying Bolshevik approaches to this country were viewed as means to check, neutralize, or split sections of the imperialist camp.

The confrontation of America and Russia in 1917–19 was not merely abrupt, it was accompanied by two contending programs for a new world order, programs derived not from the international arena alone but also from the preoccupations and perspectives of two continental societies situated on the margins of Europe. It was a confrontation, moreover, involving statesmen lacking any real familiarity with the other country. Perhaps as a consequence of this, Russian-American relations since that time—in addition to all the real differences between the two powers—have displayed the peculiar quality of two people talking past one another. The documents on Soviet-American diplomatic encounters over the last three or four decades almost invariably give the impression of a strange failure of communication, not verbal or semantic, but in basic premises.

For example, the negotiations leading to resumption of diplomatic relations in 1933 are filled with this kind of confusion. There was a good deal of talk on both sides about the presumed gains in trade and commerce, yet quite evidently this was not a primary concern of either party in establishing diplomatic relations. The Russians in that year were looking for active support against Japan, but it was perfectly clear that at that time the United States was not prepared for any such active engagement in the Far East. The United States for its part was seeking to "normalize" relations between the two countries; but the American notion of normality was not anything the Soviet Union was contemplating, as became apparent with the renewed bickering about the activities of the American Communist Party.

This mutual bafflement appears again in the negotiations held toward the end of the Second World War, in the strange history, for example, of the Declaration on Liberated Areas in the Yalta Agreement. More recently the variant meanings attributed to the term "status quo" in world politics give one a sense of having stumbled through Alice's looking glass.

While this persistent failure in communication is mutual, it would be a mistake to regard it as symmetrical.

Indeed, a recurrent fallacy in commentaries on Soviet-American relations has been the tendency to leap from recognition of the fact that the United States and the Soviet Union often are speaking at cross-purposes, and are unable to fathom one another's behavior, to the conclusion that both parties are therefore equally responsible for the tensions in international politics. This conclusion, clearly a non sequitur, can be extremely dangerous in current and future international affairs. Whatever we may feel about the adequacy or sophistication of American policies, we should not, for that reason, lose sight of the explicit and reiterated goals of Soviet policy.

It is altogether understandable that an observer of the course of Soviet-American relations in the years since 1917 might regret the passing of the old diplomacy, with its skills, its conventions of understatement, and above all its coolly professional recognition of the requirements of *raison d'état*. We should lose much needlessly were we to forget the insights and worldly wisdom gained in the history of diplomacy. And yet it is not accidental that the rise of the Wilsonian and Leninist outlooks, their challenge to the old order as well as to one another, should have resulted from the disastrous failure of the old diplomacy: its inability to check the outbreak of the First World War or to keep it within limits.

The failure of the old diplomacy was in turn the consequence of the emergence of new problems beyond the frame of the European *Staatensystem*—new geographically and in the fierce urgency of national and social issues. The failure of efforts to resurrect traditional diplomatic methods and outlooks in the interwar years and since— one thinks of the dismal diplomacy of the late 1930's in Europe or of the 1950's in colonial areas—would strongly suggest that foreign relations in the future will inevitably involve the whole of societies, that we cannot hold to the *Primat der Aussenpolitik* as an adequate formula.

Whatever the merits of the preceding observations, they have at most only set a problem, not solved it. For if we conclude that a useful historical approach to Russian-American relations requires careful consideration of the domestic histories of the two societies, we have not in this essay attempted such a consideration. An inquiry into the actual content of the American and Russian historical experiences, and the precise ways they came to influence the external relations of the two nations when they were thrown together in the twentieth century, would be a prolonged and exacting task, involving a vast array of social, economic, and cultural questions the diplomatic historian might prefer not to treat. It can be admitted that in general the diplomatic historian is correctly cautious about being drawn into a broader definition of his field; too often the results are irrelevancies or highly dubious generalizations. And yet, if we are to be serious here in speaking of historical perspective, we must be prepared to follow where the demands of our subject lead us. We may, however, also have the hope of gaining insights that, with the extension of our political and historical concerns beyond the traditional Western European frame, will serve us well.

III ✷ Russia
and the West:
Comparison and
Contrast

[1964]

COMPARISONS OF RUSSIA WITH THE "WEST" HAVE BEEN A
staple of historians and of contemporary observers for a
very long time, and no end is in sight. A recent appraisal
of Soviet developments in the decade after the death of
Stalin was devoted in part to a consideration of the prospects for "a gradual convergence of the social and/or
political systems of the West and the Soviet Union."[1] The
variety of the contributors' responses—"very likely," "necessarily uncertain," "unlikely any meaningful convergence,"
"highly improbable," "depends on what is meant by
'gradual' "—suggests an ample range of disagreement, both
in expectations for the future and in the characterization
of the contrasts underlying these expectations.

The Russians themselves have, of course, been perennially preoccupied with this act of comparison. As Sir
Isaiah Berlin observed, in speaking of the nineteenth
century:

[1] *Survey: A Journal of Soviet and East European Studies*, No. 47
(April 1963), 37–42.

Russian publicists, historians, political theorists, writers on social topics, literary critics, philosophers, theologians, poets, first and last, all without exception and at enormous length, discuss such issues as what it is to be a Russian; the virtues, vices and destiny of the Russian individual and society; but above all the historic role of Russia among the nations; or, in particular, whether its social structure—say, the relation of intellectuals to the masses, or of industry to agriculture— is *sui generis,* or whether, on the contrary, it is similar to that of other countries, or, perhaps, an anomalous, or stunted, or an abortive example of some superior Western model.[2]

Such concerns are not uniquely Russian. Americans and Canadians, colonial offspring of European culture, have spent a great deal of time meditating on their relations to the Old World; the inhabitants of the British Isles continue to have ambivalent feelings about the Continent; the Germans, though situated in Central Europe, have written at length about the significance of Germany's Eastern and Western "faces"; in Italy they say that Europe stops somewhere south of Rome; indeed, of the major European nations only the French seem not to have been much bothered by this particular problem of identification. Still, the relative intensity and persistence of the preoccupation in the Russian case, the fact that at times it has loomed as *the* question in discussions of Russian society and culture, would indicate a somewhat special problem.

It should be noted at the outset that what is involved here is not simply a nation-to-nation comparison but, rather, the relationship of one country, Russia,[3] to a more complex entity, the "West," by which is usually meant

[2] Isaiah Berlin: "The Silence in Russian Culture," in *The Soviet Union, 1922–1962: A Foreign Affairs Reader,* ed. Philip E. Mosely (New York; 1963) , 337.

[3] "Russia," of course, comprised numerous nationalities, and the term has occasioned much debate. In this essay, however, I shall

Western Europe. This latter entity, though comprising a number of nations, is assumed to have a degree of unity, the possession by its members of common features, against which Russia can be compared and contrasted. In other words, the question really means: Does Russia belong to the West or not, is it a part of the West or is it somehow alien from that cluster of nations. Historically it is clear that the pathos and passion this question has aroused derive from the issue of participation or nonparticipation. And while, as we shall see presently, the historian might prefer to deal with it in different terms, this issue still lies at the heart of most discussions of Russia and the West.

We can take, as an example, two recent articles. The one presented Russia as belonging to an East European cultural sphere quite sharply differentiated from, and opposed to, that of Western Europe: Eastern-Orthodox-Byzantine as against Western-Catholic-Roman. It urged, moreover, that the terms "East" and "West" in this setting "are so specific and meaningful that it would be unwise to introduce new concepts even as working hypotheses."[4] The second article, in contrast, was inclined to argue that while there have been periods, usually sterile ones, of Russian self-sufficiency and isolation, Russia and the West have "a common logic of development, a shared process of evolution. . . . Russian culture has no vital existence of its own apart from Europe."[5] Although the authors are addressing different themes, the trend of their thought is

---

not attempt to deal with this problem. By Russia I mean the Russian state or the culture and society of its Great Russian inhabitants only.

[4] Omeljan Pritsak and John S. Reshetar, Jr.: "The Ukraine and the Dialectics of Nation-Building," *Slavic Review*, XXII, No. 2 (June 1963), 224–6.

[5] Rufus W. Mathewson, Jr.: "Russian Literature and the West," *Slavic Review*, XXI, No. 3 (September 1962), 413, 417.

clear: one sees Russia as essentially distinct from the West, the other as linked to and dependent on it.

The disconcerting feature of this divergence—and both positions have respectable ancestries—is not simply their apparent incompatibility but their plausibility and persuasiveness when presented in the course of the authors' argument. From these, and other examples, we must suppose that in considering Russia's relation to the West we are not dealing with a simple question of fact—otherwise it would have been settled long since—but with a more subtle and troubling problem.

In the face of conflicting interpretations which do not appear to arise from crude errors of fact, one can explore at least three possible avenues of explanation: (1) one may look for the warping presence of animus or prejudice as the source of trouble; (2) one may attempt to achieve a more satisfactory "perspective" that can somehow encompass or reconcile the conflicting interpretations; or (3) one may conclude that each interpretation is substantially correct in its own context but together they are not reconcilable because they are answering quite different questions and intentions and are, in fact, operating on different planes of thought. We shall look at each of these possibilities in turn.

That an enormous amount of passion and animus has entered into comparisons of Russia and the West is perfectly obvious. One thinks, for example, of Dostoevsky's painful encounter with Turgenev in Baden in 1867. According to Dostoevsky, Turgenev "abused Russia and the Russians vilely and terribly," and told him that the fundamental point of his (Turgenev's) book *Smoke* lay in the sentence, "If Russia were to perish, it would cause neither loss nor distress to mankind."[6] In his account of the meet-

[6] Jessie Coulson: *Dostoevsky: A Self-Portrait* (London; 1962), p. 163.

ing, Turgenev, while denying that he would have expressed his intimate convictions to Dostoevsky, allowed that the latter had "relieved his feelings by violent abuse of the Germans, myself and my latest book."[7] We cannot go into the roots of this particular clash, but the passion evoked here by the Russia-West controversy is intense and unmistakable.

When Poles or Rumanians, despite the presence of linguistic or religious ties with the Russians and a fair measure of common if hardly joyful history, argue that Russia is not of the West, whereas their own nations most emphatically are, one feels that this is more than an academic classification, that it is an argument born of fear or desperation, and that the extrusion of Russia from the "West" is at the same time a call for support and assistance on the part of the Western nations. When a German author contends that the Russians, from the very beginning of their history, have been quite incapable of scientific and technological advance and have had to borrow and steal such knowledge from the West, which they hoped to overrun, one can agree with his enthusiastic translator that "this book is part of the Cold War."[8]

Undoubtedly the advent of the Soviet régime has greatly intensified passion and prejudice by placing Russia in the most violent possible antithesis to the rest of Europe: Communist Russia versus the Imperialist West. Moreover, the search for Communism's Russian roots or antecedents, a natural and perfectly proper inquiry, has led to heightened and perhaps inappropriate emphasis on those features of the Russian past that would seem to mark it off most sharply from Western Europe: the prominence that has

[7] *Ibid.*, p. 165.
[8] Werner Keller: *East Minus West = Zero: Russia's Debt to the Western World, 862–1962,* trans. Constantine Fitzgibbon (New York; 1962), p. 7.

been given in recent years to Ivan the Terrible's *Oprichnina*, the Marquis de Custine's animadversions, and the murky character of Nechaev is surely in good part a reflection of present concerns.

And yet, while we may grant that when passions are strong the door is opened to the tendentious selection and misuse of evidence, we may doubt whether this can be defined as the major source of our difficulty. For one thing, the presence of passion or prejudice itself requires explanation, and that may lead us back, in circular fashion, to tensions inherent in the Russia-West comparison. For surely the fact that Dostoevsky and Turgenev, whatever their personal differences, should have clashed so violently on this subject does point to a peculiar quality in the Russian society of the time that should have made such great artists so painfully self-conscious about the national identity. One might have reservations about certain Polish or Rumanian views of Russian-Western relations, but it remains true that these nations have had long and intimate exposure to Russia: their fear of Russia as an alien intruder is at least derived from immediate experience. As a Rumanian writer remarked not long ago, with some acerbity: "There are some who feel that personal experience of the things described, or the fact that the writer has personally witnessed the events discussed, throws a suspicion of bias upon the author. A writer, in other words, is suspect precisely because he has too great and too close a knowledge of his subject. For our part, we feel that ignorance is not a guarantee of objectivity."[9]

So while we may strongly suspect that when we run across that tired phrase "Scratch a Russian and find a Tartar" we are not likely to get much enlightenment about

[9] Constantin Visoianu, in the introduction to *Captive Rumania*, ed. Alexandre Cretzianu (New York; 1956), p. xvi.

either Russians or Tartars, it does not follow that no problem exists.[1] More than that, when we ask such a question
as whether the 1917 Revolution brought Russian history
closer to that of the West by placing it in the sequence of
the other great "modernizing" revolutions of the last three
centuries, or whether, on the contrary, it increased the
distance by destroying, or disrupting, some potentially important convergent lines of development, we find ourselves
faced with a real and quite intricate problem of historical
interpretation, one that is not reducible to animus or
partisanship.

Turning now from the role of animus, which while
making the subject more prickly does seem to be marginal
rather than central, we may consider some of the efforts
that have been made to overcome, modulate, or get around
the antithetical "either-or" of the Russian-Western relationship. It is my impression that these efforts have been
quite fruitful in new insights, although, as we shall see,
they tend to blur the Russia-West comparison or at least
remove it from the center of the stage.

The most obvious approach is to replace the Russia-
West polarity (with its overtones of an even more extreme Orient-Occident opposition) by the conception of
a European "spectrum" ranging clear across the Continent,
with changes occurring by degrees and shadings. This conception has the distinct advantage of calling in question
the picture of the "West" as a homogeneous unit, which
comparisons of Russia with the West so frequently posit.
For example, the much vexed question of the existence of
East European "feudalism" is cast in a rather different
light when we are told that "the existence of a hierarchy
is no longer thought to be a prerequisite to feudalism in

---

[1] Happily, the question of what the Russians *are* if they are not
Western is beyond the scope of this essay.

the West, largely because the neat hierarchy assumed to have existed in the West is found to have been virtually a phantom."[2] Once this simple unity of the West is dissolved and the tremendous variety of its historical experience and its institutional and cultural forms is taken to heart, then the way is open to a much more flexible and subtle series of comparisons: within and between regions of Europe, and on different levels—religious, social, institutional, and the like. Moreover, if Europe is seen as a spectrum, one can then attempt to locate the smaller nations of Eastern Europe in a more relaxed fashion; when the West, or Western Europe, is presented as a sharply identifiable unit then there always is the painful scramble to determine who will be permitted to slip in under the tent.

I have the impression that there is much to gain through comparative studies in this vein, studies that would include Russia in the spectrum. For one example, recent investigations comparing the recruitment and social composition of the higher bureaucracy in the Habsburg and Hohenzollern monarchies[3] could profitably be extended to include imperial Russia. For another, I should like to see a close historical study of the correlation, if any, between certain patterns of landholding and leasing and peasant unrest from France and western Germany eastward to Russia.

It must be admitted, however, that this picture of Europe as a spectrum, with Russia, say, at the red end, does not take care of several important problems. It does not overcome the subjective sense of sharp contrast and opposition, which, as we have seen, has played such a significant role in the making of Russia-West comparisons.

[2] Oswald P. Backus III: "The Problem of Feudalism in Lithuania, 1506–1548," *Slavic Review*, XXI, No. 4 (December 1962), 650.
[3] For example, Nikolaus von Preradovich: *Die Führungsschichten in Österreich und Preussen (1804–1918)* (Wiesbaden; 1955).

Moreover, the existence of sovereign states, of political boundaries, does mark real breaks in the spectrum, which is not a continuum, as anyone who has crossed a frontier post in Eastern Europe well knows. Finally, the fact that in the important realm of power politics Russia is usually set off, not against its immediate smaller neighbors, but against great powers farther to the West has certainly had a polarizing effect, of which the Iron Curtain division of Europe after 1945 is only the most recent and violent example. The impact of this effect upon other spheres of life and politics is very great indeed, as is illustrated by the sad history of countries and individuals that at times have sought to play the role of "bridge" between East and West. Still, for the student of history or comparative politics the "spectrum" approach does have real attractions, not least in helping to do justice to the enormous richness and multiplicity of the European scene.

A second device for tackling the Russia-West comparison has been that of the "time lag." For those inclined to seek similarities rather than contrasts the time lag is very convenient: features in the Russian scene that seem different from the West are shown to be the same, but corresponding to an earlier date in the West; opposing trends turn out to be merely tangents drawn at different points along the same curve. Thus, it is thought enlightening to say that the style of Soviet life today is Victorian or at the latest Edwardian. (Such resemblances or echoes do not, of course, necessarily imply a time lag. On a fresco from the Palace of Knossos there is a charming Cretan lady whom the archaeologists call La Parisienne: presumably the parallel, though attractive, is fortuitous.) The use of the time lag is valid only if a more or less identifiable sequence of stages is occurring and if more than one nation or culture has come to participate in this sequence, usually by borrowing and adaptation. W. W. Rostow in his study of the stages of economic growth provides an analytical framework for the succession of stages and then places the different modernizing countries in their rank in this procession. Within such a defined setting he does show that Russia experienced a time lag vis-à-vis Western Europe in achieving the famous "take-off" and in reaching "maturity." At the same time the burden of his message is the general similarity of these stages: "In its broad shape and timing, then, there is nothing about the Russian sequence of preconditions, take-off, and drive to technological maturity that does not fall within the general pattern; although like all other national stories it has unique features."[4]

The time lag has its problems, however. As Thorstein Veblen pointed out some decades ago,[5] the latecomer to a historical sequence does not simply duplicate earlier performances; there is usually a foreshortening of the stages, a leaping over of certain steps, and a lumpy mingling of the old and the new. Among the Russian Marxists Trotsky had perhaps the best sense of this feature of the time lag; indeed it underlay his thesis of permanent revolution. Despite the Marxist predilection for a unilinear view of history and its stages, Trotsky was able to observe: "The indubitable and irrefutable belatedness of Russia's development under influence and pressure of the higher culture from the West results not in a simple repetition of the West European historic process, but in the creation of profound *peculiarities* demanding independent study."[6]

[4] W. W. Rostow: *The Stages of Economic Growth* (London and New York; 1960), p. 67.
[5] In his *Imperial Germany and the Industrial Revolution* (2d edn., New York; 1939).
[6] Leon Trotsky, *The History of the Russian Revolution,* trans. Max Eastman, 3 vols. (Ann Arbor; 1960), I, 464.

In other words, the conception of the time lag, although serving to increase the comparability of nations by putting them on the same track, may actually, when refined, reinforce the appearance of individuality and uniqueness.

A study of the mingling of the foreign and the indigenous, for which the term "symbiosis" can sometimes be used appropriately, affords a third approach to the comparative study of Russia and the West. In my judgment this is probably the most fruitful of all, since it corresponds to the common sense observation that, in modern times at least, all nations are increasingly taking over or being bombarded by external influences which they must digest, naturalize, or otherwise cope with as best they can.

Two examples can illustrate the utility of this approach to a comparative study of Russia and the West. It is certainly to the Slavophiles that we owe part of our sense of Russia's difference and uniqueness. Not only were they intent upon stressing the differences, but the way they wrote and the features of the Russian scene they chose to emphasize strike Western readers as peculiarly Russian. And yet, as we know from their education and the intellectual currents that influenced them, the conceptual apparatus of the Slavophiles was borrowed directly from German idealism and romanticism.[7] Paradoxically, increased access to "Western" ideas was to sharpen the picture of a Russia-West antithesis.

Or, to take an instance from the eighteenth century, a recent essay on the education and upbringing of the Russian nobleman[8] first brings out certain "Russian" features

[7] See Nicholas V. Riasanovsky: *Russia and the West in the Teaching of the Slavophiles* (Cambridge, Mass.; 1952) .

[8] Marc Raeff: "Home, School, and Service in the Life of the 18th-Century Russian Nobleman," *The Slavonic and East European Review*, XL, No. 95 (June 1962) , 295–307.

in his childhood experience: "The Russian nobleman of the 18th century normally lacked strong roots in any particular area and had no real feeling of attachment to a specific locality and to a family estate on which his ancestors had lived for generations. . . . There is little evidence of the attachment to and the ties with the ancestral home which characterized the mentality of the western nobleman." The child was under the supervision of serf nursemaids and tutors who had no rights and very rarely any powers of discipline. From this very "Russian" setting the young nobleman was sent to a school, where he received "a completely western education which had practically submerged the Muscovite traditions of learning and education by the middle of the 18th century." The author suggests that the effect of the somewhat abstract Enlightenment education upon children with this particular background was to produce a distinct cast of mind, exceptionally rationalistic and didactic, that was to have important consequences for Russia in the next century. For our present purposes the most interesting feature of this analysis is the way in which Russian and Western influences are seen to combine to produce a personality that is neither the traditional Muscovite nor the French man of the Enlightenment but, rather, the forerunner of the nineteenth-century *intelligent*.

Such an approach to the historical evidence can be extremely productive in dealing with a number of major problems of Russian institutional and social history: the impact of the Mongol conquest in Muscovy; the effects of Peter the Great's adoption of the goals and methods of contemporary German *Polizeiwissenschaft;* the consequences of taking a peasant, the son of a serf, and dropping him into the large factory of advanced Western industrialism; or the particular combination of Russian and Western Marxist elements that went into Bolshevism.

This approach is hardly an exciting discovery; it is the familiar province of the historian. But in the present connection two points need emphasis. First, such an approach, if it is to be fruitful, must be closely related to the material at hand; the results are illuminating to the degree that they lead to a concrete historical picture. It is not an approach that yields sweeping generalizations. Second, while such study does look beyond Russia's frontiers for some of its evidence and insights, its central purpose is to advance our understanding of Russia. Comparative study is a valuable tool to that end, but comparison per se is not the goal.

Indeed, all these approaches that I have mentioned as methods of looking at Russia and the West move away from direct comparison, either by blurring the comparison through reference to a "spectrum" or by becoming an analysis of the various factors, belatedness or foreign influences, that have contributed to the formation of Russia.

Would this suggest that such a comparison is a fruitless enterprise, that we may be engaged in an impossible endeavor to answer a pseudo-problem? In one sense the answer must be Yes. If we are asked whether two objects are alike or different, we are immediately impelled to counter: "With respect to what?" or "In terms of what standard?" If we ask whether two maple leaves are alike, we can answer affirmatively if it is a question of contrasting them to oak or elm leaves, or we can answer negatively if it is a question of their being congruent or having identical vein structures. We cannot make a comparison *sans phrase*, without reference to the setting and purpose of the question.

This rather simple but tricky ambiguity in the act of comparison was well analyzed by Kant in a section of his *Critique of Pure Reason*. As he observed, some scholars are interested in and attracted by the principle of "homogeneity," others by the principle of "specification." "Those who are more especially speculative are, we may almost say, hostile to heterogeneity, and are always on the watch for the unity of the genus; those, on the other hand, who are more especially empirical, are constantly endeavoring to differentiate nature in such manifold fashion as almost to extinguish the hope of ever being able to determine its appearances in accordance with universal principles."[9]

According to Kant these differences in attitude have nothing to do with questions of fact or with the nature of reality but with method. In his rather formidable vocabulary similarity and dissimilarity are "regulative principles" —working maxims, both of which are necessary and which describe diverse tendencies and interests of human thought. Difficulties occur when we mistake their function and take them to constitute reality.

> When merely regulative principles are treated as constitutive, and are therefore employed as objective principles, they may come into conflict with one another. . . . The differences between the maxims of manifoldness and of unity in nature thus easily allow of reconciliation. So long, however, as the maxims are taken as yielding objective insight, and until a way has been discovered of adjusting their conflicting claims . . . they will not only give rise to disputes but will be a positive hindrance, and cause long delays in the discovery of truth.[1]

My mention of maple, oak, and elm leaves suggests the possibility that we might bring the Russia-West comparison into more manageable shape by establishing the criterion of genus and species, of making our comparison within a hierarchy of classification. The terms of our com-

[9] See *Immanuel Kant's Critique of Pure Reason,* trans. Norman Kemp Smith (London; 1933), pp. 537–49.
[1] Ibid.

parison—Russia, a country, and the West, a group of countries—would point to just such a classification. In some restricted but relevant areas this kind of classification can be useful. If we wish to compare the Russian language with those of Western Europe, we do have a linguistic structure locating Russian in the Slavic branch of the Indo-European languages, to which French and German, through their respective branches, also belong. Even in the more elusive field of religion we can, by tracing the course of theological disputes and schisms, construct a reasonably workable classification of the branches of Christendom and place Russian Orthodoxy in its appropriate niche.

But these classifications extend only to such relatively well-defined subjects as language and religion; we are here concerned with such vast complexes as national entities, of which language and religion form only a part. How are we to establish classifications that can enable us to make comparisons on this larger scale?

Max Planck, the originator of the quantum theory, remarked that while the introduction of order and comparison is essential to scientific treatment and that order demands classification, "It is important at this point to state that there is no one definite principle available *a priori* and enabling a classification suitable for every purpose to be made. This applies equally to every science. Hence it is impossible in this connection to assert that any science possesses a structure evolving from its own nature inevitably and apart from any arbitrary presupposition. . . . Every kind of classification is inevitably vitiated by a certain element of caprice and hence of one-sidedness."[2]

[2] Max Planck: *The Philosophy of Physics,* trans. W. H. Johnston (New York; 1936), pp. 13–14.

Such a cold douche from the austere natural sciences should make us cautious about the absoluteness of classifications in our rowdy and disheveled political and humanistic disciplines. I am entirely skeptical of any claims for a system of classification that purports to be inherent in the structure of history itself and free of arbitrary presuppositions. I find none of the principles of classification, whether based on geography or geopolitics, religion, ethnic-racial categories, social structure, or political system, to be persuasive in providing an *objective* basis for ordering and comparing such complex congeries as nations. For example, to take the familiar Orthodox–Roman Catholic division of Christendom, while granting the enormous importance of this division as a historical influence, it would appear to me, after periods of residence in Moscow, Bucharest, and Athens—all Orthodox capitals—that this religious factor is, at least in the twentieth century, altogether inadequate as a principle of classification, though obviously of value in helping to explain many attitudes.

If we concede that we are not likely to find a purely objective order of classification that will enable us to compare Russia and the West, then we are driven back to the view that difference and similarity, heterogeneity and homogeneity, are tools to serve our diverse intellectual interests. As such they are necessarily tied to, and get their meaning from, our purposes and concerns in making the comparison. This is not to say that they conveniently produce answers we feed into them, but that, depending upon the questions which we bring to bear in our comparisons of Russia and the West, we will get a multitude of answers, indicating widely varying degrees of similarity and dissimilarity, each perhaps valid in its own setting, but only there. An anthropologist interested in the whole range of humanity's social organizations would probably regard the Russia-West contrast as relatively narrow. The political theorist, working within the framework of highly articulated and sophisticated political systems, would find the contrast, say, between autocracy and democracy very great indeed, perhaps representing the extreme ranges of his particular scale.

If we could be satisfied with such a modest and circumscribed role for comparisons of Russia and the West, there would be much less acrimony and controversy on this subject. But there's the rub. As we have seen, the motives that have impelled both Russians and Westerners into such endless debate and wrangling are powerful and urgent. Although we can hold, with Kant as our guide, that attempts to make absolute comparisons will produce intellectual confusion and error, I am afraid it is certain that efforts will continue to be made to find in a comparison of Russia and the West either support for normative positions on the *political* relations of the Soviet Union and the Western Powers or the basis for a prediction on the outcome of this relationship in the future.

With respect to the range of ideological, diplomatic, and moral issues that currently divide us from the Soviet Union, I should certainly not underestimate their reality and importance or question the need for us to defend our own positions. But while we have all become used to employing the term "West" as a kind of shorthand for "our side," it would be well if we based our policies on the preservation of values and principles because we believe in them and not because they are "Western."

As for the future, I do not believe that the outcome, whatever it may be, is prefigured in the comparison of Russia and the West. If we look back to the decade or two preceding the outbreak of the First World War, we have the impression that for a brief period the old debate over Russia's relationship to the West was losing its intensity and was perhaps beginning to appear irrelevant. These were the years of that profound intellectual and cultural eruption (Einstein, Freud, postimpressionism, etc.), the consequences of which are still jolting us and which, in a half century's retrospect, seems to have been one of the great historical watersheds. Russia in its "Silver Age" entered fully and immediately into that movement, its creative talents were at the forefront, there was no significant time lag. In this breakthrough, initially on a narrow front of thought and art, the traditional Russia-West debate seemed out of place, not resolved but overtaken by new challenges and horizons. The First World War and the Russian revolutions interrupted and in considerable measure obscured this development, and, as we have seen, the old antithesis reappeared in the harsh form of Communism versus "imperialism."

While this antagonism has by no means played out, it is becoming increasingly evident that the new world adumbrated at the beginning of the century is coming on apace, and whether we prefer to symbolize it by $E = mc^2$, or automation, or the return of the repressed, or abstract expressionism, it is a strange world. While Russia and the West will probably respond to it in different fashions, there is a distinct danger that by keeping our attention focused on Russian-Western relations and comparisons we may be quite unprepared to meet the challenge of novelty. If we think of the Western tradition as a kind of comfortable interest-bearing inheritance that we can bank on for the future, we are in for serious trouble.

PART TWO

Politics and Diplomacy in Eastern Europe

IV ❦ International Relations Between the Wars

[1953]

I

THE MOST STRIKING ASPECT OF THE CONSTELLATION OF states in Eastern Europe after 1918 was that it should have come into existence at all. It is not that these states were "artificial" creations. It is, rather, that the appearance at that time of a zone of independent nation-states, from the Baltic to the Aegean, was largely the consequence of the simultaneous collapse, through war and revolution, of both Germany and Russia, an eventuality not anticipated in 1914. One cannot say what would have been the picture in Eastern Europe had either Germany or Russia emerged victorious, but certainly it would have been very unlike that which actually came about.

The continued independence of the area was dependent upon preventing either of the two great powers from gaining ascendency or from working with the other to control the non-Germanic and non-Russian peoples of the area, as they had done during much of the nineteenth century. This was a common burden of all the states of Eastern Europe after 1918. Unfortunately, it was almost their only real point of unity. The other unifying factor was that they were predominantly agrarian states, rather uncomfortably situated between a highly industrialized West and a "proletarian" U.S.S.R.

In nearly all other respects the area was marked by wide diversity. The boundaries between the different linguistic and cultural groups, often not clear, were generally not congruent either with natural boundaries or with the frontiers as they emerged after the First World War. In consequence, there were a series of territorial controversies which, in keeping the region at odds with itself, were of tragic significance. To take a few of the more critical examples: Vilna was contested by Poland and Lithuania, and Teschen by Poland and Czechoslovakia. Hungary and Czechoslovakia disputed the borders of Slovakia and Carpatho-Ruthenia. Transylvania was an issue between Rumania and Hungary. The Dobrogean quadrilateral divided Rumania and Bulgaria, and the latter was in turn in conflict with Yugoslavia over Macedonia and with Greece over access to the Aegean. In addition, of course, the great powers bordering on Eastern Europe were involved in a number of unresolved issues: Danzig, Upper Silesia, and Bessarabia, to name only three.

Accompanying and to some extent a consequence of these differences was the constant controversy over minorities. It is unjust to say that the Versailles treaties, in breaking up the old multinational empires, merely reproduced the old nationality conflicts within the new components. On the contrary, many more people than before lived within states controlled by their own nationals. Yet the solution was far from perfect. The very establishment of the national principle as the basis for the state carried with it a strong impulse to consolidate and coordinate—with resulting pressures on the minorities.

Certainly the mood of strong nationalism, often accompanied by an inner lack of self-confidence, frequently led to unfair treatment of minorities. One must admit, nevertheless, that the multinational principle, as represented in actual fact by the Austro-Hungarian Empire and the Russian Empire, did not in the years before 1914 seem to offer any real framework for constructive development. To be sure, there were many projects for the reorganization of these states, but on close examination they reveal little basis in reality.

In addition to the frontier and minorities problems, there was also the phenomenon of economic nationalism. Insofar as the restrictive effects of economic nationalism, especially the high tariffs, added to the difficulties of the region, they were symptomatic rather than a basic cause of trouble. In most instances, economic nationalism developed as a natural, if not particularly enlightened, reaction to the fact that these new states were under strong incentive to strengthen their economies as rapidly as possible. Because of many political uncertainties, they tended to proceed along the path of economic nationalism: "By ourselves alone" as the Rumanian liberals used to say. In this, of course, the behavior of the Eastern European states was not unlike that of the larger states, but the results in this area were often preposterous. For example, the chopping up of the Danube basin into a number of different tariff areas certainly was not a rational action.

Before turning to the development of international relations in this period, a further observation should be made. In comments on the vicissitudes of this part of the world, one encounters two opposing views. The first is expressed by the phrase "the Balkanization of Europe," which carries with it the implication that the stability of Europe was perennially upset by the bickering, intrigue, and petty rivalries of the small states of Eastern Europe. The other view is that the Eastern European states were behaving as well as they could under constant subjection to the machinations of the great powers who tried to use them as pawns. Both views are misleading. During the interwar period, the wisdom and stupidity of statesmen and peoples were fairly evenly distributed. It is true, of course, that the actions of the great powers inevitably had the more far-reaching effects, and in that sense their responsibility for the course of events is the greater. But one may doubt that their motives were either nobler or meaner than those of the small powers. The real trouble lay in the interplay of relations between the great and small powers, and for this all must carry a burden of responsibility.

II

It has been noted that the occasion for the independence of the Eastern European states was the collapse of both Russia and Germany in 1918. From the point of view of the new Eastern European states, the most favorable post-war situation would have been a continuation of Russian and German weakness, with these two powers at odds with one another. The worst situation would have been a strong Russia and a strong Germany working in cooperation. During the 1920's German-Russian relations were comparatively close, but both powers were weak. In the 1930's they both were much stronger, but in general hostile. In 1939 they joined forces with catastrophic results. Unfortunately, the states of Eastern Europe were not in a position to control these developments. The recovery in strength of Germany and Russia lay beyond the range of the small countries' influence, as did the course of German-Soviet relations. There were two possibilities open to the Eastern

European states: to gain support from other great powers, more specifically, the victors of the First World War; and to work among themselves in building up their collective strength.

They were ultimately unable to realize either possibility, but the failure to accomplish the first was of more consequence. In the last analysis, the great powers responsible for the outcome of the First World War and for the Versailles settlement were likewise responsible for the ordered evolution of the new peace. The reasons for their failure in this undertaking lie in a field of international relations beyond the scope of this essay. A few points must suffice. The United States, during the interwar period, was of little positive value in this connection. Great Britain, though closer to the scene, was unwilling, until the spring of 1939, to undertake major commitments respecting Eastern Europe.

The case of France was different, and one of the anchor points of European stability appeared to be France's military and other connections with the states of Eastern Europe, especially in the 1920's. Unfortunately, the French policy, particularly evident in the 1930's, of working with the states of Eastern Europe came into conflict with two of her other policies. One was the tendency to work out relations with Germany directly, or in concert with the other great powers. This pattern is traceable from Locarno, through the Four Power Pact, to Munich, and was a trend that the Eastern European states viewed with justified alarm. The other policy was the tendency to rely upon the Soviet Union, especially after 1934, as a counterweight to Germany. This was a development unacceptable to that part of Eastern European strategy which looked for support against both Germany and Russia.

Italy, the fourth victorious power at Versailles, was also

interested in Eastern Europe, but in this case the consequences were more damaging than helpful. Although Italy
was a victorious power, it had strong revisionist interests,
and the 1920's were marked by an intense Franco-Italian
rivalry in the southern part of Eastern Europe. The Stresa
Front in 1934–5 temporarily aligned France and Italy in
their opposition to German pressure on Austria, but later
Italy usually sided with Germany, although not without
certain uneasy doubts.

In general, then, France was the one great power really
committed to support the status quo in Eastern Europe,
and France, as it proved, was not enough.

Within the area itself, all the Eastern European states
had a common interest in avoiding great-power control, an
interest whose object became tragically apparent when the
whole area was dominated by Hitler after 1941. The First
World War had brought into being several formations or
groupings of the Eastern European states. However, the
beneficiaries of the war must be distinguished from the
losers. Some states were new creations, or had greatly added
to their prewar territory. Others—Bulgaria, Hungary, and
Austria—had been in the camp of the Central Powers.
Bulgaria's losses date both from the First World War and
from the Second Balkan War of 1913, in which it had lost
territory to Rumania, Yugoslavia, Greece, and Turkey. In
the case of Hungary, a strong case could be made that it,
too, was a successor state, but as a defeated power it was
obliged to sign the Treaty of Trianon. One can, perhaps,
justify each of Hungary's territorial losses to Czechoslovakia, Rumania, and Yugoslavia, on ethnic, economic, or
strategic grounds—though not all three at once—but the
cumulative effect of all these detachments was such as to
make the Hungarian cry, "No, no, never," a justifiable
response. This meant, of course, that in Danubian and

Balkan Europe, there was a profound disunity, which served to block efforts at extended common action.

North of the Carpathians a somewhat different situation prevailed. Finland, the Baltic states, and Poland were all beneficiaries of the new settlement. Unhappily, Vilna and Teschen provided, or at least symbolized, disputes which inhibited common action in that region.

III

Despite this disunity, important efforts were made to bring greater cohesiveness and unity to Eastern Europe. Of these the most important was the Little Entente, formed through a series of treaties between Czechoslovakia, Yugoslavia, and Rumania in 1920–1. The sponsors of these treaties had as a broader and eventual aim the establishment of a "great entente" extending, as expressed by Take Ionescu, the Rumanian statesman, from the Baltic to the Aegean. Nevertheless, the immediate and specific objective was more limited: the defense of the territorial settlement of the Treaty of Trianon against Hungary and opposition to any effort to bring back the Habsburgs. In the case of the Yugoslav-Rumanian Treaty, provision was also made for the defense of the Treaty of Neuilly against Bulgaria.

In the course of time a fairly extensive philosophy of the meaning of the Little Entente was formulated. The Entente became active in the League of Nations, of which the Entente members were ardent supporters. By 1926 the Entente became linked with France through a series of understandings and agreements. The statutes of the Entente were gradually enlarged to include agreements for the settlement of mutual disputes by arbitration, and later, in 1933–4, for the creation of a Permanent Council, an Economic Council, and a permanent Secretariat. All these steps were aimed at coordinating and unifying the foreign policies of the three members and at increasing their efficacy in the world as a whole.

Seen in retrospect, the Little Entente had certain short-comings. It was directed against Hungary and, despite various efforts, the rift between the Entente and Hungarian revisionism was never overcome. Perhaps too great emphasis was placed on Hungary, which was, after all, a very secondary power in these years, and probably weaker militarily than any single Entente power. At the same time, the treaties had nothing to say about meeting threats arising from great powers. There was no immediate community of interests in this regard, since each of the three members was potentially threatened by a different great power: Czechoslovakia by Germany, Rumania by Soviet Russia, and Yugoslavia by Italy. The Czechoslovakians had no direct conflicts with the Russians, the Rumanians had no direct conflicts with the Germans, and neither were at odds with Italy. This meant that the Entente was overprotected from internal, but underprotected from external, danger. This flaw became evident in the latter half of the 1930's.

To the south of the Little Entente, a Balkan grouping also came into being. The idea of a Balkan confederation was not a new one. Programs for achieving South Slav unity had been in the air from the time the Balkan states began to emerge from Turkish control. But a series of quarrels, especially concerning Macedonia, had always blocked these efforts. In the early 1930's a number of Balkan conferences were held. While significant achievements could be listed—the creation of machinery for the settlement of disputes, projects for intellectual cooperation, and even a project for a customs union—these achievements were largely procedural and technical. They did not extend to real political innovations. The Balkan Entente, formed in 1934, comprised Greece, Turkey, Rumania, and Yugoslavia, but not Bulgaria, which was not willing to accept the premise of no territorial revision. The Bulgarian position was not as intense as the Hungarian, and in certain political groups there was a real desire for South Slav unity. But it should be noted that a reconciliation on such lines would have had a doubtful reception in such a state as Rumania, which was very sensitive about being an island of Latinity in a sea of Slavs, as the phrase went. The terms of the Balkan Entente provided for defense against a Balkan aggressor only, not against a great power. The Balkan Entente was linked by two of its members to the Little Entente, but one cannot say that this association measurably increased the unity of Eastern Europe.

An extension of the Little Entente to the north was blocked by the Polish-Czechoslovakian conflict, by Poland's unwillingness to enter a grouping directed against its traditional Hungarian friends, and by a certain Polish reluctance to become committed to the preservation of the status quo south of the Carpathians. The one real link here was the Polish-Rumanian joint defense agreement, which, unlike the other arrangements, was directed against a great power, the Soviet Union.

As for the Baltic region, no great achievement can be recorded. Finland tended to orient itself toward the Scandinavian states. Poland and Lithuania did not even establish diplomatic relations until 1938, and then only under a Polish ultimatum. There was an alliance between Latvia and Estonia in 1923, and in 1934 a modest Baltic Entente covering the three Baltic states was signed, but it was not of great moment.

In general, looking from north to south, one sees the appearance of a number of groups aiming at the preservation of stability and independence in the area. Nevertheless, there were ominous gaps between and within the groups, and no sufficient measures for threats from without. The key connections, of course, were the Little Entente and the French ties with it and with Poland.

Apart from these alignments, which stood for the status quo and the Versailles system, there were certain other combinations that should be mentioned. Italy, which was in competition with France, attempted to counter the French ties with the Little Entente by the Rome Protocols of 1934 with Austria and Hungary—a clear example of the dangers of the reciprocal interplay of great- and small-power differences. Poland under Colonel Beck, had some rather ambitious plans for achieving a bridge to the West via the Scandinavian states, and to create a great Baltic bloc. But the Scandinavian states, at this time, were not entering into the power combinations of Central and Eastern Europe, and the project never got beyond some good-will tours. Finally, in 1938, Beck, with Ciano, discussed the formation of a Rome-Belgrade-Budapest-Warsaw axis, with the intent of checking German eastward expansion which was now clearly in the offing. But it was very late in the day for such a project, and it never came to any practical fulfillment.

Perhaps the most extensive, although abortive, effort to increase the security of Eastern Europe, this time in conjunction with the great powers, was the French attempt to achieve a so-called Eastern Locarno agreement. The states of Eastern Europe had been understandably disturbed by the Locarno agreements of 1925 which had seemed to settle, by international guarantee, Germany's western frontiers but which had done this at the cost of inviting German revisionism on its eastern frontiers. In 1934–5 France tried to achieve an agreement on the

Eastern territorial settlement; Germany, Russia, Poland, Czechoslovakia, and the Baltic states were to be signatories with France as a guarantor of the treaty. Germany, however, refused to participate. This led to a Polish refusal to underwrite what would then have been an anti-German combination. Eventually the project was reduced to the French-Soviet-Czechoslovakian mutual assistance agreements of 1935, which were clearly something other than a regional organization.

Apart from these various diplomatic combinations, certain other efforts were made to increase the unity of Eastern Europe. Of some interest in this respect is the International Agrarian Bureau, also known as the Green International, founded by leaders of peasant, or agrarian, parties in a number of Eastern European states in 1921. In its heyday in the 1920's it included peasant parties from Czechoslovakia, Bulgaria, Yugoslavia, Rumania, Austria, Switzerland, Poland, France, the Baltic states, and Finland. The literature of the late 1920's concerning Eastern Europe shows that this peasantist, or agrarian, movement was widely regarded as the hope of the future. Here was a movement representing a basic common interest of the area and transcending national frontiers.

Unhappily the promise in this movement was never realized, and the movement eventually collapsed. The agrarian parties were not able to dominate the domestic political scene in most of these countries, and the whole position of agriculture was undermined by the advent of the depression in 1929. A governmental effort to organize some defense of agricultural interests was made in 1930 in the form of an agrarian bloc, including Bulgaria, Estonia, Hungary, Latvia, Poland, Czechoslovakia, Yugoslavia, and Rumania. At a number of international conferences and at the League of Nations, this movement attempted to coordinate economic policy and to gain from the industrial states of Western Europe preferential treatment for agricultural exports. This effort achieved nothing tangible, and under the lash of the depression, these states were driven to a policy of *sauve qui peut*.

IV

The depression and the rise of Hitler were undoubtedly the major factors in starting the breakup of whatever cohesion had been achieved in the calmer years of the 1920's. For a time, to be sure, even after Hitler came to power, the Eastern European states showed a good deal of ability to act together. The Little Entente, together with Poland, was largely effective in protesting against the Four Power Pact of 1933. The extension of the powers of the Little Entente in 1934 and the creation of the Balkan Entente in the same year also showed a positive response to the new dangers. In the false calm of 1934 a number of voices could be heard saying that at last the Balkans had come of age and were no longer a source of European trouble. This was partly true, but somewhat irrelevant.

Unhappily, the breakdown was not far off. In 1934 Poland signed its nonaggression pact with Nazi Germany. Poland was clearly in a very difficult position and it is not hard to understand the attraction of an offer which seemed to promise an alleviation of the German revisionist campaign. The pact served, however, to increase the disunity of Eastern Europe. Although it was the basic intention of Polish policy to maintain an even balance between its two great neighbors, this agreement served in effect to bring Poland increasingly to a position paralleling that of Germany. This tendency was heightened when Czechoslovakia, by its 1935 pact with the Soviet Union, came to look eastward for support. Here again the local Polish-

Czechoslovakian conflict became involved in a more extensive and dangerous diplomatic issue.

The other states whose interests lay in the preservation of the status quo also engaged in an increasing amount of fence-mending. The Stojadinović government in Yugoslavia moved to improve its relations with Germany. In Rumania, Titulescu, who had favored a cautious *rapprochement* with the Soviet Union, was replaced in 1936, and King Carol tried with increasing difficulty to follow a policy of balance. This was a hard job, since he was being pressed domestically by the growing threat of the pro-German Iron Guard.

The events that led to the disintegration of Eastern Europe are too familiar to require more than the listing of a few of the more important: The failure of France and Britain to challenge the German remilitarization of the Rhineland left Hitler relatively free to turn eastward. The formation of the Axis and Mussolini's withdrawal of support from Austria paved the way for the *Anschluss*. And finally, of course, the Munich crisis was followed by the breakup of Czechoslovakia, in which Hungary and Poland participated. Certainly the ultimate responsibility for the collapse of Czechoslovakia must rest with the Western powers, yet it is conceivable that had the Eastern European states, above all Poland and Czechoslovakia, stood together, it might have been possible to stiffen the French spine at this fatal juncture. From Munich the road led to the crises of 1939, and eventually to the German-Soviet pact of August, which spelled the end of independent Eastern Europe.

Germany's economic penetration of Eastern Europe after 1933 was not a primary factor in the breakup of this region. While the reality of the penetration cannot be denied, for it meant much more than foisting aspirin and cameras on the Eastern European states, its importance may be questioned. This penetration did not really impair the political independence of these states until after the diplomatic situation had deteriorated greatly, and some of the German trade agreements which really bound the economies of the area were a result rather than a cause of the shift in the balance of power.

One may ask at this point about the influence of the domestic political and social problems of Eastern Europe on international relations. A good deal has been written about the failure of parliamentary and constitutional régimes in Eastern Europe, and their replacement by authoritarian régimes. Some have concluded from this that there was a tendency on the part of these régimes to gravitate toward Hitler and to refuse to have anything to do with the Soviet Union at a time when Litvinov was loudly calling, at the League and elsewhere, for collective security against aggression.

The relationship between foreign and domestic policy is always complex and debatable. In the case of Eastern Europe, however, one must steer a course between two inadequate interpretations of this relationship, which may be called the Popular Frontist and the Retrospective Vindicationist. The first, which is roughly the one described above, is not tenable. Documentary evidence that has appeared since the war makes it difficult to consider the Popular Front as anything but an instrument of Communist advance. It is quite evident that the Communists were not renouncing their ultimate aims either in Eastern Europe or elsewhere. It is also clear that the U.S.S.R. was not seriously prepared to stand up for the collective security it was calling for, although admittedly it was never required to do so. At the time of Munich, the Germans were not particularly anxious about the danger from the Soviet side. Moreover, it appears from the diplomatic memoirs of the Eastern European statesmen that they tended, as a group, to view the Soviet danger in the traditional terms of the "colossus of the East," as a perennial threat whether or not it had a Communist régime. Thus their suspicions of the U.S.S.R. cannot be reduced to a reflection of the "class conflict."

Regarding the second interpretation, it should be recognized that there was a special antipathy to the U.S.S.R. on the part of the Eastern European countries, which led to certain misjudgments of the relative dangers existing in the 1930's. Piłsudski, for example, after ordering an intelligence survey of his two powerful neighbors in 1933-4, concluded that, while both were dangerous from the Polish point of view, in the short run the Soviet Union was more likely than Germany to follow an erratic and aggressive course. This proved to be a miscalculation. One nevertheless gains the impression that a similar mood was prevalent in the diplomatic circles of Eastern Europe. This served to reduce the area of maneuverability in the final crisis and did not afford any way out of the tragic impasse of 1939.

During the war years, Eastern Europe disappeared as a region of independent states. Germany and the Soviet Union divided most of the area into spheres of influence and, with the German attack on Russia in June 1941, the whole region fell directly or indirectly under German domination. There was, nevertheless, some continuity. Among the governments-in-exile, the struggle for future independence was clear and explicit. Likewise, among the German satellites, there was a persistent attempt to maintain a degree of independence. The extent of the resistance of Hungary to Hitler has come out quite clearly since the war in the memoirs of the statesmen involved. Even such an active and cooperative Eastern European satellite leader as Marshal Antonescu seems finally to have placed his hopes on a German defeat from the West, while he continued in the effort to keep Russia at bay in the East.

It should also be noted, however, that the old frictions did not disappear. One major motive for Antonescu's entering the war, apart from the desire to recover Bessarabia, was his wish to put himself in a favorable position vis-à-vis Germany to press for the return of Northern Transylvania, which had been lost to Hungary in 1940. This old conflict continued unabated throughout the war.

It is worth noting, finally, the importance to Eastern Europe of the fact that Russia did not emerge victorious in the First World War. We do not know what such a Russian régime would have been like or how it would have treated Eastern Europe, but we do have some clues from the secret treaties and arrangements made by the Entente powers during the war. Poland, including the German and Austrian sections, would probably have been incorporated into Russia. By an agreement in 1915 Russia was to obtain Constantinople and the Turkish territory in Europe. In a Russian-French exchange of notes in February 1917, Russia was given complete freedom to determine its own western frontiers. Thus the intrusion of Russia far into Eastern Europe was a likelihood in 1914–18, and was staved off in 1919–21 only to reappear as a reality in 1945 under new and decidedly more dangerous circumstances. In this sense there had been a rather bleak continuity, of which Eastern European statesmen were far more aware than were the diplomats in Western Europe or the United States.

V

From this brief survey of international relations in Eastern Europe, it is clear that the states of the region, certainly singly and perhaps even collectively, had only a marginal control over their destiny. Traditionally they have been the objects rather than the subjects of history. This appeared less true in the twenty years between 1919 and 1939, but in an age of superpowers it will be more true than ever and their only hope will be to speak and act together.

It must be recognized that the mutual conflicts which divided the Eastern European states were not merely damaging but exorbitant in their cost. Surely the small Teschen district was not worth the struggle either to Czechoslovakia or to Poland when it is set against the disaster which overtook both and which might possibly have been averted by their common action. However, creative steps were taken by the Little and Balkan Ententes in the 1920's and 1930's toward increasing cooperation. One should not underestimate these achievements because of their ultimate failure. At the very least, they showed that the states of Eastern Europe could work together and devise an institution capable of growth and of assuming an increasing number of functions. Yet they arouse only moderate enthusiasm. One authority has said: "Both ententes made excellent beginnings, and they constituted steps in the right direction." This same authority had to grant, however, that Hungary and Bulgaria were never included, and that the stimulus for these ententes lay largely in a fear of neighboring Eastern European states.

In looking ahead, one must recognize that these national conflicts represent a major hurdle to be overcome. One cannot assume that the Little Entente eventually would have reached a stage when Hungary also would have joined. It is extremely difficult for institutions to transcend the limitations inherent in the motives for their formation, and it remains to be shown that the so-called functional approach to international organization—that is, an approach by economic, technical, or intellectual co-operation—can successfully bypass the real political conflicts that stand between nations. Any future federative or entente movement that hopes to encompass all of Eastern Europe must squarely face all political problems of a divisive nature. Only by transcending rather than disregarding the national principle can harmonious order be achieved in Eastern Europe.

V ❧ Maxim Litvinov

[1952]

MAXIM LITVINOV, PEOPLE'S COMMISSAR FOR FOREIGN AFFAIRS from 1930 to 1939, was undoubtedly the Soviet diplomat most widely and familiarly known in the West during the interwar period. At international conferences and at sessions of the League of Nations his chubby and unproletarian figure radiated an aura of robust and businesslike commonsense that was in striking contrast to the enigmatic brutality of the Politburo or the conspiratorial noisiness of the Comintern. Although he was an old revolutionary— he was born Meyer Wallach in 1876 and like Lenin, six years his senior, and Stalin, three years his junior, he assumed a *nom de guerre* while dodging the Tsarist police— to him perhaps more than to any other single person may be traced the impression that revolutionary Russia was returning to the family of nations and could be counted upon as a force for stability and peace. Indeed, the most perplexing problem in Litvinov's career is that of the relation of his role to the totality of aims and intentions of the Soviet régime.

This problem was most sharply posed in the blatant contrast between Litvinov's appeals after 1933 for collective security against Nazi Germany and the provisions of the

German-Soviet agreement of August 23, 1939. Was Litvinov really striving for the determined cooperation of the peacefully inclined powers or was Lord Lothian right in his belief that the ulterior aim of Litvinov's policy was "to maintain discord in Europe"?[1] Is it correct to assume that there was a distinctive "Litvinov policy"[2] or was his role throughout an essentially subordinate one in the Soviet hierarchy?[3] Were there important differences between Litvinov's outlook and that of the Politburo? If so, how did he survive the great purges which decimated the Foreign Commissariat; if not, why was he so abruptly retired in May 1939? Finally, did his retirement represent a real turning point in Soviet policy or was it only a tactical shift, the importance of which should not be overrated?

In attempting to come to closer grips with these questions—their definitive resolution seems impossible in the absence of evidence from the Soviet archives—this essay will consider in turn three topics: (1) the content of Litvinov's diplomatic policy, so far as it can be ascertained from his public pronouncements and recorded conversations; (2) the connection of this policy with the aims of the Politburo; (3) the relations between Litvinov, the Foreign Commissariat, and the Bolshevist high command.

[1] See his speech of April 2, 1936, in *Germany and the Rhineland* (London; 1936), p. 55.

[2] "Soviet foreign policy between 1929 and May 1939 followed the pattern of Litvinov's mind more than his chief's" (Louis Fischer: *Men and Politics* [New York; 1941], p. 127).

[3] Max Beloff, reflecting on his study of Soviet foreign policy, commented in 1950: "It is probable, too, that I did not lay enough stress upon the essentially subordinate nature of Litvinov's role" (*"Soviet Foreign Policy, 1929–1941: Some Notes," Soviet Studies* [Oxford], II [October 1950]).

I

Although it may be a matter of temperament one can detect a definite and largely consistent flavor in Litvinov's diplomatic attitude and behavior. Never the firebrand or the theoretician, he was always valued for his efficiency and practical abilities. Before the 1905 Revolution, the nickname Papasha (Little Father) was given to him by party comrades. In 1918, when hopes of general revolution were running high, when Foreign Commissar Chicherin was suggesting that the League of Nations be based on the expropriation of the capitalists of all countries and was intimating to President Wilson that the latter's government was to be replaced by a Council of People's Commissars,[4] Litvinov, writing to Wilson two months later, struck a quite different note. He attempted to explain the Red Terror as a defensive measure, protested against the intervention as leading only to the final devastation of Russia, and concluded: "The dictatorship of toilers and producers is not an aim in itself, but the means of building up a new social system under which useful work and equal rights would be provided for all citizens, irrespective of the class to which they had formerly belonged. One may believe in this ideal or not, but it surely gives no justification for sending foreign troops to fight against it, or for arming and supporting classes interested in the restoration of the old system of exploitation of man by man."[5]

One cannot be sure, of course, whether Litvinov's moderation was merely adroit diplomatic address—it was

[4] See his note to Wilson of October 24, 1918, in *Soviet Documents on Foreign Policy*, ed. Jane Degras, 3 vols. (London, New York; 1951–3), I, 112–20.

[5] Telegram from Litvinov to Wilson, December 24, 1918, Degras, I, 129–33.

clearly to the advantage of the struggling régime to per-
suade the Western powers to give up their intervention—
or whether it actually reflects the absence of revolutionary
expectation and belligerence. Louis Fischer reported Litvinov as saying to him some years later, "The prospect of
world revolution disappeared on November 11, 1918."[6]
In any event, this tone of unrevolutionary reasonableness
remained a permanent trademark of Litvinov's dealings
with the outside world.

During the years when Litvinov served as Chicherin's
second in the Narkomindel, the principal goals of Soviet
diplomacy were, after the flurry of revolution and civil
war, to achieve recognition and to increase the security of
the Soviet Union by means of treaties of neutrality and
nonaggression. The reason for these goals is evident and
requires no discussion. Less evident is the Soviet purpose
in entering the League discussions concerning disarmament, discussions which first brought Litvinov's name to
general prominence.

The initial Soviet attitude on the subject of war and
peace is stated in the Narkomindel's Appeal to the Toiling,
Oppressed, and Exhausted Peoples of Europe, of December 19, 1917: "We do not attempt to conceal the fact that
we do not consider the existing capitalist Governments
capable of making a democratic peace. The revolutionary
struggle of the toiling masses against the existing Governments can alone bring Europe nearer to such a peace. Its
full realization can only be guaranteed by the victorious
proletarian revolution in all capitalist countries."[7] As a

---

[6] Fischer: *Men and Politics,* p. 127. Litvinov's American biographer, Arthur Upham Pope, states that as early as 1920 Litvinov
had declared that the project of world revolution was impossible
(*Maxim Litvinoff* [New York; 1943], p. 334) .

[7] Degras, I, 19.

logical consequence the League of Nations was viewed as a "mere mask, designed to deceive the broad masses, for the aggressive aims of the imperialist policy of certain Great Powers or their vassals."[8] Despite this hostile attitude, Litvinov appeared at the Preparatory Commission of the Department Conference to propose "the complete abolition of all land, marine, and air forces."

Litvinov never denied these Soviet views concerning peace under capitalism. In 1922 he granted that the present social-economic structures of the majority of countries made the removal of the possibility of armed international conflict "unthinkable."[9] In 1927 he reiterated the Soviet Union's lack of confidence in the readiness and capability of capitalist countries to destroy the system of war between nations.[1] Nevertheless, this fundamental skepticism did not, in Litvinov's view, preclude the possibility of negotiating for disarmament. On November 6, 1930, he made this point quite clearly: "To us, the representatives of the Soviet Union, and exponents of definite socio-economic theories, the impossibility of removing the politico-economic antagonisms of capitalist society, and hence the ultimate inevitability of war, is perfectly clear. We believe, however, or we should not be here, that the danger of war might be considerably diminished, or made comparatively remote, by some measure of real disarmament."[2] It would appear that something which is ultimately inevitable may, however, be reduced as an imminent likelihood by appropriate action.

But was the Soviet proposal for complete disarmament such an appropriate action? Did it represent an effort, as

[8] Ibid., p. 381.
[9] *The Soviet Union and Peace* (New York; n.d.), p. 117.
[1] Ibid., p. 134.
[2] *The Soviet's Fight for Disarmament* (New York; n.d.), p. 34.

Litvinov put it, "to find a common language" with the other powers? It is easy to understand the embarrassed and irritable reaction of the other nations, which were trying—without notable success—to fit disarmament into a more general program encompassing security and arbitration. But to the charge that the Soviet scheme could not guarantee security or destroy international distrust, Litvinov simply answered that he was not offering a universal remedy ("We cannot recommend you any such panacea, for we know you would not entertain it for a moment.") .[3]

The other powers also had suspicions, though they were reluctant to express them, that the real intent of the Soviets was to weaken other states militarily and increase the effectiveness of the Communist weapons of insurrection and subversion. To this charge Litvinov replied with a mixture of frankness and disingenuousness. He stated that the Soviet government had no intention of participating with any other government in working out questions "regarding the class war or the struggle against revolution," and asked caustically if the purpose of armaments was to put down possible revolution. He also gave the customary Soviet denial of any responsibility for the actions of the Comintern.

A more serious doubt about the sincerity of the Soviet disarmament proposal arises from the basic premises of Leninism. The argument has been advanced that the Soviets by their own theory could not be advocates of disarmament: true peace is achievable only in a classless and stateless world. Such a world cannot come about by a process of peaceful evolution, but involves the establishment of the dictatorship of the proletariat. This dictatorship explicitly rests on force, of which the Red army is

[3] *The Soviet Union and Peace,* pp. 188-9.

equally explicitly a vital element. Hence, complete disarmament would be, for the Soviets, a "suicidal act."[4] This argument, however, is not wholly conclusive, since the Communist response would be that their analysis and consequent tactics were based on the real nature of modern imperialist states. If these states were to prove capable of overcoming their own nature by the act of disarmament, then the Soviet Union could likewise disarm the Red army. Such indeed was the implication in Litvinov's report to the Fifteenth Congress of the Russian Communist party:

> If the capitalist governments doubt our sincerity, they have a simple means of proving it. This means is their adherence to our programme. Let them decide on this. If they do not do this, if they cannot do this, if they do not wish to do this, then, before the whole world, against their will, they testify to the fact that a proposal for full disarmament and abolition of war can emanate only from the Soviet government; that it can be accepted and executed only when the Soviet system has been adopted by all the countries of the world, when their policies and principles will, of course, be at one with those by which the USSR is guided.[5]

In retrospect the real criticism to be made of Litvinov's stand on disarmament in the 1920's is not that it was insincere propaganda but that by viewing the world in the black and white of Communism *vs.* Capitalist Imperialism it misrepresented the significance of the relations between the non-Communist powers, and reduced them to the sinful bickerings of reprobates.[6] By making the sweeping

[4] See T. A. Taracouzio: *War and Peace in Soviet Diplomacy* (New York; 1940), pp. 266–76, for an able expression of this argument.
[5] *The Soviet Union and Peace,* p. 162.
[6] In his report to the Fifteenth Congress Litvinov said: "It may be said that on all questions considered by the Commission, a clear sharp line was drawn between us and the other delegates. It was a case of *we* and *they*. And this is as it should be."

generalization that "economic competition is the true cause of war," it falsely placed the issue of security, which could not be separated from disarmament, on an all-or-nothing basis.

With such an outlook collective security was, of course, impossible. In 1924 Chicherin had said:

> The Soviet Government therefore rejects any plan for an international organization which implies the possibility of measures of constraint being exercised by any international authority whatsoever against a particular State. . . . In the present international situation, it is impossible in most cases to say which party is the aggressor. Neither the entry into foreign territory nor the scale of war preparations can be regarded as satisfactory criteria. . . . The Soviet Government considers, therefore, that it is absolutely impossible to adopt the system of deciding which State is the aggressor in the case of each conflict and making definite consequences depend upon such decision.[7]

In 1928 Litvinov expressed somewhat the same view: "Owing to the lack of exact criteria as to what constitutes an offensive and what a defensive war, the system of regional guarantee pacts based upon mutual assistance . . . may end in something perilously akin to the prewar system of alliances and other military and political combinations."[8]

Even the innocuous Kellogg Pact was regarded with deep suspicion. Chicherin, in August 1928, flatly termed it "an organic part of the preparation for war against the USSR." Litvinov, too, intimated that the proposal to prohibit war as an instrument of national policy implied the possibility of war as an instrument for the defense of

[7] Degras, I, 432–3.
[8] *The Soviet Union and Peace*, p. 167.

"civilization" against "barbarism"—i.e., against the Soviet Union.[9] Nevertheless, after having criticized its origins, its omissions, and its reservations, Litvinov not only announced that the U.S.S.R. would subscribe to the pact but then turned it to advantage by achieving a regional reaffirmation of its terms through the Litvinov Protocol, signed by the Soviet Union and most of its Western neighbors, in February 1929. The Protocol, however, represented "negative security"; it was not a step toward positive cooperative action. When, in 1929, the United States government attempted to invoke the Kellogg Pact in the Russian-Chinese dispute in Manchuria, Litvinov brusquely rejected all efforts at diplomatic intervention and declared that the Pact did not provide any one of its signatories with the function of being its guardian. Clearly, he was not thinking of collective security at this point.

In July 1930, Chicherin, who had been in ill health for some years, was retired, and Litvinov became chief of the Narkomindel. It is generally agreed that the relations between the two men were far from friendly. Their temperaments clashed, each was suspicious of the other's intentions, and Litvinov, who, despite his amiable appearance, was not an easy person to get on with, appears to have been not overly scrupulous in his ambitions to become Foreign Commissar.[1]

With regard to a new course in foreign policy, Litvinov, on July 25, 1930, informed correspondents that his ap-

[9] Louis Fischer (*Men and Politics*, pp. 88–9) states that neither Litvinov nor Chicherin really believed that the Soviet Union was threatened with attack in 1927–8. Litvinov is quoted as saying: "That was merely idle gossip here of some people and the press. . . . It is wrong to suppose, as many of us do, that Russia is the center of all international affairs. . . ."

[1] See A. Barmine: *Memoirs of a Soviet Diplomat* (London; 1938), pp. 217–18.

pointment did not imply any change, not only because
he had been for ten years a close associate of Chicherin's
but because, under the dictatorship of the proletariat,
foreign policy was determined by the will of the working
masses and hence not subject to fluctuations.[2] Nevertheless, the German ambassador in Moscow, Dirksen, felt, or
so he related twenty years later, that his task had become
more difficult because Litvinov was not a really convinced
adherent of the Rapallo policy of German-Soviet cooperation but gave it only lip service.[3] Dirksen went on to say,
however, that Litvinov did not really deviate from the
German orientation until the Nazi seizure of power gave
him the perhaps not-unhoped-for opportunity to be one
of the first to abandon the Rapallo connection.

In fact, it was not his new post as Foreign Commissar
but, rather, developments abroad between 1931 and 1933
which led Litvinov to a new course. The process was gradual, but several stages may be observed.

The Soviet Union continued its policy of signing
neutrality and nonaggression pacts with its neighbors.
Treaties were made with Turkey, Lithuania, Iran, and
Afghanistan between 1925 and 1927. A new treaty with
Afghanistan was signed on June 24, 1931. Then, in Sep-
tember 1931 Japan launched its attack on Manchuria. On
January 21, 1932, the Soviet Union and Finland signed a

[2] M. Litvinov: *Vneshniaia politika* SSSR (Moscow; 1937), p. 59.
[3] Herbert von Dirksen: *Moskau, Tokio, London: Erinnerungen
und Betrachtungen zu 20 Jahre deutscher Aussenpolitik, 1919–
1939* (Stuttgart; 1950), pp. 94–5. Dirksen also commented: "Although he [Litvinov] almost passionately denied any deviation
from the pure Rapallo doctrine, his sympathies were with Great
Britain, where he had passed the years of his exile and met his
wife. So he had to be earnestly admonished from time to time
when he was disposed to deviate from the correct faith to the
Western heresy."

treaty which resembled its predecessors, but included a significant new clause: "Should either High Contracting Party resort to aggression against a third Power, the other High Contracting Party may denounce the present treaty without notice." This clause appeared in all subsequent Soviet nonaggression treaties up to, but definitely not including, the pact with Germany of August 1939.[4]

If this double negative—denouncing a nonaggression pact—be considered a positive step, it may be concluded that this initial move toward collective security, at least by indirection, was stimulated by the first overt aggression of the 1930's.

Litvinov, however, still challenged the possibility of improving international relations except by the path of disarmament. On February 11, 1932, at the Disarmament Conference he declared: "Security against war must be created. This security can never be achieved by round-about ways, but only by the direct way of total general disarmament. This is no communist slogan. The Soviet delegation knows that the triumph of socialistic principles, removing the causes giving rise to armed conflicts, is the only absolute guarantee of peace. So long, however, as these principles prevail only in one-sixth of the world, there is only one means of organizing security against war, and that is total and general disarmament."[5]

A year later, on February 6, 1933—that is, after Hitler had come to power—Litvinov took a different line. He expressed, somewhat reluctantly, his willingness to consider the French security proposals, and in conjunction with a French plan submitted a draft definition of aggression. He was now attempting to supply the criteria which

[4] Such pacts were signed with Estonia, Latvia, Poland, and France in 1932, and with Italy in 1933.
[5] *The Soviet Fight for Disarmament*, p. 23.

in 1928 he had said were lacking. Litvinov's original draft, which defined as aggressions declarations of war, invasions without a declaration, bombardments and naval attacks, landings and unpermitted occupations, and blockades, did not include a notable phrase, subsequently added by a subcommittee of the Disarmament Conference: "Provision of support to armed bands formed on its territory which have invaded the territory of another state, or refusal, notwithstanding the request of the invaded State, to take on its own territory all the measures in its power to deprive these bands of all assistance or protection."[6] Moreover, Litvinov's original draft in its second clause was far more vigorous than the subsequent convention in spelling out the political, military, economic, or other considerations which could *not* serve as an excuse or justification for aggression as defined: in substance, revolutionary régimes were not to be subject to retaliation for their revolutionary acts of expropriation and civil violence, "backward areas" were not to be exploited by force or penalized by gunboat assault for their actions against capitalist exploitation. It is interesting to note, in view of the publicity later given to the definition of aggression, that Litvinov said frankly, "I admit, however, that the Soviet delegation itself attributes infinitely greater importance to the second clause in its declaration."[7] Thus, the

[6] It is worth noting that when the U.S.S.R. in November 1950 presented a definition of aggression to the Political Committee of the U.N. General Assembly, it reverted to the original Litvinov formulation—i.e., without mention of indirect aggression by armed bands—and not to the revised formula accepted by the Soviet Union in 1933 and used in its treaties with neighboring powers.

[7] League of Nations: *Records of the Conference for the Reduction and Limitation of Armaments*, Series B, Minutes of General Commission, II, 238.

Soviet Union was at this time definitely less interested in establishing a criterion for aggression—which could provide the basis for collective measures—than in protecting its position as a revolutionary state in a presumably hostile world.

A modification of the convention was proposed by a subcommittee on May 24, 1933 and was accepted by the Soviets. While it fared no further at the Disarmament Conference, at the London Economic Conference Litvinov proposed that Russia and its neighbors sign this convention. The proposal was accepted, and in July 1933 a series of treaties bound the Soviet Union, Afghanistan, Estonia, Latvia, Persia, Poland, Rumania, Czechoslovakia, Turkey, Yugoslavia, Finland, and Lithuania to accept this definition of aggression.

On December 29, 1933, shortly after his return from the United States, where he had successfully negotiated for American recognition,[8] Litvinov delivered an important speech to the Central Executive Committee of the U.S.S.R. In this speech a distinct change in outlook was apparent. The era of "bourgeois pacifism" had come to an end; new and dangerous ideologies were arising. But whereas

[8] For the negotiations leading to the establishment of American-Soviet diplomatic relations and for an account of the mutually disappointing aftermath, see *Foreign Relations of the United States: Diplomatic Papers: The Soviet Union, 1933-1939* (Washington, D.C.; 1952). American-Soviet relations are not discussed here primarily because they were not of great importance to Litvinov's major diplomatic efforts. As George F. Kennan wrote from Moscow in November 1937: "When he can be found in Moscow, Litvinov has frequently shown a reluctance to discuss topics other than those he considers to be major political matters. These seem at present to be the success or failure of efforts to induce other states to take strong measures against Germany, Italy and Japan. The result is that few of the current problems of Soviet-American relations attract his interest" (ibid., p. 447).

Litvinov had previously tended to lump all capitalist states together, he now differentiated between actively belligerent powers, those that were temporarily passive but that would not mind a bit of fighting in the world, especially if it were directed against the U.S.S.R., and those powers actively interested in the preservation of peace. With regard to the latter, "I am not entering into an estimation of the motives for such a policy, but am merely stating a fact which is highly valuable to us." Moreover, while stressing that the Soviet Union was perfectly capable of defending itself, "and even the approaches to it," he went on to say that "the maintenance of peace cannot depend upon our efforts alone. It depends upon the cooperation and assistance of other countries as well. By striving, therefore, toward the establishment and maintenance of friendly relations with all countries we devote particular attention to the strengthening of relations and maximum *rapprochement* with those countries which, like ourselves, furnish proof of their sincere desire to preserve peace and show that they are prepared to oppose any violators of peace."[9]

The chief troublemakers, of course, were Germany and Japan, to whom Litvinov devoted a considerable amount of attention. He pointed out that for ten years Germany and Russia had enjoyed particularly close political and economic relations, which were advantageous to both powers. Nevertheless, relations had deteriorated beyond recognition in the course of the last year. The new German régime was showing itself openly hostile to the Soviet Union; its leaders in the past had frequently advocated an anti-Soviet policy, which they had not disavowed since they had come to power. He denied that the Nazi attack

[9] *Vneshniaia politika* SSSR (Moscow; 1937), pp. 74–96.

on the German Communists was the source of friction: "We have, of course, our own opinion of the German régime. We are, of course, sensitive to the sufferings of our German comrades, but we Marxists are the last who can be reproached for permitting our feelings to dictate our policy." He emphasized that the Soviet Union desired good relations with Germany, but that the responsibility lay with the new régime to desist from its current attitude. In concluding, Litvinov fell back upon the older view that the U.S.S.R. was, after all, surrounded by capitalist powers and had ultimately to rely upon the Red army, navy, and air force.

In passing, it is interesting to compare this speech with the one delivered by Stalin to the Seventeenth Congress of the Communist party a few weeks later, on January 26, 1934.[1] While the main lines of foreign policy were quite similar, there was a certain difference in emphasis. Stalin's speech, naturally, was more pontifical and grimmer in tone. He expounded at greater length on the reasons for the changes in the world scene, stressing as always the economic crisis of capitalism. (Litvinov had given less weight to this, and suggested such other factors as the rise of a new generation which had not experienced war.) His talk was more "revolutionary": "The masses of the people have not yet reached the stage when they are ready to storm capitalism; but the idea of storming it is maturing in the minds of the masses." While criticizing the attitude of the new German régime, he was by no means friendly to the "peaceloving" capitalist powers. He denied any new orientation: "Our orientation in the past and our orientation at the present time is towards the U.S.S.R., and towards the U.S.S.R. alone."

[1] J. Stalin: *Problems of Leninism*, 11th ed. (Moscow; 1940), pp. 470–86.

The year 1933 seems definitely to have marked a major turning point in Litvinov's diplomatic orientation. To be sure, in subsequent years Communist spokesmen would say that the Soviet Union had anticipated the mounting crisis of the 1930's and point to a multitude of statements about the precarious state of the capitalist world and the emergence of fascism. But in these earlier statements the jeremiads against the capitalist world were general volleys against all the Western Powers, just as the term "fascism" was a general epithet for quite indiscriminate use in domestic politics. The specific menace of a National Socialist Germany was something else again, and it took the unpleasant experiences of 1933 to bring Litvinov, and the Soviet Union, to the position he adopted in his speech at the end of the year.

For the next two and a half years, however, Litvinov proceeded in high gear down the road of collective security and cooperation with the peace-loving powers. These were the years when the U.S.S.R. joined the League, when mutual-assistance pacts were signed with France and Czechoslovakia, and when Litvinov made some of his most constructive pronouncements on the means to preserve peace, which he now declared to be "indivisible."

In the spring of 1934, on May 29, Litvinov was prepared to admit that "international life and particularly political events in some countries during recent years had prevented the [Disarmament] Conference from carrying out its direct task of drawing up a disarmament convention." After all, however, disarmament was only a means to an end: "Could not the Conference feel its way towards other guarantees for peace?"—a possibility he had categorically denied some years earlier. He then went on to say: "Even if there should be dissident States, that should by no means prevent the remainder from coming still more closely together to take steps which would strengthen their own security."[2]

In line with this approach was a new and amiable view toward the League of Nations. As late as December 1933 Litvinov had denied that Russia was likely to join the League in any foreseeable future, but by the following spring his attitude was quite different, and in September the U.S.S.R. obtained a permanent seat in the Council. Of course, one specific reason for joining the League was that a mutual-assistance pact with France, the negotiations for which began in 1934, could be reconciled with the Locarno Treaty only if France's partner were a member of the League.[3]

Although Litvinov was unsuccessful in persuading Germany to join in guaranteeing the Eastern European frontiers or in creating an Eastern Locarno Pact, France and Russia did achieve a mutual-assistance pact, which was signed on May 2, 1935. On May 16 a Soviet-Czech mutual-assistance pact was signed, with provisions similar to those of the French pact, but stipulating that they should come into force only if France gave assistance to the country attacked.

Although the Soviet Union was thus drawing closer to some of the capitalist powers, at the same time, in 1935 and 1936, the Fascist states struck three decisive blows at the structure of European peace: Germany's repudiation of disarmament, the Italian attack on Abyssinia, and the march into the Rhineland. While each of these events did not directly concern the U.S.S.R. and while the Soviet government did not actually take any important measures,

[2] League of Nations: *Records of the Conference for the Reduction and Limitation of Armaments,* Series B, III, 657–61.
[3] Max Beloff: *The Foreign Policy of Soviet Russia,* 2 vols. (London; 1947, 1949), I, 135.

a good deal of Litvinov's positive reputation rests on the speeches he delivered in response to these actions.

In his speech of April 17, 1935, he stated that while the Soviet Union neither favored the Versailles Treaty nor was bound by it, the German action did violate the Covenant of the League, and "one of the foundations of peace is the observance of international relations directly affecting the security of nations."[4] He agreed in principle to the right of equality of armament, but not "if a country which demands or assumes the right to arm is exclusively led by people who have publicly announced as the programme of their foreign policy a policy which consists, not only in revenge, but in the unrestricted conquest of foreign territory and the destruction of the independence of whole States."

On September 5, 1935, when Italy was threatening Abyssinia, he pointed out that while the U.S.S.R. had no interests involved, the Italian action could set a dangerous precedent: "The repetition of the precedent would certainly have a cumulative effect and, in its turn, would stimulate new conflicts more directly affecting the whole of Europe."[5]

On September 14, in speaking of the Fascist powers' technique of advocating bilateral pacts, he stated:

We know of another political conception that is fighting the idea of collective security and advocating bilateral pacts, and this not even between all States but only between States arbitrarily chosen for this purpose. This conception can have nothing in common with peaceful intentions. Not every pact of nonaggression is concluded with a view to

4 Maxim Litvinov: *Against Aggression* (New York; 1939), pp. 18–19.
5 League of Nations: *Official Journal,* 16th Year, No. 11 (November 1935), 1142.

strengthening general peace. While nonaggression pacts concluded by the Soviet Union with its neighbors, include a special clause for suspending the pact in cases of aggression committed by one of the parties against any third State, we know of other pacts of nonaggression which have no such clause. This means that a State which has secured by such a pact of nonaggression its rear or its flank, obtains the facility of attacking with impunity third States.[6]

Perhaps this statement indicates why Litvinov was not quite the man to negotiate the German-Soviet pact of August 1939.

When Germany marched into the Rhineland in March 1936, Litvinov again urged collective action: "One cannot fight for the collective organization of security without taking collective measures against the violation of international obligations. We, however, do not count among such measures collective capitulation to the aggressor."[7]

His funeral speech, on July 1, 1936, for the demise of Abyssinia was one of his best. "We are gathered here," he began, "to close a page in the history of the League of Nations, the history of international life, which it will be impossible to read without a feeling of bitterness." The League had been unable to maintain the territorial integrity and political independence of one of its members, and it was possible that the League itself would be declared bankrupt. Litvinov undertook to combat this defeatist mood and to strengthen the collective security provisions of the Covenant:

I say we do not want a League that is safe for aggressors. We do not want that kind of League, even if it is universal,

[6] League of Nations: *Official Journal, Special Supplement to No. 138,* 73.
[7] *Against Aggression,* p. 23.

because it would become the very opposite of an instrument of peace. . . .

We must educate and raise people up to its lofty ideas, not degrade the League. We must seek to make the League universal, but we must not by any means make it safe for the aggressor to this end. On the contrary, all new members and all ex-members wishing to return must read on its portals: "Abandon all hope of aggression and its impunity all ye who enter here." . . .

As for myself, I would rather have a League of Nations that tries to render at least some assistance, even if it proves ineffective, to a victim of aggression, than a League of Nations that closes its eyes to aggression and lets it pass unperturbed. . . .

In an ideal League of Nations military sanctions, too, should be obligatory for all. But if we are yet unable to rise to such heights of international solidarity, we should make it our concern to have all continents, and for a start, at least all Europe, covered with a system of regional pacts, on the strength of which groups of States would undertake to protect particular sectors from aggression.[8]

Finally, on September 28, 1936, he warned against the sense of apathy that was spreading under the impact of the Axis: "The legend of the invincible aggressor is being created even outside his country; it is engendering fatalistic and capitulatory sentiments in some countries, which gradually—sometimes even without their noticing it—are beginning to lose their independence and are becoming vassals of the aggressor. Thus begins the process of the formation of a hegemony which is to culminate in the crushing of all refractory countries by force of arms."[9]

Toward the end of 1936, however, there were signs that the Soviet Union's new policy was not proving particularly

[8] Ibid., pp. 35–45.
[9] Ibid., p. 49.

fruitful. The growing menace of Germany, Italy, and Japan was not being checked. The efforts at collective security did not develop into anything substantial, and indeed the outbreak of the Spanish Civil War introduced new strains in the relations between the Soviets and France and Great Britain. The Popular Front adopted by the Comintern did not diminish the suspicions of the non-Communist states, which continued to find that the activities of domestic Communists were a major impediment to collaboration with the Soviet Union. The great purges within Russia were under way and served to weaken Western confidence in the character and stability of the Soviet régime.

In Litvinov's speech before the Extraordinary Eighth Congress of Soviets, on November 28, 1936, a new note, or rather an old one, made its appearance. After commenting on the danger of Fascism, not as a form of government but as a source of external aggression, after stressing the specifically anti-Soviet content of the anti-Comintern pact (he clearly had very accurate information on its secret terms), Litvinov waxed bitter over the policy of nonintervention in Spain, and uttered a definite word of warning to the non-Fascist powers:

> The Soviet Union, however, does not beg to be invited to any unions, any *blocs*, any combinations. She will calmly let other States weigh and evaluate the advantages which can be derived for peace from close cooperation with the Soviet Union, and understand that the Soviet Union can give more than receive. . . .
>
> Other States, other territories are menaced most. Our security does not depend upon paper documents or upon foreign policy combinations. The Soviet Union is sufficiently strong in herself.[1]

[1] Ibid., pp. 78–9.

From this time on, in Litvinov's speeches and reported statements two distinct themes are detectable: on the one hand, a continued appeal for collective security; on the other, increasing animus against Great Britain and France and the threat of a Soviet return to isolation. The first theme needs no further development as it is largely the exposition of the principles set forth in the preceding two or three years. The second and ominous theme tends to become more and more dominant.

On February 4, 1937, Litvinov complained to the United States ambassador, Joseph E. Davies, that "he could not understand why Great Britain could not see that once Hitler dominated Europe he would swallow the British Isles also. He seemed to be very much stirred about this and apprehensive lest there should be some composition of differences between France, England and Germany."[2] On February 15 he said that "Germany was concerned solely with conquest and it was a mistake to magnify Hitler's importance by engaging in discussions of the character which France and England were projecting."[3]

In a speech to the electors of Leningrad, on November 27, 1937, Litvinov reiterated the old theme that imperialism was inherent in all bourgeois states, and was heavily sarcastic about the efforts of France and Britain to pretend that the Fascist powers were not aggressive: "I see it is a puzzle to you how experienced bourgeois diplomats could fail to understand the meaning of the aggressor's tactics. You think they are only pretending to disbelieve the aggressor's statements and, under cover of negotiations for confirmations and explanations, they are groping for a deal with the aggressor. You can think so if you like, but

[2] Joseph E. Davies: *Mission to Moscow* (New York; 1941), p. 60.
[3] Ibid., p. 79.

my position does not allow me to express such doubts, and I must leave them to your responsibility."[4]

In December Litvinov had an interview with a foreign correspondent in which he was reported, some years later, to have made the following significant remarks:

> Anti-Comintern Pact? What nonsense! Can you never look at things without your cheap bourgeois prejudice? The Anti-Comintern Pact is no threat to the Soviet Union. It is dust in the eyes of the Western democracies. . . . Ideologies mean little to the Fascist brigands. The Germans have militarized the Reich and are bent on a brutal policy of gangsterism. Those contemptible peoples, the Japanese and Italians, are following at the German heels, hoping to share in the spoils of German conquest. It is the rich capitalist countries which will fall an easy prey. The British and French peoples are soft under leaders who are blind. The Soviet Union is the last foe to be attacked by the Anti-Comintern powers. They will loot your countries, but we have the Red Army and a vast extent of territory. . . .
>
> Hitler and the generals who control Germany read history. They know that Bismarck warned against war on two fronts. They know that he urged the reinsurance policy with Russia. They believe the Kaiser lost the first world war because he forgot Bismarck's admonitions. When the Germans are prepared at last to embark upon their new adventures, these bandits will come to Moscow to ask us for a pact.[5]

According to this report, he predicted the *Anschluss* and the attack on Czechoslovakia, and pointed out that the Soviet Union need not come to Czechoslovakia's aid unless France did: "Well, France won't fight. France is through."

By the spring of 1938 Litvinov had adopted a com-

[4] *Against Aggression*, pp. 106–7.
[5] J. T. Whitaker: *We Cannot Escape History* (New York; 1943), pp. 207–8.

paratively passive role, though still affirming that the Soviet Union was ready to join in collective action to arrest further aggression, and was willing to discuss measures within the League or outside it. In March 1938 he told Davies that Czechoslovakia would probably fall because it lacked confidence in France; for that matter "France has no confidence in the Soviet Union, and the Soviet Union has no confidence in France. . . . The only thing that would prevent a complete Fascist domination of Europe was a change of government or policy in Great Britain." He appeared to envisage within the near future a Europe dominated by Fascism and opposed only by Great Britain on the West and the U.S.S.R. on the East.[6]

The prolonged Czechoslovak crisis of 1938 is far too complex for even summary discussion here. In general, it may be said that Litvinov, publicly and apparently privately, stood by the position that the Soviet Union would honor its obligations to Czechoslovakia if France came to the latter's aid. On the other hand, he repeatedly indicated that the responsibility for taking the initiative lay with France, and this included the thorny question of obtaining Polish and/or Rumanian permission for Russian troops to come to Czechoslovakia's assistance.

There does not seem to be much evidence, however, that he was expecting Russia to be required to take forceful action. It is striking that neither the British nor the German diplomatic representatives in Moscow felt that the Soviet government showed any sign of preparing itself or the Russian people for the defense of Czechoslovakia. The German ambassador, Schulenburg, commented that Litvinov's speech of June 23, 1938, showed distinct aloofness and a desire to retain freedom of action. Moreover, "the

[6] Davies: *Mission to Moscow*, p. 291.

tone of the speech has remarkably little aggressiveness and strives to leave open all possibilities. The attempt to arrive at an objective attitude toward the policy of the Third Reich is striking."[7] On August 22, 1938, Litvinov, in a conversation with Schulenburg, was quite frank in charging Germany with aggression and a desire to destroy Czechoslovakia. He went on to say, however: "If the old democratic Germany still existed, the Czech question would have a quite different aspect for the Soviet Union." While the Soviet Union approved of national self-determination and had had no part in the creation of Czechoslovakia, the threat to its independence affected the balance of power: an increase in Nazi strength would be bad for the Soviet Union.[8] According to a British report the Germans felt that in this conversation Litvinov was opening the door for a possible German-Russian *rapprochement*.[9] Schulenburg, however, did not thus interpret his conversation, and its content as reported need not lead to such an interpretation.

Was Litvinov considering the possibility of independent Soviet action even if France failed to act? This question remains somewhat obscure. In May 1938 he asked the French ambassador, Coulondre, what France, the ally of Poland, would do in case the latter, having attacked Czechoslovakia, was itself attacked in turn by the U.S.S.R. Coulondre replied that the answer was obvious, since France was also allied with Czechoslovakia and both

---

[7] *Documents on German Foreign Policy, 1918–1945: From the Archives of the German Foreign Ministry* (Washington, D.C.; 1949——), Series D, I, 924.

[8] Ibid., II, 604, 630.

[9] *Documents on British Foreign Policy, 1919–1939*, ed. E. L. Woodward and Rohan Butler (London; 1949——), 3rd series, II, 141, note 3.

treaties were defensive. Coulondre also pointed out that France recognized that Russia was not bound to move unless France intervened. Litvinov replied: "That is right, but there is another hypothesis: the case in which the U.S.S.R. for one reason or another should intervene without France having moved."[1] The question naturally presents itself, as it did to Coulondre at the time, whether the Soviet Union was envisaging military action against Poland and whether such action was possible without a preliminary understanding with Germany.

As far as the Czechs themselves are concerned, it is still not altogether clear whether, and if so how, they were led to believe that Russia would aid them even if France did not. Apparently Litvinov, through the Soviet minister in Prague, Alexandrovsky, did inform the Czech government that if the case were submitted to the League of Nations and Germany were found an aggressor, the Soviet Union would give assistance regardless of France.[2] This was clearly not a very rash promise under the circumstances. It has also been stated, though the evidence seems less satisfactory, that Alexandrovsky later informed the Czech government that the Soviet government would come to the support of Czechoslovakia as soon as Moscow was informed that the League had been seized of the case and would not wait for a decision to be reached at Geneva.[3] Some years later Beneš referred to "the fact that, in spite of the insistence of Moscow, I did not provoke war with Germany in 1938."[4] Some light on this remark may be cast by a statement in a recent Soviet work: "More than that, J. V. Stalin,

---

[1] Robert Coulondre: *De Staline à Hitler* (Paris; 1950), p. 153.

[2] Cf. Beloff: *Foreign Policy*, II, 151.

[3] John W. Wheeler-Bennett: *Munich—Prologue to Tragedy* (New York; 1948), p. 127.

[4] Letter from Eduard Beneš to L. B. Namier, in Namier: *Europe in Decay* (London; 1950), p. 284.

in conversation with K. Gottwald, said that the Soviet Union was ready to give military aid to Czechoslovakia, even if France did not do this, but on the condition that Czechoslovakia defend itself and ask for Soviet assistance. Gottwald told Beneš to that effect."[5] Although this statement requires a good deal of elucidation, it would indicate that such approaches, if made, may not have been through diplomatic channels but through the Communist party. In any event there appears to be no direct evidence connecting Litvinov with any measures more extensive than those to which the U.S.S.R. was publicly committed: the Czech Treaty and the League of Nations. Furthermore, although Litvinov told the Germans that he thought France and England would assist Czechoslovakia, he seems to have been thoroughly skeptical. On September 16, in discussing with a foreign journalist ways and means of Soviet assistance, he remarked, "This is also unrealistic. . . . They have already sold Czechoslovakia down the river."[6]

In his last major speech in the League, on September 21, 1938, Litvinov bitterly criticized the record of the last few years:

A fire brigade was set up in the innocent hope that, by some lucky chance, there would be no fires. Things turned out differently, however. Fires have broken out in defiance of our hopes, but luckily not in our immediate vicinity: so let us dissolve the fire brigade—of course not forever, but merely temporarily. Directly the danger of any fire disappears, we shall reassemble the fire brigade without a moment's delay.

He also carefully relieved the Soviet Union of any responsibility in the debacle:

[5] *Diplomaticheskii Slovar'* (1950), II, 198.
[6] Fischer: *Men and Politics*, p. 561.

At a moment when the mines are being laid to blow up the organization on which were fixed the great hopes of our generation, and which stamped a definite character on the international relations of our epoch; at a moment when, by no accidental coincidence, decisions are being taken outside the League which recall to us the international transactions of prewar days, and which are bound to overturn all present conceptions of international morality and treaty obligations; at a moment when there is being drawn up a further list of sacrifices to the god of aggression, and a line is being drawn under the annals of all postwar international history, with the sole conclusion that nothing succeeds like aggression—at such a moment, every State must define its role and its responsibility before its contemporaries and before history. That is why I must plainly declare here that the Soviet Government bears no responsibility whatsoever for the events now taking place, and for the fatal consequences which may inexorably ensue.[7]

He concluded:

The Soviet Government takes pride in the fact that it has no part in such a policy, and has invariably pursued the principle of the two pacts I have mentioned, which were approved by nearly every nation in the world [the League Covenant and the Briand-Kellogg Pact]. Nor has it any intention of abandoning them for the future, being convinced that in present conditions it is impossible otherwise to safeguard a genuine peace and genuine international justice. It calls upon other Governments likewise to return to this path.

Despite these concluding remarks it was generally felt among European diplomats that the Munich agreement did mark the bankruptcy of the Litvinov policy and that the U.S.S.R. would inevitably examine other possibilities.

[7] *Against Aggression*, p. 127.

The German reaction is particularly interesting. Counselor of embassy in Moscow, von Tippelskirch, on October 3 and 10, 1938, wrote:

> That the policy of Litvinov has suffered a complete fiasco, that the war, from which chaos and weakening of Germany were expected, has not broken out, that the policy of pacts and alliances has failed, that the collective idea has collapsed, and that the League of Nations has disappointed the hopes reposed in it, can in my opinion not remain without consequences for Soviet policy. . . .
>
> In the light of our experiences it seems to me probable that Stalin will draw conclusions about personalities from the failure of Soviet policy. In that connection I naturally think in the first place of Litvinov, who has made fruitless efforts in Geneva throughout the crisis. . . .[8]
>
> Litvinov will certainly try to convince the Soviet Government that the policy hitherto pursued by him was the only right one and that it must be continued in the future as well. . . . If I judge Litvinov correctly, he will continue to defend his policy of collective action in the conviction that Germany's growth of power . . . will lead to a change in the European balance of power in which sooner or later a definite role must quite automatically fall to the Soviet Union. . . . In other words he will continue to recommend measures against the aggressors in the hope of having more success next time.[9]

This German observer was, perhaps, unduly persuaded that Litvinov still had the opportunity to pursue his policy, or that he really felt capable of pressing it vigorously any longer. Shortly after Munich, Potemkin, Litvinov's assistant, after coldly receiving Coulondre, burst out: "My poor friend, what have you done? As for us I do not see

[8] *German Documents,* Series D, IV, 602–5.
[9] Ibid., p. 605.

any other outcome than a fourth partition of Poland."[1]
And on October 16, Litvinov himself said: "Henceforth the
U.S.S.R. has only to watch, from the shelter of its frontiers,
the establishment of German hegemony over the center
and southeast of Europe. And if by chance the Western
Powers finally decide to wish to stop it, they must address
themselves to us, for—he added throwing me a sharp look
—we shall have our word to say."[2] He then went on to
remark that he had made the following declaration to Lord
Halifax: "Once its hegemony is solidly established in
Europe, and France neutralized, Hitler will be able to
attack either Great Britain or the U.S.S.R. He will choose
the first solution because it will offer him much greater
advantages with the possibility of substituting the German
Empire for the British Empire, and, to succeed in his undertaking, he will prefer to reach an understanding with
the U.S.S.R."

In his discussions with the British after Munich, Litvinov was distinctly cool; he saw no evidence that the Western powers would cease their policy of capitulation, and
said that the Soviet Union would probably remain "aloof"
henceforth, since its interests were not directly threatened.[3]
In late March 1939, in a conversation with R. S. Hudson,
Litvinov was reported as saying: "He foresaw in the not

---

[1] Coulondre: *De Staline à Hitler*, p. 165. On September 29, 1938,
Potemkin said to Schulenburg: "The Powers now taking part in
the destruction of Czechoslovakia would bitterly regret their
submission to militant nationalism. In the first place, Poland,
for there were a 'great many' Germans in Poland; in particular
it must not be forgotten that several million Ukrainians were
living in Poland, who were already begining to 'move'" (*German Documents*, Series D, II, 998).

[2] Coulondre: *De Staline à Hitler*, p. 171.

[3] E.g., his conversation with Sir William Seeds, February 19, 1939.
British Documents, 3rd series, IV, 124.

far-distant future a Europe entirely German from the
Bay of Biscay to the Soviet frontier and bounded, as it
were, simply by Great Britain and the Soviet Union. Even
that would not satisfy German ambitions, but the attack,
he said smiling happily, would not be directed to the
East."[4]

It is true that Litvinov was willing to embark on the
final round of fruitless negotiations after the German
march into Prague, but it was clear that he displayed no
confidence in the Western powers. On May 3, 1939, he
was relieved of his post.

From this review of Litvinov's diplomatic career several
general observations may be made. In the first place, his
advocacy of collective security was limited in time; before
the rise of the Fascist powers, he denied the possibility of
such methods of providing international security. Moreover, from 1936 on there is an increasing note of isola-
tionism: if the other powers would not cooperate the
Soviet Union could follow its own interests independently.
In the second place, the idea of collective security was
restricted conceptually. Basically the world was still divided into two camps and the Fascist powers belonged to
the capitalist camp. "Peaceful coexistence" was not in the
permanent order of things, nor were the motives inducing
certain capitalist powers to be peace-loving necessarily
fundamental or enduring. Litvinov's collective security is
not to be identified with the idealism of some of his Western admirers.

On the other hand, it is difficult to find evidence that
Litvinov had any revolutionary expectations in these years
or that by his diplomacy he was bent on fomenting strife.
To be sure, the Soviet Union's total impact abroad, its un-

[4] Ibid., p. 585.

official as well as its official activities, remained troublesome and disturbing. It is also true that Litvinov's speeches
to the Soviet audiences displayed a truculent and scornful
attitude toward the capitalist world which was moder-
ated though not entirely eliminated in his diplomatic ad-
dresses to the League. Even so, his speeches on collective
security in the League and elsewhere do have a most convincing ring of sincerity and urgency. By 1938 most foreign diplomatic observers in Moscow—Germans as well as
French and English—seem to have felt that Litvinov was an
ardent supporter of the course he had advocated since 1933.

If, with the above-mentioned qualifications, Litvinov's
campaign for collective security was something real and
not merely misleading oratory on his part, then the question arises whether his views and those of the Politburo
coincided.

II

From all that is known of the structure of the Soviet state
and the Communist Party it would be absurd to assume
that Litvinov could have pursued a diplomatic course at
odds with that desired by Stalin and the inner circle of
the Politburo. Clearly the general lines of his foreign
policy had the official blessing. Nevertheless, an examination of the available record does reveal a number of instances during his career in which Litvinov was reportedly
not in agreement with his superiors. Some of the more
illuminating examples may be given, in chronological sequence:

In 1919 a British naval officer, who had an interview
with Litvinov in Reval, reported that "M. Litvinov stated
that from the first he had opposed his Government's repudiation of their external debt, as he felt certain that

such a course would tend to unify the resistance of other nations against them."[5]

In 1924, according to Christian Rakovsky, Litvinov wished to recognize Rumanian sovereignty over Bessarabia in order to settle the matter. Opposed to his view were Rakovsky, Chicherin, and Stalin, who felt it desirable to maintain Bessarabia as a "Soviet irredenta."[6]

Litvinov seems not to have been convinced of the value of Soviet and Comintern maneuvers in the colonial and Asiatic world at the expense of relations with the Western powers. He is reported as having said, in March 1929, "I think an agreement with England about Afghanistan and the East generally is possible, but the government takes a different view."[7]

In 1938 it was the opinion of the German ambassador that the new evidence of Soviet antiforeign feeling shown in the closing of numerous consulates was not Litvinov's doing: "Litvinov has to accommodate himself to this predominance of domestic policy."[8]

In January 1938 both Zhdanov and Molotov publicly criticized the Foreign Commissariat, though not Litvinov in person, for its presumed lenience with France, which was accused of harboring anti-Soviet elements, terrorists, and diversionists.[9]

In the summer of 1938 Coulondre told Schulenburg that Litvinov was willing to agree to Soviet participation in defraying expenses occasioned by the withdrawal of volunteer troops from Spain, but had encountered opposition

[5] *British Documents*, 1st series, III, 659.

[6] Fischer: *Men and Politics*, p. 135.

[7] Ibid., p. 128. See also David Dallin: *The Rise of Russia in Asia* (New York; 1949), p. 240.

[8] *German Documents*, Series D, I, 905.

[9] Beloff: *Foreign Policy*, II, 113–14.

in the Politburo. Litvinov seemed willing to cut losses in the Spanish affair, but the Politburo had prestige considerations.[1]

On March 1, 1939, Schulenburg, referring to Soviet economic negotiations with Germany and Japan, remarked that "M. Litvinov does not regard M. Mikoyan's negotiations with a friendly eye at all. If by obstinacy toward Japan he can sabotage the zealous activities of the Commissar for Foreign Trade, he will intensify rather than moderate this line of action.[2]

Louis Fischer has remarked that Litvinov "has never by word or hint approved of Stalin's pact policy with Hitler."[3] It is obvious, of course, that the German-Soviet *rapprochement* of 1939 was hardly in the spirit of collective security, that the nonaggression pact of August 23 did not contain the escape clause in the event one of the signatories attacked a third power. On the other hand, as should be apparent from the above, it is not difficult to find a number of hints of a possible German-Soviet agreement in Litvinov's private remarks from 1937 on. Still, it is worth noting that after the German attack on the U.S.S.R. in June 1941, and after Stalin in his speech of July 3 had defended the wisdom of the nonaggression pact, Litvinov, in a broadcast in English on July 8, indicated that agreements of any sort with Hitler were worthless because the Nazi gang considered themselves above all conceptions of international obligations. While commenting on the failure to organize collective resistance, he stressed Hitler's technique of dividing his prospective victims: "His strategy is to knock down his victims and strike them one by one in an order prompted by circumstances. He intended first

---

[1] *German Documents*, Series D, III, 714.
[2] Ibid., IV, 628.
[3] Louis Fischer: *The Great Challenge* (New York; 1946), p. 46.

to deal with the Western countries so that he would be free to fall on the Soviet Union." Not only was this no defense of the German-Soviet pact—which would hardly have been a tactful approach to the British and American audience at whom the broadcast was directed—but the whole line of argument was that Hitler's treachery was inevitable and predictable.[4]

Finally, evidence of Litvinov's disapproval of Soviet policy following the Second World War has been provided by two American reporters writing shortly after his death. C. L. Sulzberger stated that on April 5, 1945, Litvinov, then an isolated figure in Moscow, expressed his pessimism about East-West relations: "The situation is developing badly. First, the Western Powers make a mistake and rub us the wrong way. Then we make a mistake and rub you the wrong way."[5] Richard C. Hottelet wrote that in June 1946 Litvinov indicated to him that the Soviets would continue pressing demands on the West. "As far as I am concerned the root cause is the ideological conception prevailing here that conflict between the Communist and capitalist worlds is inevitable." He declared that the Soviet rulers would not call on him for advice and had reverted to the outmoded concept of security in terms of territory.[6]

While it is difficult to weigh the importance of these scattered examples, they do seem to have a certain consistency: in each case Litvinov appears to have favored practical accommodation with the Western powers as against moves to create or abet revolution, disturbance, or international disorder. To be sure, such an attitude would be part of his diplomatic function: his job as Foreign

---

[4] *The New York Times*, July 9, 1941.
[5] *The New York Times*, January 3, 1952.
[6] New York *World-Telegram*, January 28–February 1, 1952.

Commissar was not made easier by the Communist temptation to kick things around.

Less tangible than these evidences of disagreements on
policy but perhaps as important are the subtler indications
of a difference in emphasis and interpretation. In a political system where all action and policy are dependent on a
"party line" enunciated by the supreme authority, emphasis and interpretation are all-important, especially since the
"line" is often not wholly unambiguous. For example, the
theme which underlies Soviet diplomacy throughout most
of the interwar period—"the temporary coexistence of the
two systems"—can in practice be given two entirely different meanings depending upon the emphasis accorded "temporary" or "coexistence." Although it is perilous to draw
conclusions from purely external evidence, there appear
to be a number of respects in which Litvinov's interpretation differed from that of the Politburo—Stalin and the
rather murky figures of his inner circle.

While Litvinov always acknowledged that the possibilities of cooperation with the capitalist powers were temporary, that ultimately the capitalist system was doomed
to destruction, in the period after Hitler came to power
he recognized the Nazi menace as something requiring the
cooperative resistance of the peace-loving powers, not as
the turbulent prologue to the victory of Communism. This
mood is quite apparent in his speech of December 29, 1933.
Yet at the same time, on December 31, 1933, the official
journal *Bolshevik* could still give the following interpretation of the German situation: "In Germany the proletarian
revolution is nearer to realization than in any other country; and victory of the proletariat in Germany means victory of proletarian revolution throughout Europe, since
capitalist Europe cannot exist if it loses its heart. . . . He
who does not understand the German question does not

understand the path of the development of proletarian revolution in Europe."[7] Stalin's speech of January 26, 1934, while less far out on the limb, is much more revolution-conscious than Litvinov's.[8] One receives the impression that the Politburo was reluctant and regretful in accepting the new course.

Indeed, Litvinov as a diplomat seems always to have found the irrepressible revolutionary yearnings of the Bolsheviks an uncomfortable problem. In a letter to an English negotiator in December 1919, he said: "From the point of view of the vital interests of both countries there should be no obstacle to the establishment of real peace, excepting the bogey of revolutionary propaganda. If formal guarantees from the Soviet Government on this point be considered insufficient, could not means of preventing this propaganda be devised without barring the way to mutual representation?"[9]

The change in the Comintern line at the Seventh Congress in 1935 did not really eradicate this difference. Although Litvinov's diplomatic policy of "collective security" and the Popular Front are often identified, it is doubtful whether this identification should be pressed too far, even though both had Stalin's approval in some fashion. A reasonably attentive reading of Dimitrov's speeches at the Seventh Congress can dispel the popular notion that the Comintern had now really concealed its hard revolutionary core. Certainly, the energetic behavior of the Comrades under the new line caused Litvinov perpetual embarrassment. In 1936, for example, Coulondre pointed out to him that the interference of the Comintern in

[7] Quoted in David Dallin: *Russia and Post-War Europe* (New Haven; 1943), p. 62.

[8] See above, p. 89.

[9] *British Documents*, 1st series, III, 740.

French internal affairs was imperiling the Franco-Soviet
pact. In response, Litvinov—after assuring him that the
Soviet Union had no intention of interfering and that the
Soviet ambassador in Paris had received instructions to
that effect, which he would make even more precise—was
obligated to fall back on the old claim that the Comintern
had nothing to do with the foreign policy of the Soviet
government. Coulondre felt, however, that Litvinov was
fully aware that this customary disclaimer of responsibility
for the Comintern carried no conviction. "But the question went beyond him. It concerned the other side of the
double ladder on the top of which sat Stalin alone."[1]

Although Litvinov frequently expressed disapproval and
suspicion of the capitalist nations and, in the years after
1936, was extremely critical of the policies of France and
Great Britain, he does not seem to have been so deeply
imbued with that xenophobia which has increasingly
blighted the perception of Soviet leaders. It should not be
forgotten that he lived a decade in England, from 1908 to
1918, during which time he settled rather thoroughly into
a middle-class existence and married an English wife.

With regard to Germany, while Litvinov certainly subscribed to the general line that the Soviet Union did not
desire bad relations with Germany and would welcome a
resumption of cordial relations should the German government drop its menacing attitude, he does not seem to have
shared the enthusiasm which a number of Russians and
Germans had for the Russo-German connection. Dirksen,
as mentioned earlier, felt that Litvinov was not a true be-
liever in the Rapallo policy and was pro-English at heart.
In March 1936, following the march into the Rhineland,
the Soviet statements concerning Germany seemed to dis-

[1] Coulondre: *De Staline à Hitler*, pp. 32–3.

play some confusion. On the one hand, Litvinov in the League castigated Germany's recent actions in very sharp terms; on the other, Molotov said to a French editor: "The main trend among our people, the trend which determines the policy of the Soviet Government, considers an improvement in relations between Germany and the Soviet Union possible. . . . The participation of Germany in the League of Nations would be in the interest of peace and would be favorably regarded by us."

"Even of Hitler Germany?" asked the French journalist.

"Yes, even of Hitler Germany."[2]

While there may be no logical contradiction between the two Soviet statements, they have a quite different flavor.

The German-Soviet pact of 1939 inevitably created the suspicion that some Soviet leaders, including Stalin, were always eager for a *rapprochement* with Germany and had made secret contacts with Hitler even during the period of so-called collective security. Coulondre, who said that he was convinced that Litvinov was, like himself, "a sincere worker for the Franco-Soviet entente within the framework of the League of Nations,"[3] also commented, "I am not even sure that during all that period of my mission in the U.S.S.R., certain clandestine contacts had ever ceased between Moscow and Berlin."[4] He was of the opinion that something was definitely in preparation in the spring of 1937, only to be dropped in April.[5] The former Soviet intelligence officer, Krivitsky, professed to know that in the spring of 1937 an agreement had been drafted by Stalin and Hitler, with one David Kandelaki as the

[2] See Beloff: *Foreign Policy*, II, 51–4.
[3] Coulondre: *De Staline à Hitler*, p. 32.
[4] Ibid., p. 45.
[5] Ibid., p. 125.

intermediary, but had broken down.[6] This source also stated, however, that the Commissariat for Foreign Affairs had no part whatever in this undertaking.

In general, even after one has made deductions for the fact that Litvinov, as a diplomat dealing with the outside, capitalist world, was likely to adopt a less revolutionary stance than Communists dealing with Communists or, perhaps, dictators with dictators, there still seems to remain a not unimportant difference between the diplomatic policy advocated or desired by him and the temper of the Politburo, a difference occasionally showing up in specific disagreements but more persistently if less tangibly in shadings of interpretation and emphasis. These, however, form a sufficiently coherent pattern to warrant the conclusion that there was a tension of ideas within the monolithic framework of the Soviet government. If so, is it possible to form any notion of the political or bureaucratic relations behind this tension?

III

Diplomacy as such did not stand very high in the hierarchy of instruments developed or revamped by the new Soviet

---

[6] W. G. Krivitsky: *In Stalin's Secret Service* (New York; 1939), pp. 225–6. The thesis that Stalin was, all along, seeking for a deal with Hitler encounters difficulties in having to explain all the anti-German steps taken by the Soviet Union between 1933 and 1938. Krivitsky contended that the entry into the League, collective security, the pact with France, the intervention in Spain were all undertaken with a view to making Hitler find it "advantageous to meet his [Stalin's] advances." This seems a singularly roundabout way to achieve a *rapprochement*. Still, this tactic of trying to win an ally by making things uncomfortable for him is not unknown in the history of diplomacy. William II and Holstein tried to woo Britain by the threat of a continental bloc against it.

order. Foreign considerations tended to rank below domestic considerations during most of the interwar period, and even in the field of foreign relations the diplomatic arm lacked the prestige of the revolutionary and the military arms. At the same time, because of the peculiar sensitiveness attaching to foreign policy decisions there came to be "a particularly close, direct, and continual relationship . . . between the Politburo and the Narkomindel in the conduct and control of foreign affairs."[7] Consequently the post of People's Commissar for Foreign Affairs did not, in itself, carry a great deal of weight in the Soviet system.

Nor did Litvinov, despite the fact that he was an "old Bolshevik,"[8] rank high in the Party. He was never in the all-important Politburo, though he was a member of the Party's Central Committee for a number of years. Two reasons may help to explain why he was never admitted to the inner circle despite his obvious ability and long record as a party member. He had not returned to Russia from England to participate in the Bolshevik Revolution. From the very first he was concerned not with the establishment of the revolutionary state but with its relations abroad. Moreover, even before the Revolution he seems to have been valued primarily as a competent technician. In Lenin's references to him during the war as "our legal representative in the International Socialist Bureau," the term "legal" is charged with the characteristic double

---

[7] Julian Towster: *Political Power in the USSR, 1917–1947* (New York; 1948), p. 162. Towster points out that in the late 1920's, while nearly all the governmental organs were scheduled to report before the Politburo, the Narkomindel apparently was not, presumably because decisions concerning foreign issues were continuously on the agenda of the Politburo itself.

[8] He joined the Russian Social Democratic Labor party in 1898 and was on Lenin's side when the latter formed the Bolshevik faction against the Mensheviks in 1903.

meaning of being official and public but not really part of the illegal or extralegal revolutionary core. While part of his function as Chicherin's second in the 1920's may have been as Bolshevik guardian over a former Menshevik,[9] it is doubtful whether in the long run his party status was any higher than that of his predecessor; in the opinion of the German ambassador who worked with both men, it was lower.[1]

Consequently, neither as People's Commissar nor as a Party member was Litvinov in a position to follow his own policy or even to initiate policy. Indeed, late in his career he is reported as remarking rather sourly: "You know what I am. I merely hand on diplomatic documents."[2]

It is, therefore, difficult to see just how Litvinov was in any position to differ significantly with the Politburo. Moreover, Litvinov's term in office overlapped the years of the Great Purges, in which, so it seems, even half-formed or possibly-to-be-formed disagreements were sufficient to destroy a man. Yet Litvinov retained not only his health but his post.

His success in surviving the purges was something of a surprise and miracle to contemporary observers. He was an old Bolshevik; old Bolsheviks were dropping like flies. He headed the Foreign Commissariat; the Foreign Commissariat and the embassies abroad were swept clean. The former Soviet diplomat Alexander Barmine comments on Litvinov's "inexplicably surviving all his friends and collaborators": "Two of Litvinov's four assistants were executed, the third was put in prison and the fourth disappeared. His old friends and personal protégés, Ambassadors

<hr />

[9] See, for example, Simon Liberman: *Building Lenin's Russia* (Chicago; 1945), p. 111.

[1] Dirksen: *Moskau, Tokio, London,* p. 94.

[2] Fischer: *Men and Politics,* p. 497.

Yurenev and Rosenberg, disappeared also. Almost all the
heads of departments of his ministry and the leading diplomatic personnel abroad, gathered and trained by him
over fifteen years, were shot. But Litvinov continued to
smile enigmatically. 'They were traitors; all is well!' Was
he so confident because he deemed himself indispensable,
or did he have to keep a good face because his family
were held as hostages?"[3] Litvinov does seem to have been
jolted by the arrest of his assistant, Krestinsky,[4] but in
general his recorded remarks indicate approval of the
purges as a necessity to rid the Soviet Union of treasonous
elements.

Inasmuch as the underlying intent of the purges remains
one of the major riddles of Soviet history,[5] it is impossible
here to unravel their meaning in the Foreign Commissariat. While some observers have been inclined to regard
the diplomatic housecleaning as a preparation for the
agreement with Hitler, the part played by foreign policy
considerations is by no means clear beyond the fairly obvious fact that people with foreign contacts and foreign
experiences were frequent victims, but this may have been
for reasons other than the direction of foreign policy itself.
The effect of the purge was to reduce even further any
independence of action or decision on the part of foreign
service officials, an increasing number of whom apparently
were attached to the NKVD, and to leave Litvinov a
general without an army.

[3] Alexander Barmine: *One Who Survived* (New York; 1945), p.
121.
[4] Davies: *Mission to Moscow*, p. 262.
[5] Two authors, with firsthand experience in the purges, have
enumerated seventeen theories which have been advanced to
explain the purges: F. Beck and W. Godin: *Russian Purge and
the Extraction of Confession* (New York; 1951). With unusual
reserve they do not pretend to know the answer.

As to Litvinov's own survival, a few comments may be made. In the first place, he may have been fortunate in the fact that while an old Bolshevik he had *not* been one of the inner circle which made the Revolution, and consequently had not become enmeshed in the struggle for power within the Party, a struggle which produced a very high death-rate among the contestants. Moreover, so long as the policy of "collective security" was officially upheld by the Soviet Union, Litvinov's removal or disappearance would have had unfavorable foreign repercussions. By the time he was dropped the purges had subsided. Finally, it is clear that Litvinov must have possessed in some sense or another Stalin's confidence. It is difficult to believe that for all his international political value he could have survived those years of unimaginable suspicion had Stalin not had confidence in his personal as well as his political loyalty. The thesis, however, that Litvinov really believed that Stalin was purging the Foreign Commissariat to rid it of a Fascist fifth column seems quite unlikely, especially since the course of the purges generally started with a suspected chief and spread out through the ranks of his associates and subordinates. Nor does the contrary thesis that Litvinov and Stalin were clandestinely retooling the Narkomindel for a German *rapprochement* carry conviction; besides making utter nonsense of Litvinov's public policy it increases the difficulty of accounting for his dismissal.

The conclusion that seems able to deal with these confused and contradictory problems most satisfactorily is the one which sees Stalin as always having several strings to his bow. If one assumes that he was capable of considering simultaneously two separate and even conflicting lines of policy, not making up his mind in advance but waiting to see how events developed, then it is possible, perhaps, to reconcile the elements of difference discussed above and the fact that Litvinov was not a victim of the purge.

According to this interpretation, which is the most this essay can attempt to offer, there were at least two contending lines of foreign policy within the Politburo, and perhaps within Stalin's own mind, in the 1930's: one, the "Litvinov policy," of which Litvinov himself was not only the agent but probably also the advocate and possibly even the formulator (even in a monolithic state ideas cannot all originate at the apex of the pyramid); the other, the policy which emerged with the pact of August 23, 1939, and acquired explicit characteristics in the two years following. Stalin, while perhaps inclined toward the second, was willing to give the first a trial, especially since no other possibility appeared profitable after 1933: the revolutionary line had brought few results and did not fit well with domestic developments; the Rapallo connection seemed impossible with Hitler's Germany behaving in an exceedingly unfriendly fashion. On the other hand, the "Litvinov policy" depended upon achieving results. When these failed to come about, the balance—whether between persons in the Politburo or between ideas in Stalin's own mind—would swing away from it. Thus, Litvinov's warnings after 1936 that "collective security" could be wrecked if the Western powers did not change their ways may be regarded as a reflection of a decision still in suspension in the Politburo, a forewarning of a course which he himself may not have favored but which was in the cards if collective security failed.[6]

[6] When discussing the possible failure of collective security, Litvinov often indicated that the U.S.S.R. might do well to return to isolation. The Molotov-Ribbentrop Pact was scarcely a return to isolation but, as it proved, a decision to collaborate in aggression (the purely defensive interpretation of Russia's ad-

This interpretation also seems able to meet the question of Litvinov's resignation on May 3, 1939. The terse Soviet announcement merely stated that his resignation had been at his request because of ill health. Since the war, however, the official Soviet explanation has been that in the spring of 1939, when the international situation was deteriorating, when the Soviet Union was threatened with a hostile combination of capitalist powers, "it was necessary to have in such a responsible post as that of People's Commissar for Foreign Affairs, a political leader of greater experience and greater popularity in the country than M. M. Litvinov."[7]

While this statement is true in the sense that the authority of the Politburo was now concerned with the immediate direction of foreign relations, it does not suggest the possibility of a change in policy. At the time, quite naturally, the Soviet government and its representatives abroad assured the other powers that the switch in Foreign Commissars meant no alteration in the direction of Soviet policy. These assurances were received with justified skepticism, however, and one of the most interested parties, Hitler, later said, "Litvinov's dismissal was decisive."[8] To

vances during the period of the pact seems inadequate in light of the documents published in *Nazi-Soviet Relations, 1939–1941: Documents from the Archives of the German Foreign Office*, ed. R. J. Sontag and J. S. Beddie [Washington, D.C.; 1948], esp. pp. 258–9). Hence in his occasional predictions that the Germans would seek a pact with the Soviet Union, Litvinov may have been predicting a development which he himself did not approve.

[7] *Falsifiers of History*, Supplement to "New Times" (Moscow), No. 8 (February 18, 1948), 9. See also *Diplomaticheskii Slovar*, II, 162, 675.

[8] "Notes on Hitler's Conference with his Commanders-in-Chief, August 22, 1939," *Documents on International Affairs 1939–46*, I, 446.

be sure, Stalin's speech of March 10 at the Eighteenth
Congress of the Communist Party had served to pave the
way, as had the remarks on April 17 by the Soviet am-
bassador in Berlin.[9] Nevertheless, it can be concluded that
Litvinov's retirement was a very important step in the
German-Soviet *rapprochement,* if only because he was a
Jew and had come to symbolize the effort at collective
security against German aggression.

While Litvinov's retirement certainly facilitated the
German-Soviet negotiations which led to the pact, was it a
mark of "no confidence" in him or his diplomacy? His
American biographer, whose account of the event was obtained directly from Litvinov during the latter's ambassadorship in the United States during the war, denies that
he was discharged or abruptly dismissed. According to this
account, Litvinov, after Munich, decided that a *rapprochement* with Germany was necessary, that he was an obstacle,
and suggested his own retirement. The resignation took
place untheatrically after a series of conferences with
Stalin, and Litvinov himself proposed his friend Molotov
as a successor.[1]

This interpretation has Litvinov's authority for its
authenticity. And while it is true that he was, in 1942–3,
an official representative of the Soviet government and
therefore not likely to stress conflicts in the conduct of
Soviet diplomacy, it is also true that he was often surprisingly frank in such matters and not inclined to allow
personal concerns to flavor his thinking. Nevertheless,
there are certain difficulties with this interpretation. The
postwar Soviet explanation seems to imply, quite ungra-

[9] *Nazi-Soviet Relations,* pp. 1–2.
[1] Pope: *Litvinoff,* pp. 441–2. The author is grateful to Pope for
his letter explaining that Litvinov had personally confirmed this
account of his resignation.

ciously if the change had been marked by full harmony, that Litvinov was not a big enough man for the job. The picture of Litvinov, not a member of the Politburo, nominating the powerful Molotov to be his successor, appears incongruous. Moreover, there is some evidence that Litvinov was in disgrace with fortune and Stalin's eyes. Early in May 1939 the unusually communicative and perhaps unreliable, Soviet chargé in Berlin, Astakhov, told Coulondre that for six months Litvinov's fall had been foreseeable, since he and Molotov were no longer in accord, and Stalin, while esteeming him, did not like him.[2] After his retirement he seems to have received a cold shoulder at Soviet public functions.[3] In a speech on August 31, 1939, Molotov criticized those "shortsighted people even in our own country who, carried away by oversimplified anti-Fascist propaganda, forgot about this provocative work of our enemies [the machinating Western European politicians],"[4] a remark that may be interpreted as a slap at Litvinov. On February 20, 1941, Litvinov was dropped from the Central Committee of the Communist Party for "inability to discharge obligations."[5]

It is possible, then, that Litvinov was under a cloud;

[2] Quoted in Georges Bonnet: *Fin d'une Europe* (Paris; 1946), p. 184.

[3] It may be worth mentioning that the daughter of a former NKVD official attached to the Foreign Commissariat has written that immediately after Litvinov's resignation and replacement by Molotov her father was purged as a part of a general though unexplained house-cleaning in that ministry (Nora Murray, née Korzhenko: *I Spied for Stalin* [New York; 1951], pp. 116–29.

[4] V. M. Molotov: *The Meaning of the Soviet-German Non-Aggression Pact* (New York; 1939), p. 8.

[5] According to Pope: *Litvinoff*, p. 460, this step was taken because "Stalin was determined to give no offense to the Germans." In that case it is difficult to see why Maisky, Soviet ambassador to Great Britain, should have been elevated to alternate membership on the Central Committee at the same time.

that Stalin had weighed his policy and found it wanting. At the same time he was not officially damned, partly because the policy connected with his name had been Stalin's also, at least nominally; partly, it would seem, because he might still be useful should circumstances change, as they did in June 1941. Still, the remainder of his career is an anticlimax. During his brief ambassadorship in the United States from 1941 to 1943 he was not the leading figure he had been in the 1930's. After the war he sank again into obscurity. At his death on December 31, 1951, he was a minor Soviet hero—with members of the Foreign Ministry as pallbearers, but no one from the Politburo. In the second volume of the *Soviet Diplomatic Dictionary,* published in 1950, the favorable but brief biography of Litvinov occupies 92 lines, as compared with 54 for Chicherin and 292 for Molotov. Stalin's accomplishments as a diplomat were, of course, too vast for inclusion or comparison.

IV

In retrospect Litvinov's "collective security" can be seen to have been largely a phrase, never a reality. Neither the Soviet Union nor the Western powers were ever really guided by the principle of common action against the rising danger from Germany; both ardently hoped that the hurricane, if it developed, would not come in their direction. The "appeasement" policies of France and Great Britain have been thoroughly criticized by disapproving citizens of those states. There was also, however, a corresponding tendency in Russia which sought a reconciliation with Nazi Germany. This tendency was naturally less apparent so long as the major force of Hitler's propaganda was directed against Soviet Communism.

Even Litvinov's position appears reasonably clear and unambiguous only during the short span from 1933 to

1936—before Germany was equipped to fight a war. After it was clear that the Third Reich was, willy-nilly, going to become a powerful military state, Litvinov's pleas for collective measures were interspersed with warnings of a Soviet return to isolation. By the time of the Munich crisis his support of collective security was form without content: he was sure that France and England would not move; the French, the British—and the Germans—were equally convinced the Russians would not move.

Nor, in the long run, did Litvinov's efforts to "find a common language" between the Soviet Union and the rest of the world succeed. This failure needs no emphasis today. Indeed, Litvinov may have been a cause for deepening the rift. The atmosphere of practical cooperativeness that he created partly concealed but in no way softened the hard core of the Stalinist régime. As a result, collisions with that hard core were not only bruising but carried the additional sting of disillusion.

Still, after this has been said and after one recognizes that future documentary revelations may further darken the picture of Soviet policy between the wars and present Litvinov in a more doubtful light, the late Foreign Commissar does have claim to two things of lasting significance: his ideas and his acumen as a diplomat. Regardless of the aims of Soviet foreign policy or of Litvinov's connection with those aims, the ideas he expressed in his major League speeches are important in themselves. Indeed, whole paragraphs describe, in mood as in content, the tasks facing the world today in its effort to check the new danger of Soviet expansion. His ability to detect the major trends in the 1930's and to anticipate the course of events indicates an extraordinary understanding of that decade. A recent historian of the League of Nations has remarked on Litvinov's role in that organization:

No future historian will lightly disagree with any views expressed by Litvinov on international questions. Whatever may be thought of the policy and purposes of his government, the long series of his statements and speeches in the Assembly, the Council, the Conferences, and Committees of which he was a member between 1927 and 1939 can hardly be read today without an astonished admiration. Nothing in the annals of the League can compare with them in frankness, in debating power, in the acute diagnosis of each situation. No contemporary statesman could point to such a record of criticisms justified and prophecies fulfilled.[6]

While one might quarrel with the inclusion of the years 1927–33, it is difficult to disagree with this conclusion for the six years between Hitler's coming to power and Litvinov's retirement from the diplomatic scene.

[6] F. P. Walters: *A History of the League of Nations*, 2 vols. (London; 1952), II, 712.

VI ❧ The Diplomacy of Colonel Beck

[1952]

AMONG THE PUBLIC FIGURES OF COUNTRIES OVERRUN BY NAZI Germany, Colonel Józef Beck, Poland's Foreign Minister from 1932 to 1939, has probably received the least sympathy. Despite his determined resistance to Hitler's threats in the crisis leading to the outbreak of the Second World War, he has been remembered as one of the Piłsudskian *epigoni,* as the man who refused to work with the Little Entente or the League of Nations, who pursued, in substance, a pro-German policy after 1934, who joined in the dismembering of Czechoslovakia, and, finally, as the man whose stubborn refusal to enter any combination with the Russians contributed to the failure of the Anglo-French-Soviet negotiations of the spring and summer of 1939.

After Poland's defeat and Beck's internment in Rumania, the world heard little of him. He died in obscurity, of tuberculosis, on June 5, 1944. Less than a year after his death the war of which his country was first victim came to an end, but Poland soon fell under the domination of the power that Beck always felt to be the ultimate enemy. This retrospective vindication of his Russian policy, the postwar publication of Polish, French, German, and British evidence bearing on his activities, and the recent appearance of Beck's own diplomatic memoirs[1] suggest a reappraisal of this controversial and rather elusive figure.

I

Although it has been said that Beck lacked diplomatic training,[2] it is doubtful whether his shortcomings as a statesman can be attributed to amateurishness. He did not, it is true, come to the Foreign Ministry from a career in the Diplomatic Service, but he was not lacking in experience. At the time of his fall, he was dean of European Foreign Ministers in terms of uninterrupted occupation of his post. Born in Warsaw in 1894, educated at the polytechnic school in Lwów and the *Exportakademie* in Vienna, he participated in the First World War as one of Piłsudski's legionnaires. During the period of confused fighting following the Russian Revolution and the collapse of Germany he seems increasingly to have been chosen for diplomatic missions, official and clandestine. In 1922 Piłsudski sent him as military attaché to the Polish legation in Paris. After a year he was abruptly recalled under un-

---

[1] Colonel Joseph Beck: *Dernier rapport: Politique polonaise 1926–1939* (Neuchâtel; 1951). Although these memoirs, three memoranda dictated between 1939 and 1943, are fragmentary and were intended as preliminary drafts, they are sufficiently complete to provide many insights into Beck's own view of his diplomatic role. Supplementing these, and of considerably greater value as a record of Polish foreign policy, is the journal of the Under-Secretary of State for Foreign Affairs, Comte Jean Szembek: *Journal, 1933–1939*, trans J. Rzewuska and T. Zaleski (Paris; 1952). This latter was published while the present essay was in galley proof and could be utilized only through a few footnotes.

[2] L. B. Namier: *Diplomatic Prelude, 1938–1939* (London; 1948), p. 438.

pleasant but somewhat obscure circumstances with, perhaps, a permanent feeling of rancor for certain French circles.[3]

Following his return from France he entered the Polish War College and appeared to be moving toward a military career. As an active participant in the *coup d'état* of 1926, however, he entered the circle of Piłsudski's close collaborators and was the Marshal's *chef de cabinet* between 1926 and 1930. Some time before 1930 Piłsudski is reported to have said to an official of the war ministry: "Do not count on Beck; you will never have him. M. Beck is not going to make his career in the army. M. Beck will go to Foreign Affairs, to be charged with responsibilities of high importance."[4] In December 1930 he became Under-Secretary of State in the Foreign Office and in November 1932 Minister of Foreign Affairs, replacing August Zaleski. For the next seven years he directed Poland's foreign policy, as Piłsudski's agent until latter's death in 1935, then largely on his own.

On the other hand, the French ambassador, Léon Noël, who found Beck "one of the most unusual, in certain respects one of the most mysterious, and above all one of the most interesting persons it has fallen to me to be associated with," was probably correct in his observation that Beck showed many of the characteristics of the young man who had climbed the ladder too rapidly and easily.[5] He was unduly confident in his own opinions and decisions.

---

[3] Léon Noël: *L'Aggression allemande contre la Pologne* (Paris; 1946), pp. 106–7. Noël, French ambassador in Poland from 1935 to 1939, adds, however: "It is not necessary to have recourse to this explanation to have the key to his policy in general and to his policy toward France in particular."

[4] Beck: *Dernier rapport*, p. xix.

[5] Noël: *L'Aggression allemande*, p. 20.

Moreover, he was of the generation of those who were twenty in 1914, a generation inclined to be self-consciously proud of its own "realism." Certainly, this tall, elegant, and rather Mephistophelean figure conveyed an impression of hardness without depth.

Noël also felt that while Beck had a talent for diplomacy, his experience in military intelligence accentuated a tendency to employ *deuxième bureau* techniques in his conduct of foreign policy. All his fellow diplomats found him evasive, uncommunicative, and tortuous in his methods. One of Noël's colleagues remarked that when Beck had occasion to speak the truth, one noticed it at once.[6] His own memoirs, however, do not wholly support this impression of elaborate deviousness. Indeed, he seemed to operate on surprisingly simple premises, and was irritable rather than conspiratorial in his reluctance to explain or discuss his actions. Many of his more roundabout maneuvers were made largely because they seemed to represent correct diplomatic form.

For, curiously enough, Poland, a new or at least resurrected state, displayed a distinctly old-fashioned diplomatic wardrobe. While the interwar diplomacy of the Western powers exhibits the powerful impact of political and public pressures, and while the diplomacy of Poland's two great neighbors, Germany and the Soviet Union, was but one branch of the foreign activities of an ideologically imbued totalitarian order, Beck's diplomacy had Metternichean overtones.[7]

To a degree, of course, this continuation of cabinet

---

[6] Ibid., p. 22, note 1.

[7] Beck, for example, thoroughly admired the "meticulous British protocol" surrounding the coronation of King George VI as the ideal atmosphere for diplomatic contacts and conversations (*Dernier rapport*, p. 128).

diplomacy was a reflection of Polish society and government. Poland's rather hectic experience with untempered parliamentarianism was brought to an end with Piłsudski's return to power in May 1926. The constitutional structure remained for a time, and even some parliamentary activity, but under the stern supervision of the old Marshal. The new constitution which came into effect in 1935 was distinctly authoritarian. Following Piłsudski's death, his associates, the "Colonels," governed in a quasidictatorial fashion. The régime was not Fascist or totalitarian, but, as one Pole said, merely carried on the spirit of the former gentry, "We are Poland."[8] In the confused circumstances of Polish domestic politics after Piłsudski's death, it would be difficult to say what might have been the eventual outcome of this system. In any event, it is clear that the government was not responsible to the Diet, the *Sejm,* and that Beck was able to retain his post, as were President Mościcki and Marshal Śmigly-Rydz, throughout successive changes in the Cabinet.

The setting in which important decisions on policy were reached is described in a passage in Beck's memoirs:

Marshal Piłsudski, in the spring of 1934, suggested to the President of the Republic of Poland that he convoke a conference on foreign policy, chaired by the President himself, and at which all the public figures who, since 1926, had performed the functions of Prime Minister should take part. The conference was held in the Belvedere Palace. . . . By the wish of the President it was the Marshal who opened the conference; he declared that this form of conference, bringing together the men who had assumed the responsibility for all the affairs of the country, appeared to him

[8] Władysław Grabski: *Idea Polski* (Warsaw; 1936), quoted in Raymond Leslie Buell: *Poland: Key to Europe,* 3rd edn. (New York; 1939), p. 99.

to be very useful at moments of great decisions or important events. Comparing this sort of conference with analogous and permanent institutions of other countries, in particular with the privy council of the King of England, of which the members were designated and convoked by the King himself, he vigorously urged the President to institute the custom.[9]

Beck, who thoroughly approved of this procedure, continued the practice of calling together the inner circle from time to time to discuss the foreign situation and the action to be taken. Apart from these conferences and infrequent statements to the Diet, Beck directed his foreign policy as he saw fit. The outcries of the opposition seem to have carried little weight in determining or altering his line of action. To be sure, as in all such situations, there were tensions and conflicts within the ruling oligarchy: Beck had been a rival of his predecessor Zaleski; no love was lost between the Foreign Minister and the inspector general of the army, Śmigły-Rydz, upon whom the greater part of Piłsudski's mantle had fallen and who seemed much more aware of the German military threat; friction between Beck and his subordinates was not infrequent. Even these intramural clashes, however, do not appear to have influenced Polish foreign policy markedly in the years after 1932.

It would seem, then, that the rather perverse course of Polish diplomacy under Beck is not to be explained by the fumblings of the inexperienced or by the vagaries of public opinion and party politics. For an understanding of Beck's policy it is necessary to go further: to examine the extremely difficult and complex foreign problems which Poland faced in the second decade of its independence and to follow the line of Beck's reasoning in his effort to resolve or contain them.

[9] Beck: *Dernier rapport*, p. 61.

II

Without question, geography has set the most difficult problems for Polish foreign policy. While the term "natural frontiers" has been badly misused—after all, the Rhine was singularly unsuccessful in delimiting French and German territory, and the ridge of the Carpathians failed to bring agreement between Rumanians and Hungarians—it is true that, except for the comparatively limited stretches of the Baltic Sea and the Carpathians, Poland lacked any striking geographical boundaries. More important than the topography, however, were the confused historical background of Poland's political frontiers and the intermingling of nationalities and languages. It is simply not clear where Poland begins and ends.

Rendering perilous the confusion over frontiers was the fact that Poland was wedged between Germany and Russia, both much more powerful and populous states, both with a record of partitioning Poland, and both, in the interwar period, with open or suspected designs on territory Poland had acquired from them. It cannot be overlooked that Poland's existence as an independent state resulted from a coincidence which could not have been anticipated in 1914: the collapse through defeat and revolution of both Russia and Germany. In consequence, Poland's security was inevitably endangered by the recovery and growth of either or both of these powers; if they should regain their strength and pursue a policy of close cooperation, Poland was, in all likelihood, doomed. In the last analysis, Poland's security as a state depended upon Russia and Germany being comparatively weak, as they were in the 1920's, or having hostile relations, as they did in the mid-1930's.

Poland, unfortunately, was not in a position to create or

to maintain either of these conditions, which were determined by factors largely beyond its control. Hence, the task of Polish diplomacy was twofold: first, to seek where it could a means of counterbalancing the potential menace of its two powerful neighbors; and second, to render as secure as possible its position within the unstable framework of German-Polish-Soviet relations. The great question was whether these two lines of policy could be harmonized or whether the pursuit of one would threaten the attainment of the other.

In theory, protection against German and/or Soviet pressure might be obtained through an international order collectively securing the integrity of nations, through the creation of an intermediate bloc of states lying between Germany and Russia and similarly threatened by their recovery or *rapprochement,* or through alliances with other great powers. In theory likewise, Poland's relations vis-à-vis Germany and Russia might be best served by judicious balancing between the two, or by drawing closer to one or the other, depending on the circumstances. These possibilities and the position taken by Beck and the Polish régime toward them will be considered in the following pages.

III

Inasmuch as Poland's reappearance as an independent state was intimately associated with Wilson's Fourteen Points and the Versailles treaties, it might seem axiomatic that Poland should have been an ardent upholder of the Versailles system and of the League of Nations, which was to be the basis for a new international order. Such was not Beck's attitude, however. He regarded Wilson as an opinionated reformer who had contributed to the unfortunate practice of incorporating *exposés de motifs* in the treaties at the end of the First World War. An admirer of the "old diplomacy," he felt that a treaty should deal only with concrete issues: if a nation lost a war, it should be forced to make certain concessions, but without argument or justification. The Versailles treaties, however, which he saw as the work of parliamentarians, not diplomats, were filled with explanatory clauses open to rebuttal and debate. In Beck's view this weakness in the formulation of the treaties was important in paving the way to war in 1939.[1] While it can be argued that the Versailles phraseology dealing with such items as disarmament, "war guilt," and so on, did provide a convenient wedge for the German revisionist counterattack, this argument is not without danger to a state such as Poland, which had been dismembered by the old diplomacy and was brought back into existence, in part at least, because of a widespread revulsion against this method of carrying on international relations.

Beck's second major criticism of the treaty was "the complete absence of a well established hierarchy defining the degree of importance of the different clauses of the treaty."[2] Citing Piłsudski as his mentor, as he usually did, he contended that the territorial settlement was of the highest importance, limitation of German armaments next, and then, of much less significance, all the other clauses. Sanctions and collective measures should have been designed and reserved for the protection of the vital clauses; instead there had been a fruitless expenditure of energy on issues of secondary importance, and the indispensable portions of the treaty were gradually undermined. In retrospect this criticism appears largely justified.[3]

While Beck was critical of the Versailles treaties, he was

[1] Ibid., pp. 48, 251–2.
[2] Ibid., p. 252.
[3] For a discussion of this point see R. F. Harrod: *The Life of John Maynard Keynes* (London; 1951) , pp. 269–70.

definitely hostile to the League of Nations, to the "spirit of Geneva," and to the statesmen who rested their hopes in that organization, particularly the representatives of other successor states active in the League, Beneš of Czechoslovakia and Titulescu of Rumania. The absence of the United States, he argued after his fall, had effectively deprived the League of its universalism and nullified its claim to represent a new international order. One may suspect, however, that this contention was a rationalization for the real basis of his dislike of the League: the pretensions of that body to concern itself with the internal affairs of the middle and small states, especially through such agencies as the International Labor Organization and the minority treaties. This meddling had the effect of disorganizing their internal stability and rendering them vulnerable to the propaganda of the aggressive powers: "It is enough to study the political campaign and propaganda undertaken by the Third Reich while preparing the invasion of Eastern Europe to realize the support which it constantly found in the debates of Geneva and in the interpretations of the treaties on the protection of minorities."[4] Moreover, Beck felt that the League put the small and middle powers in a particularly difficult situation. They were forced by the great powers "to make unforeseen friends and enemies in connection with questions which had nothing in common with their own interests."[5]

It is not possible here to go into Poland's internal affairs, but there is little doubt that much of Beck's touchiness concerning the League stems from Poland's minority question, which was a source of continual friction with its neighbors and of domestic discord. About 30 per cent of Poland's population was made up of non-Polish minorities,

[4] Beck: *Dernier rapport*, p. 256.
[5] Ibid., p. 266.

a large number of whom were Ukrainians. With the Soviet Union's entry into the League in 1934, Beck "deemed that the moment had come to finish with the question of the treaty on minorities. It was, in effect, inadmissible that the representative of the Soviet Union could discuss and decide the internal affairs of Poland."[6] With evident plea‑ sure at causing a stir, Beck, in September 1934, announced to the Assembly of the League of Nations that, "pending the introduction of a general and uniform system for the protection of minorities, my Government is compelled to refuse, as from today, all cooperation with the international organizations in the matter of the supervision of the appli‑ cation by Poland of the system of minority protection."[7] Since he neither expected nor desired the minority treaties to be converted into a general system applicable to all countries, he was, by this unilateral act of denouncing an international obligation, flatly rejecting the competence of the League to concern itself with Poland's minorities.

Beck also resented another function of the League that intimately concerned Poland: its supervision of the Free City of Danzig, which the Treaty of Versailles had taken from Germany but had not given to Poland. The real danger to Poland here was, of course, Germany. Never‑ theless, Beck was pleased with the difficulties the League High Commissioners were having with the growing Nazi domination of Danzig and proud of his ability to straighten out affairs by direct negotiation with the Third Reich. In reflecting on a minor crisis in 1936 Beck later commented: "The roles were thus reversed: It was no longer the League of Nations which protected Poland at Danzig, it was Poland

---

[6] Ibid., p. 71.

[7] League of Nations: *Official Journal, Special Supplement No. 125. Records of the Fifteenth Ordinary Session of the Assembly* (Geneva; 1934), 43.

which had to defend the League of Nations in the Free City. This corresponded, moreover, to the reality of things which Geneva, up to then had so obstinately refused to see."[8]

By this policy on the minorities question and Danzig, Beck was, in effect, removing them from the sphere of international concern to that of direct German-Polish relations. In 1939 this transfer had dire consequences when Hitler began his assault on Poland with precisely these issues. Still, Beck could reply, "And what would the League have done to protect Poland in 1939?"

On the one occasion when the League undertook collective measures against aggression—its imposition of sanctions against Italy—Beck was lukewarm about the whole affair: the dispute was far from Poland; he approved of Pierre Laval's efforts to avoid a break in French-Italian relations; he wanted to maintain Poland's coal exports to Italy; he mistrusted the ideological overtones of collective security;[9] and he was bored and irritated by the tenor of Titulescu's anti-Italian tirades in the "little world" of Geneva. Indeed, Poland was the first power to drop sanctions. In a letter to the President of the Council of the League, on June 26, 1936, Beck, after emphasizing that the adoption of economic sanctions was a "sovereign decision" for each state to make, declared that since further measures were useless Poland was terminating its application of sanctions. In his memoirs he said that this action was not intended to hasten recognition of the Italian annexation, but was simply a response to the fact that "un-

[8] Beck: *Dernier rapport*, p. 123.

[9] In a conversation with Anthony Eden on October 9, 1935, Beck remarked that "sanctions should not lead to a reinforcement of the action of the Second International, which was patronized by the Third" (*Dernier rapport*, p, 290).

fortunate Abyssinia had already ceased, *de facto,* to exist as an independent country."[1]

In retrospect the sanctions episode was a sorry one, which failed to check Italian aggression and contributed to driving Mussolini toward Hitler. It is painful, though, to hear a Polish statesman employ the "ceasing to exist" argument, when the soul of Poland's survival has been its obstinate refusal to admit the loss of national existence.

It is clear that the realist Beck placed very little confidence in the League of Nations as a defense for Poland. In considering the unhappy fate of those smaller states which did embrace the "spirit of Geneva" with such ardor, one may admit he had reason for his skepticism. After all, the League was not an independent supranational authority, nor could it enforce the peace unless the great powers, France and Great Britain—not to speak of the absent United States—exerted their power on its behalf. This they did not do; a far greater responsibility for the failure of the League attaches to them than to Colonel Beck's scornful attitude. It cannot be said, however, that his activities in this field were of any positive value in the preservation of the peace or of international responsibility in those darkening years.

IV

In the absence of an international body, the maintenance of peace, in the century preceding 1914, had come to be regarded as a function of the "Concert of Europe," the great powers of the continent. During the interwar years one can follow a thread of attempts to reconstruct this Concert, from the Locarno treaties of 1925, through the Four Power Pact of 1933, to the Munich Conference in

[1] Ibid., pp. 107-8.

1938, attempts to settle major problems by consultation and agreement among Great Britain, France, Italy, and Germany (the Soviet Union was not included).

Beck's attitude toward this approach to international security is not difficult to guess. If he was scornful of the League, he saw these efforts as a positive menace in their aim of settling affairs to the satisfaction of the great powers, but in disregard of the middle and small states. He quoted with approval Piłsudski's blunt comment on Locarno that "every good Pole spits with disgust at the name." By the Locarno agreements, two categories of frontiers in Europe had been created, and in Beck's opinion Germany was thereby solemnly invited to attack to the East for the price of gaining peace in the West.

The Four Power Pact, while eventually reduced to a rather vague and innocuous statement, aroused great indignation in Poland. Other middle and small states of Eastern Europe were equally alarmed, but upon learning of the eventual terms of the agreement, were willing to accept it. This compliance on the part of the Little Entente enraged Beck, who said that Europe had three categories of states: great powers, middle and small powers with a will to pursue their own policy, and client states. Putting Poland in the second category—he always denied that Poland was a great power in the sense of having worldwide interests—he was intent on maintaining an independent course against the infringements of the great powers and the submissiveness of the client states.

Since the Little Entente powers had dropped their opposition to the revised pact, the Polish government felt obliged to show its displeasure alone; and Piłsudski and Beck consequently arranged that the newly appointed Polish ambassador to Italy should announce his resignation on the ground that Italian policy in pressing the

POLITICS AND DIPLOMACY IN EASTERN EUROPE · 140

Four-Power agreement was contrary to the international interests of his country.

This particular technique of taking abrupt action to indicate disapproval of some international move potentially affecting Poland became characteristic of the Beckian diplomacy and greatly contributed to his reputation for deviousness. In fact, Beck had a rather simple pride in this "style" of Polish diplomacy, fast ripening into a tradition. The sudden harshness of his last moves against Czechoslovakia in September 1938 were in part occasioned by this same intention to register a protest against the Four-Power decisions at Munich.

Unquestionably Beck had every reason to be suspicious of the "Concert of Europe." It was a danger to the independence of the smaller states. Nevertheless, to assume this attitude was to raise a difficult problem, for if both the old principles of the Concert and the new principles of the League were rejected, as they were by Beck, what alternatives remained for a state which was neither so situated nor so powerful as to be able to stand in splendid isolation?

Beck did not provide any satisfactory answer to this question. He insisted that states should mind their own affairs, and he spoke of the advantages of bilateral agreements between nations to settle mutual problems without infringing upon the rights of others. But quite evidently, such principles are only desiderata, which a professed realist like Beck could not find sufficient in a world of contending powers, and on occasion he quite flagrantly contradicted his maxims. In practical terms, of course, the refusal to rely on the League or to admit the benefits of great-power paternalism meant that Poland must acquire allies, either among the states of Eastern Europe or in the West.

V

That the states of Eastern Europe had much to gain from a policy of cooperation and mutual assistance against the German and Soviet dangers seems more than obvious. Unfortunately, throughout most of the interwar period, Poland's relations with two of its immediate neighbors, Lithuania and Czechoslovakia, were far from cordial, and this condition made it impossible for Poland either to create a solid Baltic bloc or to cooperate with the Little Entente.

The conflict between Poland and Lithuania arose from the Polish seizure of Vilna after the First World War. Although its population was largely non-Lithuanian, Vilna had been the capital of the medieval duchy. Its loss was not recognized by the Lithuanian régime, which refused to establish diplomatic or economic relations with Poland. Despite occasional feelers, this anomalous relationship between two states once intimately connected continued up to March 1938.

The re-establishment of diplomatic relations with Lithuania is one of the oddest examples of Beck's diplomatic technique. While anticipating and accepting the German-Austrian *Anschluss*, Beck felt, nonetheless, that it would be "dangerous to remain entirely passive in face of the German expansion."[2] It was necessary to give proof that

---

[2] Ibid., p. 149. In December 1936, in a conversation with Szembek, Beck said he was expecting a crisis to develop in Central Europe. In such a situation, Poland had five choices, of which two were unacceptable: passivity or an alliance with Czechoslovakia against Germany. The other three were: (1) to occupy Teschen, permit Hungary to take Ruthenia, and gain a common frontier with the Magyars; (2) to take Kaunas; (3) to occupy Danzig (Szembek: *Journal*, p. 220). Apparently Beck felt he would have to do something, no matter in what direction.

Poland was alert and able to react swiftly. At the same time, since the action in Austria did not directly affect Polish interests, "our response should be very prudent."

While mulling over these thoughts, he received word that, in a frontier incident, Lithuanian guards had killed a Polish soldier. He grasped this occasion and, on March 17, 1938, arguing that in such tense times it was dangerous for Lithuania to refuse diplomatic recognition to Poland, sent a forty-eight-hour ultimatum demanding, mildly enough, resumption of normal relations. Certain sectors of Polish opinion urged more extreme measures against Lithuania and the abrupt action raised further doubts about Beck as a responsible diplomat, but it appears that his real intent was the symbolic gesture of demonstrating that Poland, too, could issue ultimata. In actual fact, the action did not lead to further trouble, and Polish-Lithuanian relations showed signs of improvement. But by 1938 it was very late.

Much more serious was Poland's conflict with Czechoslovakia, arising out of the rival claims for Teschen. The Poles felt that the Czechs had obtained, in 1920, an unfairly large part of this district at a time when Poland had been fighting the Bolsheviks. While the Teschen issue was the focus of irritation, Beck had more far-reaching reasons for disliking the Czech state. He objected to Czechoslovakia's alliance in 1935 with the Soviet Union and claimed that the Comintern was using Prague as a headquarters for anti-Polish activities. Beneš's work at the League aroused his scorn, and he held that the Czechoslovak régime's much advertised "liberalism" was but a façade for a classic "police state"[3] governed by an innately brutal nationality.[4]

[3] Beck: *Dernier rapport*, p. 52.
[4] Ibid., p. 171.

Moreover, the existence of the Czech state as such did not appeal to Beck. Marshal Piłsudski was accustomed to say that there were two states which would not survive, Austria and Czechoslovakia; the only important point was to know which would disappear first. Beck obviously subscribed to this analysis. In December 1931, before he was Foreign Minister, he and Piłsudski decided to increase the aid sent the Polish minority in Czechoslovakia and to be more energetic in educating and organizing it.[5] There is little use in seeking consistency between Beck's own highly sensitive attitude toward external interference with Poland's minorities and this policy of aiding and propagandizing the Polish minority in Czechoslovakia. The divine right of one's own nationality is rarely a principle admitting of reciprocity.

When the Four Power Pact was under negotiation in 1933, Piłsudski did approve of some confidential negotiations with the Czechs, but this brief attempt at *rapprochement* collapsed with Czechoslovakia's willingness to accept the pact as finally drafted. In the following year he ordered practice maneuvers for Polish military operations to assure the acquisition of Teschen in the event Czechoslovakia should disintegrate or capitulate in face of Germany.[6] The Polish régime was not interested in the maintenance of Czechoslovakia, regarded it as a doomed state, and was solely concerned with seeing to it that Poland gained its appropriate share of the remains.

With such an attitude toward Czechoslovakia, Poland was not likely to enter the Little Entente. Beck, however, had further objections to this bloc. He observed quite correctly that each of the Little Entente members was potentially threatened by a great power—Czechoslovakia

[5] Ibid., pp. 9–10.
[6] Ibid., p. 83.

by Germany, Rumania by Russia, and Yugoslavia by Italy
—yet the Entente was, in fact, directed solely against
Hungary, which was militarily weaker than any of its
three neighbors. Consequently, the Entente provided for
no united defense against aggression by a great power;
and Beck had no desire to join an anti-Hungarian combination, since an improvement of Polish-Hungarian relations was a major aim of his foreign policy. He concluded
that Poland had no reason to concern itself more intimately with the affairs of the small powers south of the
Carpathians. The 1921 Polish-Rumanian alliance, directed
against the Soviet Union, was the one Eastern connection
which seemed to him to meet a real problem.

His attitude toward Czechoslovakia also influenced
Beck in rejecting the French effort to create an Eastern
bloc in 1934. While his major objection to this project,
as will be seen presently, lay in his ambition to maintain
a balance between Germany and Russia, he did not wish
to enter any agreement which would oblige Poland "to
guarantee the Czechoslovakian frontiers."[7]

Beck was not lacking in plans, however, for an organization of the Eastern European states. In the first place, he
had hopes for a Baltic-Scandinavian bloc. Poland as a
Baltic Sea power should develop its ties with the advanced
and more enlightened Scandinavian states: "The bridge
which united Poland with the Occident and our western
friends passed, for me, by way of the Baltic and the solid
Scandinavian nations rather than by the artificial combination of the Little Entente south of the Carpathians."[8]
In pursuit of this project, he made several goodwill tours,
including one in the critical summer of 1938. The basic
difficulty in the way of this bloc was, of course, that the

[7] Ibid., p. 73.
[8] Ibid., p. 154.

Scandinavian states, for all their stability, were on the sidelines of the European power conflict and still pursued a policy of neutrality and noninvolvement.

A second project, which Beck worked on when the expansion of Germany began to appear alarming, was the creation of a Rome-Belgrade-Budapest-Bucharest-Warsaw connection. In March 1938, on the eve of the *Anschluss,* he had several conversations in Rome with Mussolini and Ciano. After assertions on both sides that they did not intend to pull chestnuts from the fire for other powers—a common figure of speech that passed for diplomatic sophistication in those years—there was mutual agreement that while an understanding with Germany was a necessary part of Italian and Polish foreign policy, efforts should be made to strengthen ties with Hungary, Yugoslavia, and Rumania, presumably as a check to overly great German domination.[9]

In support of this program Beck became increasingly anxious to establish a common frontier with Hungary. Just as the eastern prolongation of Czechoslovakia was, in part, strategically designed to give that country and Rumania common frontiers, so in the late 1930's, especially after Czechoslovakia's future seemed problematic, Beck's advocacy of Hungary's claims in Slovakia and Ruthenia was aimed at providing a geographical basis for increased cooperation between Poland and its "best neighbor."

A serious obstacle, of course, to Beck's rather jejune project was the fact that Hungary and Poland's ally, Ru-

[9] Ibid., pp. 145–8. See also Galeazzo Ciano: *1937–1938 Diario* (Bologna; 1948), pp. 127–9. While Beck found Ciano, underneath his theatrics, a precise and accurate agent for his father-in-law, Ciano felt that Beck was not very strong, rather rambling, and imprecise.

POLITICS AND DIPLOMACY IN EASTERN EUROPE · 146

mania, were bitterly antagonistic. Beck did his best to patch up relations between these two states but without success. In mid-October 1938, after Munich, he proposed to the Rumanian ambassador that, in the event of Czechoslovakia's further disintegration, Hungary and Rumania should divide Ruthenia between them. A few days later, in a visit to King Carol, he elaborated on this proposal. While not overlooking Rumania's old ties with Czechoslovakia, he urged that, if Hungary and Rumania took such an action in concert, their mutual relations would improve, Rumania would gain an additional rail connection with Poland, and, incidentally, Poland and Rumania would be rid of a center of Ukrainian agitation unsettling to their minorities. Carol, however, declined the offer, and Beck was subsequently outraged to learn that the Rumanian Foreign Minister, Petresco-Comnène, had spread the story that Poland was attempting to lure Rumania into aggression against Czechoslovakia.[1]

Apart from such complications, Beck's scheme for an Italian–Eastern Europe bloc had two fatal drawbacks. In the first place, by basing his plans on Italy and Hungary rather than on the Little Entente, he was fostering the forces making for territorial revision of the Versailles system and weakening those defending the status quo. In so doing, he was undermining the very arrangement which had enabled Poland to make its reappearance as the largest state in eastern central Europe. In the second place, Germany was the most powerful and active of the revisionist nations. It is therefore difficult to see just how a Rome-

[1] For Beck's account of this episode, see *Dernier rapport*, pp. 172–5; for the views of the Rumanian Foreign Minister, whom Beck called a perfect imbecile and who suspected Beck of secret aggressive agreements with Germany, see N. Petresco-Comnène: *Preludi del grande dramma* (Rome; 1947), pp. 276, 283–94.

Budapest-Warsaw axis—Belgrade and Bucharest in this connection merely represented the wreckage of the Little Entente—could be the instrument to check German ambitions. By 1938 Germany was in a position to overshadow and outmaneuver any such combination, as was made clear by the absolute worthlessness of the common Polish-Hungarian frontier which was achieved by the Hungarian absorption of Ruthenia in March 1939.

But, if Beck's program may be dismissed, it must be admitted that in all probability no arrangement by the Eastern European states could have assured the security of the area, even had their statesmen been far wiser and more self-restrained. Apart from the internecine quarrels, which were perhaps an inescapable by-product of the same spirit of national self-determination which created these states from the destruction of the old multinational empires, this unhappy area, by its history, its geography, and its low economic and industrial level, was scarcely in a position to maintain itself against external aggression or internal strain. Beck may certainly be criticized for his contribution to the disastrous confusion which afflicted this area in the 1930's, but the fact remains that the responsibility for Eastern Europe ultimately rested with the victorious powers of the First World War.

VI

If Poland's defense against Germany and Russia was not to be obtained through association with other states in Eastern Europe, the remaining alternative was the support of other great powers. The United States in the interwar period was of little value. Great Britain's position until the spring of 1939 was summarized by Sir Austen Chamberlain's private remark in 1925, that, "for the Polish corridor, no British Government ever will or ever can risk the bones of a British grenadier."[2]

There remained France, upon which had been placed far too great a burden for the preservation of the Versailles system. A Franco-Polish alliance was, at the end of the First World War, an obvious development. France favored a strong state on Germany's east and had worked for a large Poland at the Peace Conference. France mistrusted the revolutionary intentions of the new Soviet régime and supported Piłsudski in repulsing the Red army from the gates of Warsaw in 1920. The two nations, in February 1921, signed an accord which included a provision for mutual assistance and contained a secret military convention covering a German attack against either signatory or a Polish-Soviet conflict.[3] When the Locarno treaties created a distinction between Germany's eastern and western frontiers, France attempted to compensate for this shortcoming by signing a further treaty of guarantee with Poland on October 16, 1925.

Poland, however, profoundly mistrusted the trend toward Franco-German cooperation during the Stresemann-Briand era and was not enthusiastic about France's support of the Little Entente. France, for its part, found the Piłsudski régime after 1926 a trying and truculent ally. These strains were greatly sharpened after Hitler came to power. Each state seemed to the other to be inclined to come independently to terms with the Third Reich, France through the Four Power Pact and Poland through its 1934 agreement with Germany.[4]

[2] From a letter cited in F. P. Walters: *A History of the League of Nations*, 2 vols. (London; 1952), I, 284.

[3] General Gamelin: *Servir*, 3 vols. (Paris; 1946–7), II, 225, 466.

[4] For a discussion of Poland's motives in signing the agreement with Germany see below, section VII, p. 159.

In April 1934 the French Foreign Minister, Louis Barthou, visited Piłsudski. The conversation turned to Germany:

"I have had enough of these concessions; the Germans must be made to feel that we will no longer yield an inch," M. Barthou declared.

"You will yield, Messieurs, you will yield," the Marshal answered. "You would not be what you are if you did not yield."

"How can you suspect us of such a thing, M. the Marshal?"

"Perhaps you yourself do not wish to yield, but then either it will be necessary to dismiss you, or parliament will vote against you and defeat you."[5]

Commenting on this visit Beck later wrote: "It was always the same thing: the Marshal wished to intensify the purely military cooperation in face of the German menace, whereas the French sought to drag us into their own combinations in South-East Europe, combinations which had scarcely any connection with the German problem, the only decisive problem in the event of war."[6]

From the Polish point of view, then, the French were failing to stand up to the Germans but at the same time were busy building elaborate diplomatic constructions in Eastern Europe which the Poles could not welcome and in which they refused to participate.

From 1934 on, as France sought to include Russia in its security arrangements, this situation grew worse. Beck regarded Russia's admission to the League of Nations as a great mistake, since Russia lacked practically all the qualities which were demanded of League members.[7] The

[5] Beck: *Dernier rapport*, p. 59; Szembek: *Journal*, p. 5.
[6] Beck: *Dernier rapport*, p. 60.
[7] Ibid., p. 68.

project for an "Eastern Locarno," which was in theory to be an extensive pact of guarantee and mutual assistance organized by France and Russia but open to Germany, was seen by Beck as merely a means of pushing the states of Eastern Europe into the arms of Russia and then to tie this group to French policy.

It is rather strange that, after criticizing the Locarno treaties for creating a disequilibrium in Europe, Beck should have opposed a similar system of guarantees for the East. His position, however, was expounded at some length in a memorandum to the French government, drafted in September 1934. In the first place, Poland had finally succeeded in signing pacts with Germany and Russia; these, he hoped, would relieve the malaise troubling Eastern Europe. The main point, however, was that an Eastern Locarno required the presence of Germany: "Our principal thesis was that the participation of Germany in this pact represented for us a condition *sine qua non* for the maintenance of our policy of equilibrium between the two great powers which we had for neighbors."[8] Since Germany refused to join, Beck was not going to endanger his new pact by taking part in a combination that would have an anti-German bias.

While Beck respected Barthou as the last of the French statesmen who vigorously defended France's interests, he was somewhat relieved, after the latter's assassination, to find that Laval put far less pressure on Poland for an eastern pact. In Beck's view the real troublemaker in France was the "all powerful influence of the bureaucracy of the Quai d'Orsay," for which he repeatedly indicated his dislike.

After the project for an Eastern Locarno collapsed,

[8] Ibid., p. 74.

France pursued the more restricted objective of a mutual-assistance agreement with the Soviet Union, with which was associated a Soviet-Czech pact. When Laval passed through Warsaw in May 1935 on his way to Moscow to sign this agreement, Piłsudski was unable to see him; the old Marshal was dying. From that point on, Beck's and France's ways tended to part: France attempted in a rather halfhearted fashion to build up a defense system with Russia and Czechoslovakia, Beck relied upon the security given him by his pact with Germany.

The melancholy story of French-Polish relations during the next three years has been told at some length and with much feeling by the French ambassador in Warsaw, Léon Noël. In his view, Piłsudski, while having no respect for French democracy, was firmly attached to the principle of the French alliance. Beck, on the other hand, was definitely anti-French in his policy. He restricted the Franco-Polish alliance to the narrow terms of common action in the event of an actual attack by Germany but did not seek to concert with the French in the more general area of foreign policy.[9]

French criticism of Beck loses some of its point, however, if one considers the crisis of March 7, 1936, when Germany denounced the Locarno agreement and sent its forces into the dimilitarized Rhineland. Seeing this move as a definite test of force by Hitler and also as a test of the value of the Franco-Polish alliance, Beck without waiting for any word from Paris, summoned the French ambassador and requested him to inform his government that Poland intended to live up to her treaty obligations. So at this decisive moment, which was probably the dividing line between possible peace and eventual war or German hegemony, the Polish response was prompt and apparently

[9] Noël: *L'Aggression allemande*, pp. 104, 115–16.

unequivocal. Some French diplomats were of the opinion that Beck made this proposal because he anticipated no French action. This supposition, while quite possibly correct, is not wholly relevant.[1] France's failure—for which Great Britain bears its share of responsibility—to act on this fatal occasion gives a certain plausibility to Beck's subsequent actions. If France was unable to take measures to prevent the remilitarization of the Rhineland, a step which inevitably meant that Germany would eventually be free to strike in the East without fear of immediate invasion from the West, the states in Eastern Europe were unavoidably driven to an attitude of *sauve qui peut*. It must be added, however, that in his memoirs Beck says that it was difficult to believe that the Germans could be prevented, in the long run, from militarizing the Rhineland. He felt, though, that since Germany was taking a serious gamble, Hitler "was ready to accord significant political concessions to assure the success of his action."[2] In other words, Beck was less concerned with the strategic import of the act, which he felt the French could have accepted if given an adequate compensation, than with the diplomatic method employed. He feared that an unchallenged *fait accompli* would give Hitler inflated ideas.

The immediate consequence of the events of March 1936 was increased French-Polish mistrust. By the autumn of that year Noël was suggesting that Śmigły-Rydz, who was

---

[1] Szembek, who saw Beck after the meeting with the French ambassador, recorded in his journal: "Beck then expressed the opinion that the violation by Germany of the demilitarized zone did not constitute for us a *casus foederis*. . . . He does not think that war will result. France, without the support of England, will surely not move, and Great Britain is neither sufficiently prepared nor sufficiently armed to risk a conflict with Germany" (Szembek: *Journal*, p. 167).

[2] Beck: *Dernier rapport*, pp. 113–14.

to visit France to conclude a military and financial agreement, be told quite frankly: "The French Government is
wholly disposed to aid you, but you know, rightly or
wrongly, the French have no confidence in M. Beck; the
Chambers and French opinion will refuse, we fear, to permit the grant of an important loan to Poland so long as
he retains the foreign affairs portfolio."[3] Noël had reason
to believe that Śmigły-Rydz did not care for Beck's diplomatic policy, and the French government, apparently, was
inclined to accept his suggestion. As it turned out, however,
the French government did not press for Beck's removal,
primarily, it seems, because of reluctance to make what
would be construed as an anti-German gesture. This mood
of rather irresolute hostility on the part of France served
only to confirm Beck in the course he was following.

By the time of the Czechoslovakian crisis in 1938 France
was in the unhappy situation of seeing one of its alliance
partners, Czechoslovakia, increasingly threatened by another, Poland. Nevertheless, while the French were properly indignant over Beck's actions, France itself was guilty
of forcing Czechoslovakia to yield to Hitler. Indeed, an
extremely vicious circle had developed. A common Polish-
Czech front of resistance to Germany in 1938 might have
driven France to a support of its commitments; on the
other hand, Beck's belief that France was not going to oppose Germany helped keep him on his anti-Czech course.
Noël states that Beck had said to him several times during
the first days of his stay in Warsaw: "We have no illusions,
we know very well that our alliance with you is unilateral;
if you were attacked by Germany Poland would march to
your aid, because it would be in its interest; but the reverse is not true; we do not forget the press campaigns

[3] Noël: *L'Aggression allemande*, p. 140.

in France on the theme: we shall not fight for the Corridor."[4] In May 1938, when the French government proposed that Poland join the French and British ambassadors in warning Berlin against the use of force, Beck, while refusing to associate himself with this move, referred to the Polish attitude of March 7, 1936, and declared that Poland "was ready to honor its obligations as an ally of France."[5] As the crisis became more acute, Beck, in a conference with other Polish leaders, gave the following analysis of the situation: (1) the Czechs would not fight; (2) the Western powers were not prepared, either morally or materially, to come to their rescue. He went on to say, however, that "if my basic hypothesis was contradicted by the facts, it would be necessary, within a period of twenty-four hours, to modify completely the policy of Poland, for, in the event of a real European war against Germany, we could not be on the side of the latter, even indirectly."[6] As it turned out, both of Beck's premises were correct.

More fateful than this deterioration of the Franco-Polish alliance was the fact that the alliance itself, by the late 1930's, no longer had the strategic significance it possessed in the 1920's, when Russia was recovering from revolution and civil war, when Germany was disarmed, and when France had the most powerful army on the continent. France alone was no longer able to counterbalance the growing power of Germany, nor, as it later proved, were France and Britain together. Consequently, Poland's secu-

[4] Ibid., p. 252. On the other hand, in January 1935, Beck told Szembek that he did not think there was any chance that France might denounce her alliance with Poland, since such an action would amount to suicide on the part of France (Szembek: *Journal*, p. 32).

[5] Beck: *Dernier rapport*, p. 319.

[6] Ibid., pp. 162–3.

rity was more and more coming to depend upon the marginal influence it had in balancing itself between Germany and Russia.

VII

In a conversation with Pierre Laval, in January 1935, Beck explained the basic premises of Polish foreign policy by saying:

> Polish policy rests on the following elements: it follows from our geographical position as well as from the experiences of our history that the problems to which we must attach decisive importance are those posed by the relations with our two great neighbors, Germany and Russia. It is therefore to these problems that we must devote the greatest part of our political activity and of our modest means of action. History teaches us: 1) that the greatest catastrophe of which our nation has ever been victim has been the result of concerted action by these two powers, and 2) that in this desperate situation there was not to be found any power in the world to bring us assistance. . . . Another conclusion which imposes itself is that the policy of Warsaw should never be dependent upon Moscow or Berlin.[7]

To meet this difficult situation Beck, in theory at least, tried to pursue a policy of even balance between the two states. For example, in 1934 he timed a visit to Moscow to match the signing of the German-Polish pact. He insisted that his policy was clear and unequivocal and that having closer relations with one of the powers than with the other "would fatally drag us into a political activity or even into armed conflict which would not be justified by any vital interest of Poland and the only result of which

[7] Ibid., p. 283.

would be to transform our territory into a battlefield for foreign interests."[8]

While one may accept Beck's view that this was a reasonable position for Poland to take, the policy of balance leaves certain questions unresolved. It did not in itself prevent Germany and Russia from working together at Poland's expense. Moreover, while Beck contended that his diplomacy was based on "extremely simple" principles, it is not surprising that other nations found it increasingly complicated. The simple intention of riding two horses at once can lead to some exceptionally strenuous acrobatics. The real difficulty with Beck's desire to remain midway between Moscow and Berlin was its failure to indicate what should be done in the event one state was moving off on a clearly aggressive and revisionist tangent, whereas the other, for the time being at least, was not. In classical balance-of-power theory, a state trying to maintain itself between two more powerful states should move toward the less aggressive. In Beck's hands, however, the idea of preserving a balance seemed to mean that, if Germany took an aggressive action, Poland should respond by an act perhaps half as aggressive. There are several reasons for this rather peculiar behavior, which inevitably brought Beck closer to the Germans and further from the Russians.

A number of authorities have said that in 1933, upon Hitler's coming to power, Piłsudski offered to join the French in an action against Germany and that, only after being rebuffed and after witnessing the conclusion of the Four Power Pact, was he impelled to turn to Germany for the nonaggression pact of January 1934. The evidence for this offer, reports of which began to circulate as early as the summer of 1933, is elusive, however, and the present

[8] Ibid., pp. 37–8.

author is doubtful of its authenticity.[9] A proposal for preventive war is not mentioned in Beck's own memoirs, nor does it correspond to his retrospective interpretation of Polish views at the time.

According to Beck, Piłsudski had attentively examined the "pros and cons and all the odds of a preventive war before taking the decision to negotiate with Germany. There were obviously many elements to consider in this connection. In the military field the Marshal estimated that the weakest point in our army was the high command. The weakness of our eventual allies at this period made us abandon the idea of a preventive war, and what happened later, at the time of the occupation of the demilitarized zone of the Rhine by German troops, amply confirmed the estimate of the situation."[1]

Apart from these negative considerations, it is unlikely that Beck or Piłsudski felt Hitler to be an immediate menace. Beck records that Piłsudski did not think Hitler's coming to power meant the pursuit of a more violent anti-Polish policy, and he advised Beck, in making a speech before the Polish Diet, not to attach importance to the excitement of the European press but to be calm, firm, and moderate.[2] In his speech of February 15, 1933, Beck confined himself to saying: "Our attitude with regard to Germany will be exactly the same as Germany's attitude toward Poland. Speaking practically, more depends on Berlin in this respect than on Warsaw."[3]

[9] For a further discussion of this point see the Note at the end of the essay, p. 174.

[1] Beck: *Dernier rapport*, p. 66.

[2] Ibid., p. 24.

[3] Józef Beck: *Przemówienia, Deklaracje, Wywiady, 1931–1937* (Warsaw; 1938), pp. 58–9. The German translation, *Beiträge zur europäischen Politik, Reden, Erklärungen, Interviews, 1932–1939* (Essen; 1939) includes Beck's speeches up to January 1939.

At the same time, however, the victory of the Nazis had increased tension in Danzig, the "barometer" of Polish-German relations. Piłsudski felt a vigorous step was needed and quickly moved to reinforce the Polish garrison at the Westerplatte. But, as Beck put it, the warning of this abrupt measure "was perfectly understood in Danzig and Berlin," which adopted a conciliatory attitude. The question then arose whether Poland was in a position "to profit from the internal revolution of the Reich to ameliorate our neighborly relations with that country."

The reasons for Polish optimism on this point appear in a memorandum Beck prepared in the autumn of 1933. His conclusions were as follows: (1) the National Socialist movement has a truly revolutionary character; (2) at all times reformers have wanted to reinvestigate old problems; (3) all reformers are primarily concerned with internal changes, and for that they need a period of external calm; (4) Hitler is more or less an Austrian, in any case not a Prussian; no Prussian figures among his direct collaborators; and this fact creates a new situation, since the old Prussian traditions were chiefly responsible for the anti-Polish feeling in Germany; and (5) the Hitlerian movement is the last act of the national unification of the German people. The conclusion drawn was that "we found ourselves before a unique occasion for redressing our situation in the European balance."[4]

---

[4] Beck: *Dernier rapport*, p. 29. The same line of thought appears in the introduction to the "Polish White Book": "There seemed a possibility that the National Socialist revolution might force German opinion to accept the idea of a rapprochement with Poland, though this had been impossible under the Weimar Republic. The Hitler regime transferred the power in Germany to men who had not come from Prussia, the land of traditional hatred for Poland" (Republic of Poland, Ministry for Foreign Affairs: *Official Documents Concerning Polish-German and Polish-Soviet Relations, 1933–1939* [London; 1940], p. 3).

In the spring and summer of 1933, Hitler, publicly and privately, gave reassurances to the Poles that he had no intention of violating existing treaties or stirring up trouble in Danzig. In November, the Polish government explained to Hitler that Poland's security was founded on direct relations with other states and on collaboration through the League of Nations. Since Germany had now withdrawn from the League, the Polish government wished to know whether there was any chance "of compensating for the loss of this element of security, in direct Polish-German relations."[5] From this opening, the path led directly to the signing of the nonaggression agreement of January 26, 1934; and there is no indication in Beck's memoirs that, after getting a favorable German response, Piłsudski turned once more to France before signing the agreement.

Without doubt, Beck himself was much pleased with the German pact, which he regarded as the greatest and most valuable achievement of Polish foreign policy.[6] After Piłsudski's death, he paid a cordial visit to Berlin and was able to reassure the Nazi leaders that Polish policy would not change with the Marshal's passing. Commenting on that visit, he wrote later: "It will doubtless be very interesting one day to study to what degree the complete reversal of German policy several years later can or should

[5] Poland: *Official Documents*, p. 17. On October 1, 1933, Piłsudski called a conference to discuss the situation created by Germany's departure from the League. He ordered a report on the state of German rearmament. He also wanted to ask the French what information they had on the subject, and added: "It is necessary to draw the attention of the French to the fact that this work is secret, that we are not journalists nor in the service of journalists, and that we are not sounding the alarm." He concluded by saying that he had not yet formed an opinion with regard to German rearmament (Szembek: *Journal*, p. 2).

[6] Szembek: *Journal*, p. 41.

be attributed to Hitler himself, in what measure eventually it was owing to the overly great ease with which his imperialist policy went from success to success, or, finally, if and to what point it had its origin in a reaction of the Old Prussian spirit in the interior of Germany itself."[7]

Here seems to be the real clue to Beck's policy vis-à-vis Germany. While no pro-German, he was definitely attracted by, and had confidence in, what he thought to be the Hitlerian foreign policy.[8] He had no illusions that it was a static policy, but he thought it was based on nationalist principles. Consequently, he expected an attempt to take over Austria and, subsequently, action against Czechoslovakia; but he was quite willing to accept these developments as not imperiling Poland.

Beck never felt that he was becoming a German satellite or compromising the independence of Poland's foreign policy.[9] He did not join Germany in an anti-Bolshevik or

[7] Beck: *Dernier rapport*, p. 101.

[8] In a conversation with Anthony Eden on April 2, 1935, Szembek remarked: "In any event, for the Poles there is no doubt that of all the possible regimes in Germany the present Hitlerian regime is the most satisfactory; the proof is that we have arrived at an understanding with it. A socialist or communist regime would inevitably entail a return to the Rapallo policy; the German Nationalists, . . . quite apart from their Russophile tendency, would, if they came to power, be most hostile to Poland. Hitler is the only German statesman, who has wished, and known how to reach, an understanding with us. For these reasons, it is impossible for us, or at least very difficult, to join any action whatsoever which is directed against Hitler and the policy which he represents" (Szembek: *Journal*, pp. 55–6).

[9] The difficulty, however, of maintaining this independence in practice is shown by a remark of Szembek's to the Polish ambassador to Russia in December 1938: "It is exceedingly hard for us to maintain a balance between Russia and Germany. Our relations with the latter are entirely grounded on the belief of the leading personalities of the Third Reich that, in the future con-

anti-Russian crusade, although he was gratified whenever the Nazis told him of their dislike, not merely of Communism, but of any Russian state, whatever its complexion. As early as the autumn of 1934, Göring had thrown out some hints that Poland might well join Germany in an anti-Russian agreement, but Piłsudski "cut short this conversation by declaring that Poland, a country bordering Russia, had to adopt toward that power a moderate and calm policy and could not adhere to any combination of the sort to revive tension on our eastern frontiers."[1] Beck appears to have held to this view in the face of subsequent hints and offers.[2]

Some authors, Polish and of other nationalities, have gone so far as to argue that the chief fault of Beck's diplomacy was not the German connection, which was actually Piłsudski's responsibility, but the fact that, having achieved it, he did not then ride it for all it was worth. It is difficult to guess how such a venture might have turned out. In the short run, gains in the east might have compensated for the loss of Danzig and control over the Corridor. But, at the end of this road lay Machiavelli's warning: "A prince ought to take care never to make an alliance with one more

---

flict between Germany and Russia, Poland would be the natural ally of Germany. In these conditions, the good-neighbor policy, which has its origin in the 1934 accord, could easily appear to be but a pure and simple fiction" (Szembek: *Journal*, p. 386) .

[1] Beck: *Dernier rapport*, p. 34.

[2] For example, in his conversations with Ribbentrop in January 1939, Beck explained the impossibility of Poland's joining the Anti-Comintern Pact. At the same time, he was on sufficiently close terms with the Germans to discuss with them the problems which might arise if internal pressures in Russia should lead to a war or if the Soviet Union should break up into national States. He did not, however, think that either eventuality was likely in the near future (Szembek: *Journal*, p. 413) .

powerful than himself for the purpose of attacking others, unless necessity compels him . . . because if he conquers, you are at his discretion."

Even Beck's unpleasant performance at the time of the Munich crisis was not planned in concert with the Germans. Western diplomats as well as many Poles felt, in the summer of 1938, that Poland's *rapprochement* with Germany was "degenerating into an undignified imitation of the small fish that seek their meat in the wake of the shark."[3] Nevertheless, Beck insisted he was pursuing an independent policy. As he later expressed it:

I formulated on the part of Poland a simple and at the same time very supple demand. I declared we demanded simply that, if the government of Prague decided to make concessions to other countries, our interests should be treated in exactly the same fashion. When the diplomats asked me to define our demands or claims, I categorically refused to do so and affirmed that Poland did not have the intention of dismembering the Czechoslovak state or of taking the initiative in an attack against this country, and that, consequently, it did not feel called upon to give a rigid precision to its claims. That if, however, the Czechoslovak state, a veritable mosaic of nationalities hitherto governed by methods of brutal centralisation, had the intention of revising its policy or its regime in order to take better account of the interests of a particular national group, we could not admit that the Polish minority, which was grouped in a very compact manner in a region situated on our frontier, should be less well treated than any other ethnic group.[4]

Having taken this "most favored nation" attitude, Beck was bound to be evasive when queried by the French or British ambassadors. The Germans, however, were equally

[3] *British Documents*, 3rd series, I, 431.
[4] Beck: *Dernier rapport*, p. 159.

uncertain of his intentions. On July 1 the German ambassador, Moltke, reported on a conversation with Beck: "As usual, when he wishes to avoid definite statements, M. Beck said a great deal without saying anything of importance." Moltke doubted that Poland would side with France if it intervened, but he would not assume that Poland would be on Germany's side: "Poland will . . . always act exclusively according to her own interests."[5] In September Moltke denied rumors that he had been trying to influence Poland. "Practical cooperation already exists and great emphasis on this point would not be advisable in view of M. Beck's disposition. . . . It is correct to say that Beck attached great importance to achieving Polish aims as far as possible independently and that he is trying particularly to avoid giving the outside world any impression of dependence on Germany."[6]

The basic danger in Beck's "supple" policy was that the more Germany raised its claims, the more he was obliged to raise his. As the dispute moved beyond autonomy for the Sudeten Germans to the right of self-determination and plebiscites, Beck came to demand equivalent treatment for the Polish minority.[7] When the decision was reached to cede certain Sudeten territories without a plebiscite, the Poles in turn demanded frontier revision without plebiscite.[8] By September 21 the Polish government was pressing hard on the Czechs, denouncing the 1925 Polish-Czech convention dealing with minorities and demanding rapid action. To the Czech appeal for negotiation, the Poles responded even more peremptorily, in part because of a belief that the Soviet note of September 23, threatening to

[5] *German Documents*, series D, II, 449–52.

[6] Ibid., pp. 973–4.

[7] Ibid., p. 811.

[8] Ibid., p. 849.

cancel the Polish-Soviet nonaggression pact, was somehow related to the Czech notes.[9]

Then came the Munich Conference at which the dispute was suddenly taken over by that old enemy of Polish diplomacy, the Four Powers. Germany gained its demands; Poland was not even invited to the meeting. Beck decided that an immediate reaction was in order and asked for a march on Teschen as a "protest against the Munich proceedings." On September 30 he sent a twelve-hour ultimatum to the Czechs, the text of which, as Beneš subsequently remarked, was "almost identical with the ultimatum which Hitler sent to Beck himself a year later with respect to the solution of the question of Danzig.[1] This was not Colonel Beck's finest hour.

The first inkling that Polish-German relations were up for review came shortly after Munich when, on October 24, Ribbentrop proposed to the Polish ambassador a general settlement of issues between Poland and Germany. This settlement included the reunion of Danzig with the Reich, an extraterritorial road and railway across Pomorze, a guarantee of frontiers, joint action in colonial matters, and a common policy toward Russia on the basis of the Anti-Comintern Pact.[2] Beck's response was conciliatory but held that "any attempt to incorporate the Free City into the Reich must inevitably lead to conflict."

According to Beck, writing in October 1939, the turning point in his own mind concerning relations with Germany was his interview with Hitler on January 4 of that year. To

[9] Beck: *Dernier rapport,* pp. 163–4. It was agreed by British and German observers alike that the one thing likely to push the Poles explicitly into the German camp was the appearance of Russian interference.

[1] Letter from Beneš to L. B. Namier, April 20, 1944, in Namier: *Europe in Decay* (London; 1950) , p. 285.

[2] Poland: *Official Documents,* p. 47.

his alarm he noted "new accents" in Hitler's remarks. The Chancellor, while continuing to propose German-Polish cooperation, now "treated with levity the ideas which he and German propaganda had hitherto elevated almost to the level of a religion."[3] Still unwilling to revise his estimate of Hitler, Beck thought that perhaps the Führer was still inclined to be cautious but that Ribbentrop, "a dangerous personality," was urging a reckless course. Upon his return to Warsaw, Beck felt sufficiently alarmed to tell Mościcki and Śmigły-Rydz that these shifts in the German mood might presage war. Ribbentrop visited Warsaw later in the month, but the conversations were not fruitful. Beck refused to give way on Danzig or Pomorze despite suggested compensation in Slovakia and even mention of the Black Sea.[4]

With the German occupation of Prague and Memel in March, the situation deteriorated rapidly. If Poland's Ukrainian problem had been relieved by Hungary's taking over Ruthenia, this gain was far outweighed by Germany's annexation of Bohemia and Moravia and its virtual military control over Slovakia, which, as General Jodl said, now made it possible to "consider the Polish problem on the basis of more or less favorable strategic premises."[5] By March 28 the German ambassador was accusing Beck of wanting "to negotiate at the point of a bayonet." To which Beck replied: "That is your own method."[6]

Thus, Beck's efforts to maintain good yet independent relations with Germany had come to failure. His basic

[3] Beck: *Dernier rapport*, p. 182. See also Szembek: *Journal*, p. 407.

[4] Beck: *Dernier rapport*, p. 186; Poland: *Official Documents*, pp. 54–8.

[5] Cited in Royal Institute of International Affairs: *Survey of International Affairs, 1939–1946: The World in March 1939* (London, New York, Toronto; 1952), p. 291.

[6] Poland: *Official Documents*, p. 69.

error was a misreading of the Nazi movement and of Hitler's personality. That he was deeply chagrined by this turn of events, which undid his whole diplomatic strategy, is not surprising.[7] It was reported that, after his highly popular speech of May 5 in which he courageously stood up against the German menaces, "in a fit of rage [he] had thrown a whole pile of congratulatory telegrams into a corner."[8]

Whatever Beck's personal feelings, it was clear that if he was to resist Germany he had to look abroad. Britain, and secondarily France, were the powers to which he necessarily turned. But, as has been observed above, by the spring of 1939 it was far from certain that Britain and France were capable of rescuing Poland. Polish-Soviet relations now assumed decisive importance.

VIII

Although Piłsudski and Beck declared that their policy was to keep Poland evenly balanced between Germany and

[7] For an illuminating picture of Beck's mood and outlook at this time, see the account of a train journey with him by the former Rumanian Foreign Minister, Grigore Gafencu: *Last Days of Europe* (New Haven; 1948), pp. 26–53.

[8] According to the Polish Under-Secretary of State, Mirosław Arciszewski, who is reported to have given this information to the German ambassador, Beck was not happy about the Anglo-Polish declaration of mutual assistance, was forced to make his address of May 5 because of the Führer's speech of April 28, and was exasperated by the Polish public's enthusiastic reception of it. "M. Beck even now basically favors the previous policy" (*Dokumente zur Vorgeschichte des Krieges,* herausgegeben vom Auswärtigen Amt der deutschen Regierung [Basel; 1940], p. 253). It is difficult to tell whether this statement actually represented Beck's views, since it was designed for German ears. Moreover, on several occasions Arciszewski seems to have gone beyond his instructions and acted on his own.

the Soviet Union, Polish diplomacy was in practice perceptibly off-center. Piłsudski brought with him the deep anti-Russian feelings of his revolutionary and wartime career. To these were added a justifiable suspicion of Bolshevik intentions and a concern about the large Ukrainian and White Russian minorities in Poland's eastern provinces. As in many states bordering on Russia, the outcome was a conviction on the part of the government, so pervasive as to be almost unspoken and undebated, that no positive and fruitful relationship with the Soviet Union was possible.[9] In the 1920's a Polish ambassador returning from Moscow reported to Piłsudski that he had not tried to settle conflicts of little importance but had, rather, sought to ameliorate general relations between the two countries. The Marshal interrupted him to say, "Now, that is curious. I should have done exactly the opposite."[1] While Beck always stressed the importance of an independent Polish policy and the value of bilateral negotiations, he was not enthusiastic about dealing bilaterally with the Soviet Union. When discussing in his memoirs the negotiations leading to the Polish-Soviet pact of 1932, he observed that Poland's traditional policy demanded "solidarity with all the western neighbors of Russia."[2] There was no equivalent sense of a need for solidarity with Germany's eastern neighbors when it came to negotiating with that power.

Certain steps were taken, however. Poland (along with Estonia, Latvia, and Rumania) signed the Litvinov proto-

[9] The government's view was not identical with that of Polish opinion in general. In March 1936 Szembek remarked: "Polish opinion is thoroughly hostile to Germany and, in contrast, is favorable to France and even Sovietophile. I consider that it is indispensable to make the principles of our foreign policy popular" (Szembek: *Journal*, p. 172).

[1] Beck: *Dernier rapport*, p. 6.

[2] Ibid., pp. 10–11.

col on February 9, 1929, the Polish-Soviet pact of non-aggression of July 25, 1932, and—with Russia's other neighbors—the London convention for the definition of aggression of July 3, 1933; and, in 1934, Beck made his trip to Moscow to balance the signing of the German-Polish pact.

Within the next two years, however, Polish-Soviet relations fell off greatly. In July 1936 the new Polish ambassador in Moscow, Grzybowski, was received by Krestinsky, Litvinov's deputy, with blunt words: "The political relations between us could not be worse. We are working to increase the prestige of the League of Nations, and for collective security; we are combatting all forms of aggression and all forms of fascism. At the present time we are pursuing an anti-German, anti-Italian and anti-Japanese policy. Poland is pursuing a diametrically contrary policy, tending to weaken the League of Nations, combatting attempts to realize collective security, supporting Italy and sympathizing with Japan. Poland is within the orbit of German policy."[3]

Grzybowski, of course, denied this interpretation and his rather rueful comment on this meeting must sound familiar to those who have had occasion to deal with the Soviet Union: "Irrespective of Polish policy, the Soviets constantly interpreted it so as to contrapose it to their own policy."[4] Nevertheless, it is true that Beck disapproved of the Soviet entry into the League of Nations, regarded collective security as a Communist device, and was highly critical of France and Czechoslovakia for signing treaties of mutual assistance with the U.S.S.R. Indeed, the more

---

[3] Poland: *Official Documents*, p. 195.
[4] Grzybowski himself, however, was not pleased with Poland's Soviet policy, which he regarded as uselessly hostile. See his remarks in December 1938, Szembek: *Journal*, pp. 386–7.

one considers the course of Polish diplomacy the more this deep-rooted and altogether natural mistrust of Russia seems to give a distinct flavor to Polish attitudes on almost all issues. Beck said at the end of his career: "In the course of the twenty years of my political activity in the field of foreign affairs, I acquired the conviction that the essential element which created divergences between Polish policy and French policy was not the German question but, invariably, the manner of viewing the Russian problem."[5] Beck not only regarded the Soviet Union as a dangerous power but he denied that it could serve as a counterweight to Germany, notwithstanding the mutual hostility of these two powers in the 1930's. In 1937 he and Winston Churchill informally discussed this issue while relaxing at Cannes but were unable to agree. "I could not avoid the impression," Beck later wrote, "that this eminent statesman lived too much on his memories of the preceding war and that he was too inclined to consider Russia as a relatively important counterweight to German dynamism. I tried to make him understand that Europe could not have the least confidence in Soviet Russia and that we, its neighbors, had more evidence than anyone for judging the Russian phenomenon with skepticism."[6]

When Beck went to London in April 1939 to negotiate the British-Polish mutual-assistance pact, he felt he should state Poland's position on having Russia as an alliance partner. Poland, he said, had no confidence in Russia or in the ends it pursued. It had had experience with Tsarist imperialism and with Communist imperialism, and they came to the same thing. However, in face of the German menace, there was no point in rebuffing Russia; one should

[5] Beck, *Dernier rapport*, p. 193.
[6] Ibid., p. 127.

at least be assured of its neutrality. Though doubtful of its achievement, he would not oppose an English-French-Soviet entente, but such an accord could not impose new obligations on Poland. He would be satisfied if an arrangement were made whereby, in case of war with Germany, arms could be sent to Poland via Russia and Russia could provide raw materials.[7]

The involved story of the unsuccessful efforts by the British and French to reconcile this position with the mounting demands of the Russians in the abortive negotiations of the spring and summer of 1939 cannot be told here. There is no question, however, that the Polish refusal to agree to the presence of Soviet troops on Polish soil was, as a debating point at least, an important factor in the breakdown of the negotiations. The reluctance of the Poles to make this concession is certainly understandable, nor is it by any means certain that a greater show of cooperation on their part would have deflected the Soviet Union from its pact of August 23 with Germany. Nevertheless, the utterly negative quality of Polish-Soviet relations appears very clearly in a set of conditions laid down by the Polish ambassador in a conversation with Molotov in May 1939:

We could not accept a one-sided Soviet guarantee. Nor could we accept a mutual guarantee, because in the event of a conflict with Germany our forces would be completely engaged, and so we would not be in any position to give help to the Soviets. Also we could not accept collective negotiations, and made our adoption of a definite attitude conditional on the result of the Anglo-Franco-Soviet negotiations. We rejected all discussion of matters affecting us other than by the bilateral method. . . . I indicated our favorable attitude to

[7] Ibid., p. 193. See also British comments on Polish attitude toward military cooperation with Russia, in *British Documents*, 3rd series, IV, 428, 453.

the Anglo-Franco-Soviet negotiations, and once more emphasized our entire loyalty in relation to the Soviets. In the
event of conflict we by no means rejected specified forms of
Soviet aid, but considered it premature to determine them
definitely. We considered it premature to open bilateral
negotiations with the Soviets before the Anglo-Franco-Soviet
negotiations had achieved a result. [The ambassador continued:] M. Molotov made no objection whatever.[8]

Indeed, there seemed to be very little to say.

Interestingly enough, Beck was quite pleased that Molotov had replaced Litvinov, whom he regarded as the "notorious enemy of our country." "It was possible to suppose
that the anti-Polish complex peculiar to this man, who was
by origin a *litwak*, had disappeared with him."[9] Just as
Hitler, an Austrian, was to alter the anti-Polish bias of the
Prussian tradition, so, presumably, Molotov was to rid
Soviet policy of the anti-Polish prejudices of the *litwak*
Litvinov.[1] Here again Beck's own nationalism was misleading him. By reducing foreign policy to such motives
he was unable to grasp the basic drives of either the Nazi
or the Soviet dictatorship.

For a brief period, it is true, Molotov adopted toward the
Poles an attitude of "the greatest courtesy." The Soviet
government offered to supply them with war materials; the
Soviet press urged resistance to German demands. In retrospect, of course, this amiability, which continued until
the German attack, appears altogether sinister: intended
at first to conceal the German-Soviet *rapprochement* and
then, perhaps, to prolong Polish resistance in the event
France and Great Britain failed to declare war on Germany.

[8] Poland: *Official Documents*, p. 208.

[9] Beck: *Dernier rapport*, p. 200.

[1] Beck described the *litwak* as the "worst of the Jewish types,
deported from Russia to the Polish provinces and who, at Vilna
or at Bialystok, offended Polish ears with his Russian jabber"
(*Dernier rapport*, p. 139) .

In this instance, however, Beck's position did not change. To the last he refused to have Soviet troops on Polish territory;[2] and the most he would concede was that, after hostilities had started, he might agree to re-examine the question with a view to possible Soviet-Polish cooperation.

IX

Beck's diplomatic career ended in complete disaster. All his policies turned against him. The nonaggression pact with Hitler did not prevent a German assault; the disintegration of Czechoslovakia weakened rather than strengthened his southern frontier; his refusal to admit Russian soldiers to Polish soil did not keep them from overrunning eastern Poland in September 1939. Nor was this just bad luck. His views on the art of diplomacy, his estimate of the international situation, and his analysis of political motives were filled with inconsistencies that inevitably led to self-defeating policies.

He was not just an opportunist, though the charge of unprincipled opportunism has been laid against him. He adhered, rather arrogantly and purblindly, to a set of axioms which he took to be the Piłsudskian heritage and which made up in their obvious preoccupation with the Polish national interest what they lacked in coherence and universality. But, unlike Churchill, who was fighting against the current and whose speeches of the 1930's have the real mark of prophetic insight, Beck was engulfed in the currents of his time, and his prophecies tended to be self-fulfilling ones which his own activities and outlook helped bring to pass.

[2] In mid-August 1939 Beck said to Noël: "Nothing assures us that, once they are installed in the eastern parts of our country, the Russians will participate effectively in the war" (Noël: *L'Aggression allemande*, p. 423) .

Still, when all this has been said, an appraisal of Beck cannot be wholly negative. For all the errors of his policy, he was not one of the really malignant creatures of the decade. Contrary to widespread contemporary belief, he was not in league with Hitler, even though the two often appeared to be working in collaboration. Even in the case of his least defensible action, the ultimatum to Czechoslovakia, he was, to a large degree, the victim of his own "most favored nation" formula; the movement of events which drove him to such an unfortunate action came from the interaction of German aggressiveness and the wobbling retreat of the Western powers, France and Great Britain. He did not like Czechoslovakia, but he did not plot its destruction.

Nor can one say that he contributed greatly to the disaster that overtook Europe, except in the sense that his actions fed into a vicious circle which intensified and compounded the weaknesses of the existing international order. The League of Nations was indeed a weak reed, though attitudes such as Beck's helped make it so. Russia was indeed a dangerous and unpredictable power, though Beck's policy toward Russia did nothing to make it less dangerous or unpredictable and seemed to provide a rationale for Soviet actions in 1939. In this respect, he is highly symptomatic of the 1930's. The feeling, so apparent in his memoirs, that there were no feasible alternatives, was characteristic of a general European mood which was creating, and being created by, the approaching catastrophe.

In one regard, however, Beck definitely deserves respect. When the final test came, he did not yield. In a desperate situation, partly of his own making, he took an unprovocative but courageous stand. The result, to be sure, was a horrible war, the outcome of which was not real peace and which had tragic consequences for Poland during and after the hostilities. For this reason there has been criticism for his not allying with Hitler, just as there have been those to rebuke Great Britain for not having been shrewd enough to let Poland fall as it had let Czechoslovakia fall. Whatever the results of such policies, one thing would have been missing in the future: the will to defy. Even in the painful situation of the world today, it is heartening to know that this value was not permitted to drain out of the life of nations as it threatened to for a time in the 1930's.

These considerations, however, extend beyond the horizon of Beck's career, which stopped in September 1939. By the end of his life he was far removed from politics and diplomacy. In August 1943, only ten months before his death, he wrote to his daughter-in-law:

> Reading what you report to me, I have had the impression of a kind of doubling of my personality. Here am I, taking care of my lungs, which are in a pitiable state, and, there, a phantom moves about the world, another Józef Beck with whom I have had no relations for four years. He goes this way and that, engages in conflicts, is attacked, is spoken of in books. He is a solid enough type, since he has moved about so long without my aiding him in anything. What a strange spectacle! I ask myself if someday I shall have the possibility and the desire to meet him again in this world or whether I shall abandon him to his own devices.[3]

NOTE ON POLISH PROPOSALS
FOR PREVENTIVE ACTION
AGAINST GERMANY

A number of writers and diplomats have referred to a proposal, or proposals, for preventative action against Germany which Marshal Piłsudski is said to have made to the French shortly after Hitler came to power. There seems

[3] Beck: *Dernier rapport*, p. xxiii.

to be no authoritative contemporary evidence, however, and the stories are not altogether consistent.

The Communist journalist "André Simone" stated that, in March 1933, Piłsudski informed the Daladier government of the alarming progress of German rearmament and proposed to France that the Hitler régime be crushed by a "preventive war." Daladier demurred, then refused. The offer was repeated in April, but there was no response (*J'Accuse: The Men Who Betrayed France,* New York, 1940, p. 53). This account seems to be the source of substantially the same story which appears in J. W. Wheeler-Bennett, *Munich, Prologue to Tragedy* (London, New York, 1948), pp. 283–4. The emphasis here upon Piłsudski's concern over Germany's rapid arming is in conflict with Ambassador Noël's statement that Piłsudski believed Germany would require a generation before being ready to make war (*L'Aggression allemande contre la Pologne,* pp. 67–8).

Pertinax stated that in April 1933 Poland proposed a preventive war, knowing that it would not be taken up, as a preliminary to its move toward Germany (*Les Fossoyeurs,* New York, 1943, II, 83).

The Polish journalist Stanisław Mackiewicz wrote that in March 1933 Piłsudski deliberately tried to start a war with Germany. While granting that no evidence had been found in Poland of a memorandum addressed by Piłsudski to Daladier, he contended that Piłsudski's reinforcement of the Polish garrison on the Westerplatte was intended as a provocative act (*Colonel Beck and His Policy,* London, 1944, p. 15). Beck, in his memoirs, interpreted this move as a warning to Germany of Poland's alertness, not as a provocation (*Dernier rapport,* pp. 25–7).

L. B. Namier has written that on three occasions, in March and November 1933 and again in March 1936, the

Poles suggested to France armed action against Germany; he adds that Piłsudski's initiative in 1933, though authentic, cannot be easily documented (*Diplomatic Prelude, 1938–1939*, London, 1948, p. 97, note 3). With regard to the November effort: "Piłsudski was sounding Paris once more about common action against Hitler. The talks were confined to military channels—the first approach was made through General d'Arbonneau, French Military Attaché in Warsaw. The result was negative . . ." (ibid., p. 15). Apparently the source for this statement was Józef Lipski, Polish ambassador in Berlin, who wrote to Namier: "After the German Ambassador, von Moltke, had on November 27 presented to Marshal Piłsudski the German draft of a non-aggression pact, I was instructed by Colonel Beck to keep the matter strictly secret, and that also towards the *corps diplomatique*. Piłsudski, who personally dealt with the problem, would not sign a pact with the Germans before sounding Paris once more about jointly taking decisive action against Hitler, which was a further reason for his instructing me to preserve absolute silence" (L. B. Namier, *Europe in Decay*, London, 1950, p. 282, note 1). Lipski elsewhere makes the same point: "Piłsudski se rendait clairement compte des possibilités militaires de l'Allemagne. La preuve en est qu'il me chargea d'employer devant le dictateur du Reich l'argument de la force. Hitler le comprit et proposa à Piłsudski un pacte de non-agression. Étant en possession de l'offre allemande, le Maréchal fit encore une fois des ouvertures à la France, suspendit les pourparlers avec Berlin, et partit pour Wilno. Cette fois encore Paris ne manifesta aucune volonté d'action" (J. Lipski, *Sprawy Międzynarodowe*, No. 2–3, 1947, p. 15, quoted in Beck, *Dernier rapport*, p. 32, note 1).

Against this rather scattered evidence is the fact that there appears to be no mention of any Piłsudskian proposals in 1933 in the documents the Germans captured in Warsaw, in Léon Noël's memoirs, in the volumes thus far published by the French parliamentary commission of enquiry (*Les Événements survenus en France de 1933 à 1945*), or in Beck's three memoranda written between 1939 and 1943 (*Dernier rapport*). If Beck's interpretation of Piłsudski's point of view is to be trusted, the Marshal, in 1933, did not regard the Hitler régime as a serious threat, though he seems to have given some theoretical consideration to the advisability of preventative action. Apparently, military intelligence studies made in 1933 and 1934 (see p. 159, note 5, above) led the Polish régime to believe that neither Germany nor Russia was in a condition to undertake any immediate military action. Beck, however, felt that of the two Russia was the more likely to risk an adventurous undertaking (*Dernier rapport,* pp. 65–6). His view was shared by Under-Secretary of State Szembek, who said to Eden in April 1935: "We have, however, arrived at the conclusion that the policy of Soviet Russia is to a certain degree hysterical, in any event less logical, and consequently less calculated than the policy of the Third Reich; it is for that reason that we consider we are threatened by surprises more from the side of Russia than from the side of Germany" (Szembek: *Journal,* p. 55). If such was the case it would be both unnecessary and dangerous to move against Germany.

VII ❧ Politics in a Small State: The Balkan Example

[1960]

IN HIS INTRODUCTION TO A RECENT STUDY HUGH SETON-Watson remarks: "Of all my travels I think the most enlightening were in the Balkans, whose combination of intellectual subtlety and crudity, of tortuous intrigue and honest courage revealed more truths about the political animal man than are to be found in most textbooks of political science."[1] This curiously revealing quality of Balkan politics has been experienced by many Western visitors and has undoubtedly been an important, if not always conscious, motive for further study of—and often passionate identification with—the tangled vicissitudes of this area.

There are perhaps two principal reasons why the life of the Balkans seems to provide such insights into the nature of politics and politicians. The first is the peculiar combination they present of the familiar and the unfamiliar, the recognizably European and the specifically Balkan. It

[1] Hugh Seton-Watson: *Neither War Nor Peace: The Struggle for Power in the Postwar World* (New York; 1960), p. 15.

is this, one may suppose, that leads to the impression of startling contrasts in behavior which Seton-Watson mentions. To the attentive Western observer the phenomena of Balkan politics give fuller meaning and clarity to one's whole political vocabulary, to such terms and categories as law, representation, party, leadership, or community. It is not that political life is more primitive or simpler but, rather, that the shift in meaning and emphasis gives us a stereoscopic sense of seeing politics in three dimensions.

One of our principal imports from the Balkans has been its rich treasury of political aphorisms, jokes, and cartoons. These pungent commentaries about political life gain their force and clarity precisely from this dissonant quality: a sharpened sense of reality through a distortion of familiar appearances. This effect is not the result just of difference. We do not seem to get the same *political* perceptions from a study, say, of the Nilotic tribes of the Sudan or even of the advanced cultures of Eastern Asia: there the dissimilarities are too great.

A second reason is the sense, perhaps an erroneous one, that these smaller political entities in the Balkans are somehow more graspable than such vast political complexes as the United States or the highly articulated societies of Western Europe. It often seems, in studying the politics of the Balkans, that there are only a relatively small number of people who count politically. At times a single individual could almost stand for a social category. Mr. X and Y, by their ownership of the only two steel plants in the country are, in effect, Heavy Industry. A group of people arguing in one corner of a room at a reception are the Intellectuals. Count K is the archetype of all *éminences grises,* and so on. This is undoubtedly an optical illusion that could lead to some dangerous simplifications, and yet, by following the actions of a relatively manageable number of people, one does get a vivid sense of the movement of politics.

Strangely enough, however, this illuminating quality of Balkan politics seems, in the final analysis, to cast light on other areas more than on the Balkans themselves. As Seton-Watson suggests, the Balkans have been important to him for a general understanding of man and politics. Certainly one feels a more acute perception in dealing with American and Western European politics after some exposure to Balkan politics. And yet Balkan politics themselves remain obscure. The whetstone stays dull though it sharpens the knife.

The reason is not particularly mysterious: study of the Balkans forces us to pay more critical attention to the meaning and application of analytical categories that were, on the whole, developed in our own societies, and hence makes better tools of them. But the Balkan reality itself, the extent to which it can be explained by these tools, remains uncertain.

So it is that the Balkans have been a marvelous training school for political scientists and diplomats,[2] and yet our understanding of Balkan politics still leaves much to be desired. We can hardly claim a satisfactory grasp of many vital features of Balkan politics in their evolution during the past century and a half: the actual functioning of political institutions, the full meaning of elections and electoral

2 I am grateful for Joseph Rothschild's observation in his comment on the first draft of this essay: " 'The Balkans as a testing ground' is not, of course, a new image. In the non-academic world, for example, a significant proportion of American governmental and semi-governmental personnel at present attempting to cope with the problems of the Afro-Asian countries received its training, so to speak, for such work in the Balkans, which have thus retrospectively become the original underdeveloped area. Soviet Russian foreign missions manifest a similar tendency."

procedures, the reality and measure of public opinion, the background and recruitment of political leadership, and indeed the whole relationship of national political structure to peasant communities or local politics.

Yet it is clear that there is no easy answer for this difficulty, which confronts the Balkan student of Balkan affairs as much as it does his Western colleague. Indeed, the Balkan scholar may suffer an additional disadvantage. In times past at least, he was obliged to go to the West to pick up the tools of political and historical analysis, which he then brought back to apply to his own nation. Often this meant that he might not be as surefooted and critical about these Western tools as his Western colleague; at worst there was the temptation to use them as magical devices for purposes of incantation and ritual. All students of the Balkans have, in their reading, encountered the disconcerting phenomenon of a Balkan scholar using some wholly inapposite formula or principle from a Western writer to buttress an observation about the local scene, feeling that somehow this provided weight and authority for his position.

There is probably no solution except much more spade work at the level of raw data, whether of the written word or as immediate experience, and through it the development of appropriate tools of analysis and classification. We may be reluctant to realize how culture-bound our measuring instruments are in the social sciences. But it is well to recognize that we do not possess universal measurements, on deposit in some bureau of standards and applicable to all societies, but that there has been a close interplay between our intellectual categories and the societies out of which they have emerged as a means of ordering and controlling experience.

Given this perspective, the present essay could hardly hope to present any general interpretation of Balkan politics. Nor, regrettably, was it possible here to attempt even a modest contribution to the spade work that is so necessary. Rather, in the hope of stimulating future exploration, it is limited to some speculations on a single but possibly fruitful question: the influence of the Balkan states' position as "small powers" in the nineteenth and twentieth centuries upon the operation of their domestic political systems and upon the style and attitudes of the politicians themselves. It is the thesis of this essay, at least as a hypothesis warranting testing, that this factor of smallness has had significant and continuing effect.

On the face of it there would be good reason to suspect the existence of such an influence. Their relatively small size and population, the proximity of far larger and more powerful neighbors, their location in a region of prolonged and intense international pressures, and the fact that from their very origin as independent sovereignties the histories of the Balkan states have involved relations between great powers and small powers—all this would suggest more than casual consequences for domestic politics.

And yet these consequences are not as easy to identify and demonstrate as it might seem. For one thing, it is always hard to sort out and evaluate the possible causes for anything so complex as a pattern of political life. Obviously many features of Balkan politics may be entirely unrelated to the size of these states; at least two other important influences are present: the impact of the West and the domestic social structures. Moreover, the wide diversity of political behavior within the different Balkan states, not to speak of other small powers, would indicate that, whatever the influence may be, it can find a variety of expressions.

There is, of course, no lack of easy generalizations about this presumed relationship between small-power status and

domestic politics, but it is doubtful whether these advance
our understanding very much, if only because most of
them have arisen from an effort to place some kind of
blame for the frequently untidy state of Balkan affairs.
Thus, spokesmen for the Balkan states, taking off from
Lord Acton's too frequently quoted observation about
the corrupting effect of power, have been inclined to
argue that the greed and ambition of the large neighboring
states have constantly thwarted or upset the efforts of the
Balkan states to establish orderly political communities.
This argument is not without weight. It is not difficult
to cite occasions when invasions or periods of occupation
completely upset domestic political life. The periods of
Nazi and Soviet occupation or hegemony are but recent,
and spectacular, examples. Nevertheless, this argument is
not wholly persuasive. In the first place, the historical
image it creates of great-power policies and appetites is
overly simplified and does not do justice either to the complexity of considerations that have determined the foreign
policies of great powers or to the ambiguous effects of
great-power intervention. It was, after all, a Russian occupation that brought the first constitutional instruments,
the *Règlements Organiques,* to the Danubian Principalities. Moreover, it is by no means certain that the ups
and downs of Balkan political life are attributable to these
external influences. For example, it is doubtful that the
breakdown of constitutional régimes in Balkan states
during the interwar period is directly or chiefly the consequence of great-power interference. It has been suggested
that the international developments leading to the *Anschluss* and the destruction of Czechoslovakia prompted King
Carol II to establish his dictatorship in the spring of 1938.[3]

---

[3] See, for example, Emil Ciuria's essay in *Captive Rumania,*
ed. Alexander Cretzianu (New York; 1956), pp. 12–13.

While the climate of the times probably encouraged such a step, Carol had not been a friend of the parliamentary system and his move to personal rule antedated the downfall of Austria. In the case of the somewhat earlier establishment of authoritarian régimes in Yugoslavia and Bulgaria, however, the reasons appear to have been largely domestic.

In contrast to the picture of the Balkans as Sisyphus laboring vainly against inroads by the great powers, there is the theme of Balkan "immaturity" and "irresponsibility." Proceeding from the view that impotence, not power, corrupts, it is argued that, because of the long experience of subjugation and dependence, Balkan politics in the emerging national states were chaotic, chauvinistic, and lacking in measure and balance. Hence, the great powers, by necessity concerned with areas of potential danger, were obliged to come in as troubleshooters, whether competently or incompetently. Again, this argument has some weight. One can think of the efforts of the European powers to handle the Macedonian problem, of the intervention in 1878 to remove discriminatory provisions in the Rumanian constitution, of the labors of the Conference of Ambassadors during the First Balkan War, of the insistence upon minority protection in the treaties after the First World War. And yet, this picture of the Balkans as juvenile delinquents is equally unfair and rather less attractive aesthetically.

When confronted with such conflicting interpretations it is tempting to say "the truth lies somewhere in between." But this is to say little, if anything. If we examine the thesis that the possession of power corrupts, and its reverse, that being impotent corrupts, the only middle ground between the two appears to be "it all depends," and we are likely to conclude that somehow the problem was put wrongly in the first place.

On reflection it would seem that we are misplacing ethical categories when we attribute vice to great powers and virtue to small powers, or the reverse. The possession of power in itself means nothing unless it is placed in the complex setting of the purposes for which it is employed and its function in providing a correspondence between national responsibilities and national capabilities.

When we speak of great powers and small powers, what do we have in mind? A difference in degree or a difference in kind? Are the relations between the Balkan states and the neighboring great powers simply a case of weaker and stronger, or is there a significant qualitative distinction to be made, expressible in such terms as "dependence" or "tutelage"? One has the sense that more than mere degree is involved, but it seems difficult to arrive at any simple formulation that can tell us, without gross historical simplification, what makes a small state "small" and a great power "great." It is true, of course, that in the nineteenth century the structure and practices of the European states system, and the relative ranking of the powers, were such that a fairly clear line was drawn between those states that "counted" and those that did not. And certainly the subjective views of the statesmen themselves were influenced by such diplomatic custom. Even so, it is not easy to define the real difference between, say, Italy's and Rumania's status in the alliance system that had its center in the power of imperial Germany. Moreover, the claims that Ionel Brătianu made for Rumania at the Versailles Conference were essentially those of a power demanding "equal status," and while not wholly successful, he was remarkably adept, despite the organization and procedural devices of the conferences, in acting as something other than the spokesman for a "small" power. It must be granted, however, that his success in this instance lay in the fact that not only Austria-Hungary and Germany, but also Russia were in a state of collapse or internal convulsion.[4]

The Foreign Minister of Poland in the 1930's, Józef Beck, attempted a definition by means of a threefold distinction: at the one extreme the world powers, self-sustaining and with interests extending far beyond their own frontiers; at the other extreme dependent small powers, client states unable to hold their own and requiring the support of the large states; and in between such a state as Poland, self-reliant but without global or imperial interests and concerned only with problems in its immediate neighborhood.[5] This convenient definition, while having the merit of pointing out the significant fact of differences in the extent of responsibilities, will hardly do. Poland, in fact, could not be self-sustaining; nor is it realistic to assume that even a very small power can be indifferent to developments far beyond its own frontier, since they may come to affect it. Ethiopia and Spain, so it turned out, could not safely be considered as beyond Poland's range of proper concern.

Perhaps the most we can say is that a small power is (and is so regarded by others and itself) a state lacking any hope of successfully defending itself against a great power, unable through its own resources to take the initiative in determining the course of international politics, and only marginally capable of throwing effective weight in the scales of the balance of power. On the whole, the small state is an object rather than a subject in international relations, and its resources, manpower, and territory, while of value

[4] For a discussion of Brătianu's role, see Sherman David Spector: *Rumania at the Paris Peace Conference* (New York; 1962).

[5] Colonel Joseph Beck: *Dernier rapport: Politique polonaise 1926–1939* (Neuchâtel; 1951), p. 270.

to the great powers as assets to be gained, or withheld from others, are not of sufficient magnitude in themselves to permit an independent role. In this respect its position is like that of a pawn in a chess game, not in the usual sense that it may be moved about and sacrificed by the player (all chess pieces, except for the king, are so manipulated by the player), but in the limitations in the *types* of moves it can make vis-à-vis the major pieces.

It is true of course that even the limited capability of a small power may, under special circumstances, be of considerable importance. Joseph Rothschild has suggested[6] that "in certain marginal but crucial situations such as a delicate balance between hostile alliance systems, a small state, its relative weight having been automatically increased by the general equilibrium, may exercise exorbitant blackmail power over its big ally by threatening to commit suicide." One may wonder, however, whether this opportunity for exploiting—whether through blackmail or tilting the scales—an evenly balanced great-power stand-off is as great, objectively or subjectively, as it may appear. While Brătianu made a number of paper gains between 1914 and 1916 through exploiting the "balance" between the Central powers and the Entente, he was able to cash in on these only because of the temporary destruction of any coherent balance of power in 1918–19. It might be argued that Prince Milan of Serbia took the plunge into war against Turkey in 1876 because of a stalemate among the great powers, and yet his actual reason for doing so seems to have been chiefly his fear of losing his throne if he failed to take action. On the whole one may doubt whether the threat of suicide by a small power has been, in fact, frequently resorted to, or even seriously contemplated. It

[6] In his valuable comment on the original draft of this essay.

does not ring true psychologically, and such an imputation of motives seems, rather, to represent a transferal of the fears that may be held by a great power regarding its small ally.

Apart from these marginal situations, there is little doubt that this relative inability, through their own resources, to determine, or even effectively to contend for, a favorable situation for themselves in the international scene does strongly influence the diplomatic style and strategies of small powers.[7]

On the level of technique we can observe a variety of devices: Balkan diplomacy has discovered an astonishing assortment of ways to stall for time; the maneuvers of Bulgaria and Rumania in the First World War are most instructive in this regard. The reliance upon legalisms, often with the most marvelously ingenious hair-splitting, is necessary both to ward off the brute pressures of the great powers and also to have a case "for the record" in the event of catastrophe. One can trace this distinctively protective function of legalisms from the partitions of Poland[8] —and Poland's status in the years just before and after 1773 shows many striking parallels to the situation in the Balkans a century or more later—down through the aftermath of the Soviet occupation of Eastern Europe in 1945. Balkan statesmen are often skillful at what is called, in alpinism, "chimneying": working one's way up a crevice between two opposing cliffs by wedging oneself between both sides. Such devices are in some measure, of course, the stock in trade of all diplomats, but, as Mrs. Fox observes,

[7] For a thoughtful discussion of the role small powers can play in international crises see Annette Baker Fox: *The Power of Small States: Diplomacy in World War II* (Chicago; 1959).
[8] Herbert H. Kaplan: *The First Partition of Poland* (New York; 1962).

while they usually are "of peripheral importance to the great power, supplementing its military strength, they may be essential to the small state, substituting for the military power which it lacks."[9]

Perhaps of more fundamental importance than the techniques are the *kinds* of policy choices that have been open to the Balkan states. In speaking of the diplomacy of the great powers we refer to such possible policies as "splendid isolation" or "intervention," "gaining hegemony" or "redressing the balance of power," "forming a coalition" or "operating through the European Concert." Now obviously none of these majestic choices has had much meaning for the Balkan states (except, of course, in the setting of intra-Balkan diplomacy, where there has been a real, if limited, game of power politics within the larger European framework). Their practical choices have been of a different order. While Montenegro, thanks to its terrain, could at times be "isolationist," all other states were too exposed to be able to withdraw from the field of encounter. The ideal situation for a Balkan state was, of course, to have the great powers in its immediate neighborhood either seriously preoccupied elsewhere or in a state of collapse— as in 1919—but such situations were infrequent and temporary and lay beyond the power of the Balkan states themselves to bring about. If the great powers were locked in stalemate, the best hope of the Balkan states was to have a partial "power vacuum" in their area, which would give them a degree of real, if precarious, independence. Indeed, it was such a continuing stalemate that gave the Balkans the opportunity to emerge as independent states in the nineteenth century. Had either Russia or Austria-Hungary been unhampered the outcome would have been different.

[9] Fox: op. cit., p. 185, note 4.

The danger of the stalemate, of course, was that the great powers might try to resolve it, not by permitting a low-pressure buffer zone, but by partition. The specter of an Austrian-Russian agreement to divide the Balkans along a north-south line hung over the peninsula through much of the nineteenth century and into the twentieth, and reappeared briefly in the abortive Nazi-Soviet negotiations of November 1940. Although there were always serious difficulties in the way of such a partition, it can certainly not be dismissed as having been an evident impossibility.

If one great power or grouping of powers came to be in the ascendency, it was incumbent upon the Balkan states to climb on the bandwagon or at least to be ready to hedge. Thus, in the 1930's we find King Carol in Rumania and Prince Paul and Stojadinović in Yugoslavia working to improve their relations with the ascendent power of Nazi Germany, even though their countries were beneficiaries of the Versailles settlement. And while at the time these steps were often attributed to political or ideological affinities, the evidence seems reasonably clear that the guiding impulse was in the realm of foreign policy.

But the action of coming under the aegis of a great power, either as protection against another great power or to avoid isolation, was always in danger of producing the situation against which Machiavelli warned: "A prince ought to take care never to make an alliance with one more powerful than himself for the purpose of attacking others, unless necessity compels him, as is said above; because if he conquers, you are at his discretion, and princes ought to avoid as much as possible being at the discretion of anyone."[1]

Certainly the smaller powers who felt compelled to join

[1] Niccolò Machiavelli: *The Prince*, Chapter xxi.

the Axis found themselves in this uncomfortable plight, and the successes of the Third Reich, so long as they continued, promised only to diminish the real independence of its small allies.

It is not inevitable that a small power will follow this path, even though the penalty for not doing so may be catastrophe. One apparently spectacular exception was the *coup d'état* of General Simović in March 1941, at a time when Hitler was master in Europe, an act which Winston Churchill hailed with eloquence: "Early this morning the Yugoslav nation found its soul. . . . This patriotic movement arises from the wrath of a valiant and warlike race at the betrayal of their country by the weakness of their rulers and the foul intrigues of the Axis powers."[2]

While the immediate result was a crushing German attack, one may feel that this *beau geste* by Yugoslavia is unmistakably at variance with the prudential concerns of small-power diplomacy outlined above. But the case is not a simple one. After the *coup d'état* the new government attempted to remain on good terms with Germany, and indeed one may wonder whether the purposes of the *coup* were those Churchill attributed to it. It can be argued that they arose more from domestic differences and were not chiefly an expression of foreign policy.[3] Even so it remains a remarkable event, and one that we must consider again presently in connection with domestic politics.

It is true, of course, that the foreign policies of the Balkan states have been strongly influenced, and complicated, by intra-Balkan relations; it was never just a question of relations between great and small powers. Indeed, it may

---

[2] Winston Churchill: *The Second World War*, 6 vols.; III: *The Grand Alliance* (Boston; 1950), 168.

[3] For a discussion of this see Jacob Hoptner: *Yugoslavia in Crisis, 1934–1941* (New York; 1962).

be suggested that the perennial precariousness of international relations in the Balkans is a consequence of an overlapping of two power systems: the competition of the great powers for influence in this strategic area and the mutual rivalry of the emergent Balkan sovereignties, which could lead to common action between two or more Balkan states as in 1876 and 1912, or to conflict, as in 1885, 1913–18, and 1941. This double set of wheels within wheels often led to a clashing of gears which made it difficult to achieve even a clear-cut lineup of powers and hence to rather dangerous uncertainty at all levels. For example, Austrian hostility to Serbia after 1908 suggested a *rapprochement* with Bulgaria, Serbia's rival in Macedonia; but such a *rapprochement* was not compatible with good Austrian-Rumanian relations because of the Rumanian-Bulgarian conflict over southern Dobrudja, itself an item in the internal Balkan power balance. Such curious self-contradictions may be found in the efforts of all the powers, great and small, to devise a consistent policy or set of alliances.

Still, despite the undoubted importance of small-power relations and their ability to set off conflicts, these relations, whether positive or negative, always lay under the shadow of the great powers, which were seen as being ultimately decisive. It is worth noting that the Balkan alliance of 1912 was explicitly under the aegis of Russia and, though events turned out otherwise, was not intended to stand as a self-sufficient entity. After the First World War the two combinations affecting Balkan states, the Little Entente and the Balkan Entente, were not directed against any great power. There was clearly the sense that the arithmetical sum of capabilities of the small states did not add up to great-power status.

In general, then, the foreign-policy choices before the Balkan states have been difficult and dangerous and within a frame of alternatives different from that of the great powers. This in turn seems to have produced, or at least contributed to, a different outlook on the nature of international politics. For whereas a larger power may have the hope of its foreign policy corresponding to its general political preferences in choosing friends and enemies, this is a luxury a small power cannot afford except at serious risk to its national existence.

Consequently we find the diplomacy of the Balkan states driven to two polar, but related positions, which we may call the "cynical" and the "utopian." On the one hand, since the small state must be sensitive to the shifting tides of power, be ready to abandon one ship and try to climb aboard another, this necessarily results in a rather special view of the world. It is nicely expressed in the Balkan diplomatic saying: "We have three kinds of friends: our friends, our friends' friends, and our enemies' enemies." It is also observable in the wisdom of the Cypriot saying: "When the rock falls on the egg—alas for the egg! When the egg falls on the rock—alas for the egg!"

It is frequently a cause of real misunderstanding between great powers and their small allies. Thus, as Mrs. Fox has observed:

In World War II, when the small states' leaders did examine their position in the balance of power, their perspectives on Germany and Russia almost without exception differed from those of the West and not primarily for ideological reasons. For them Germany was a valuable counterweight against the equally threatening Russians, and they were quite unable to obtain acceptance of this idea in the West, even as they failed every time in their several efforts at mediation to shorten the war. The longer the war lasted, the more precarious did they view their position, for they regarded the threatened extinction of Germany and the expansion of Communist Russia as two sides of a single catastrophe. Because of their views on the dual character of the war, they could not share the Western Allies' preference for final, unconditional and total victory over Germany.[4]

The present author recalls a conversation he had with a Rumanian officer in Bucharest in the late autumn of 1944. The officer urged that since Nazi Germany was clearly facing defeat, the United States should at once make peace with it and join in a common alliance against the Soviet Union. To an American, at this time, such a proposal seemed shocking; from the perspective of Rumania this was only the course of common sense.

As against this rather hard-bitten view of international politics and preoccupation with power, we also find a "utopian" position which attempts, in a way, to escape from the uncomfortable world of power politics that is so perilous to the small state. This position has found its most striking, and at times constructive, expression in the support given by statesmen of small powers, including the Balkans, to the League of Nations and to the United Nations, and more particularly to the efforts to devise ways of controlling aggression. One thinks at once of Beneš, Titulescu, Politis. It would be interesting to have a full picture of the contribution of such men—in ideas, formulas, and formulations—to the various efforts to outlaw war, define aggression, and develop the scope of international law. It must be considerable. One has the impression, too, that scholars from the Balkans have been relatively active in developing approaches to international affairs—functional, economic, or legal—that seek to blunt or circumvent the problem of power.

[4] Fox: op. cit., p. 182.

The use of the term "cynical" and "utopian" for these two polar positions should not be taken to suggest that they are somehow distorted or inappropriate. They are not. In the first place, they are derived from the realities of the situation in which the Balkan states found themselves and represent an effort to achieve an adequate response to that situation. It would be inappropriate for a Balkan statesman to try to model himself after a Palmerston or a Lord Salisbury. Moreover, inasmuch as the situation of small powers —the problem of the weaker coping with the stronger—is an important part of the totality of international politics, the insights and attempted solutions of the statesmen of the Balkans are of more than local interest. They can be most illuminating to any student of international affairs.

But if, in the realm of Balkan foreign policy, we find these significant consequences of smallness, the further effects on Balkan domestic politics are less obvious. Indeed, the question may be raised whether there is any necessary connection between behavior in external affairs and behavior at home. The statement is often made that the one colors the other; for example, that if a society embarks on an aggressive or warlike foreign policy, this will cast a shadow over domestic practices, or, conversely that a democratic society, if it is to be true to itself, must work for, or at least not against, freedom and independence in the world at large. But this may represent a misplaced notion of unity and consistency. An unscrupulous politician may be a good husband and kind father, and it is possible to argue that there is no simple correlation between political behavior on different levels. As Barrington Moore has put it: "The connection between the internal organization of a society and its foreign policy is a complex question that cannot yet be answered on the basis of simple formulas. Athens engaged in foreign conquest perhaps more than did warlike Sparta, and the Japanese, despite the militaristic emphasis of their society, lived in isolation for centuries until the time of their forced contacts with the West."[5] Marxists have gone further to argue that, in the capitalist world at least, there is an inverse relation: that domestic liberty is possible only because of exploitation and aggression beyond the frontiers. In this "safety-valve" view nineteenth-century English liberalism can be understood only in connection with Ireland, India, and a colonial empire.

While we cannot attempt here to resolve this problem in its general form, it is clear that we must be careful in drawing broad conclusions about domestic Balkan politics from any selected set of examples. Still, it may be worthwhile to examine one or two examples, if only to raise some questions.

In 1907 Rumania experienced a violent peasant uprising. Among radical and reformist political groups in the country, whether populist or Socialist, there was great sympathy for the unhappy situation of the Rumanian peasantry and much criticism of the existing social and political order. And yet, when the explosion occurred, the principal concern of these groups was for the quick re-establishment of domestic order, for the simple reason—as they stated explicitly—that if the revolt got out of control Rumania might face an occupation by one of the neighboring great powers, Austria or Russia.[6] This attitude on the part of Rumanian political radicals stands in sharp contrast to those radicals in Russia who were defeatists at the time of the Russo-Japanese war, precisely because an

[5] Barrington Moore, Jr.: *Soviet Politics—The Dilemma of Power* (Cambridge, Mass.; 1950), p. 396.
[6] Henry L. Roberts: *Rumania: Political Problems of an Agrarian State* (New Haven; 1951), p. 19.

external disaster might increase revolutionary possibilities at home. It may be that the Rumanian radicals lacked the zeal and intense political convictions of their Russian counterparts, but it seems more likely that the difference is a reflection of the size and vulnerability of the two countries. Rumania's tribulations as a small, exposed power were something not even the radicals could neglect or overlook.

No nation, no matter how large and secure, can be completely indifferent to the external repercussions of domestic events. Nevertheless, the weight given to this consideration can obviously vary enormously from country to country.

In Rumania at least this inhibiting or dampening effect of worry about foreign affairs appears to be a fairly consistent strand in domestic politics. In the nineteen-twenties the National Peasant Party was quite sensitive to charges by the Liberals that its reform program threatened to weaken the country's standing internationally; in the late 1930's and early 1940's the democratic opposition to the dictatorial régimes of King Carol and Antonescu was restrained by the dangerous developments abroad.

A close examination of each of the Balkan countries would probably reveal traces, more or less important, of this same kind of preoccupation. It is interesting, for example, that in the nineteenth century the emerging Balkan states, of whose ebullient nationalism so much has been made, should nearly all have placed non-native rulers on their thrones. Whether the reason was fear of local rivalries (and the Obrenović-Karadjeordjević feud in Serbia showed the dangers of competing native dynasties) or the felt need to secure useful connections abroad, the presence of foreign monarchs would suggest a continuing, if not easily defined, connection between the operation of the domestic political system and external concerns. For a time, in Greece, the political groupings themselves were known as the French Party, or the British Party, or the Russian Party—a fairly clear sign of the lack of autonomy of local politics.

From these examples one is tempted to draw the conclusion that in the Balkans, with their perennial vulnerability to, and relative helplessness against, external dangers, domestic politics could not be played as an autonomous or self-contained game, that there was, rather, a tendency to restrain or inhibit the force of political and social impulses. Unhappily for this conclusion, political caution and moderation can hardly be regarded as the hallmarks of Balkan domestic politics. The Balkans have a rich history of violent and intemperate political actions, many of them in complete disregard of foreign considerations. The Simović *coup d'état* of 1941 has already been mentioned, as a striking, even reckless, example of flying in the face of common prudence. The overthrow of rulers, the occasional rashes of political assassination, the presence of political parties having extreme programs and advocating extreme measures to achieve these programs—all these would seem to have little to do with the cautious concerns of a small power. Moreover, the intensity and expression of such impulses have been noticeably different in each of the Balkan states.

Nevertheless, there may be some connection between these two antithetical types of political behavior. Just as in the field of foreign policy there appear to be underlying bonds between what we have called "cynical" and "utopian" outlooks, so in domestic politics we may suggest that extreme prudence and extreme recklessness are not unrelated, that they are opposite responses to the perils, frustrations, and harassments of political action within a weak state under constant external pressures that may at any time limit or destroy freedom of action, even domestically.

It would require careful historical investigation to trace and identify all the cumulative consequences of this condition, which has certainly prevailed throughout the independent existence of the Balkan states and, in a different form, during the period of Ottoman hegemony. It is perhaps not fanciful to see its effects in the very style and comportment of many Balkan politicians, those alternations in behavior that Seton-Watson referred to in the introduction cited above. One is tempted, too, to speculate about such men as Ionel Brătianu, Nikola Pašić, or Thomas Masaryk, men of commanding personality and vigor, who could surely have played major roles in world history had their stage of action been a great power. What were the effects on such men, and upon their behavior as political figures, of this limitation to their role? In Brătianu's dealings with the diplomats representing the great powers one can sense an almost constant irritation. Did this in turn find expression in political relations at home? Unfortunately, these questions can only be raised here, not answered.

If we turn to the question of violence and intemperance, it is clear that the Balkans, for all the familiar stereotypes of terrorism, factionalism, conspiracy, and *coup,* have no unique claim to these forms of political action. While some of them may have indigenous roots going back to the heroic outlawry of the Ottoman era, others are derivable from French Jacobinism, German Marxism, and Russian anarchism. Nor can we point to political assassination as a characteristic peculiar to Balkan history. Around the turn of the twentieth century, for example, there was a widespread rash of assassinations which included the Balkans but many other nations as well: President Carnot of France (1894); Premier Canalejas of Spain (1912); King

Carlos of Portugal (1908) ; King Umberto of Italy (1900) ; the Empress Elizabeth of Austria-Hungary (1898) ; Minister of the Interior V. K. Plehve and President of the Council of Ministers P. A. Stolypin of Russia (1904, 1911) ; King George of Greece (1913) ; King Alexander of Serbia (1903) ; Premier S. Stambulov of Bulgaria (1894) ; Minister of War Mahmud Shevket Pasha of Turkey (1913) ; and, to round out the picture, President McKinley of the United States (1901) .

As for the last forty years, it has been great powers, not the small, that have established some of the most hideously violent forms of government known to history.

In other words, we cannot simply identify political violence and intemperance with the Balkans as small, insecure powers. They obviously have shared the varying impulses toward violence, whether rational or irrational, prevailing in the world at large. Nonetheless, within this more general pattern of behavior the fact of smallness does seem to give a special and possibly distinguishing flavor to such actions. Three examples may be offered for consideration.

As we have observed, during much of their modern history the Balkan states as weak powers were clients of neighboring great powers, in a condition of greater or less dependence. Under these circumstances domestic disputes, whether dynastic, oligarchic, or party-political, often led to efforts by the opposition to gain support from outside—at the Porte, in St. Petersburg, or in Vienna. In consequence the dividing line between opposition and treason could easily become blurred, more so than in the case of a great power where the necessity, or the temptation, to look to outside support was by its nature less compelling. The hectic politics of the Principalities in the Phanariot period, of Bulgaria in the years after 1878, of Serbia before 1903, provide numerous examples of this phenomenon, for which the term "treason" is not wholly appropriate and yet which clearly had a disturbing effect on local politics. The twentieth century, of course, has presented us with new forms of political treason identified with the totalitarian movements of the Left and the Right,[7] and it is not easy to say whether in the interwar years the Balkan states, enjoying somewhat more independence than before 1914, were more seriously afflicted than other European nations with this particular manifestation of political pathology. One has the impression that some of the extreme Fascists or Communists in the Balkans were perhaps less inhibited in contemplating or undertaking treasonous activities than were their counterparts in Western Europe, but this is a subject for further inquiry.

A second set of examples may be found in those instances where the freedom of domestic politics is curtailed or suppressed, perhaps brutally, for the sake of defending the nation's security, only to have it turn out that the latter effort is not equal to the task in any event. The resultant sense of futility may then feed back into a further poisoning of domestic politics. A poignant example is King Carol's overthrow of the parliamentary system and the establishment of a "strong" monarchy, an act followed shortly by the militarily unopposed territorial losses of 1940. The frantic and savage turmoil that led immediately to the Antonescu dictatorship was certainly in part a reaction to this double frustration, itself a consequence of Rumania's impotence vis-à-vis Soviet Russia and the Axis powers.

A third and related set of examples comprise those actions which seem to emerge from a desperate mood of rebellion against the hopeless lack of correspondence between ends and means, between purposes and capabilities, actions whose rational purpose is singularly difficult to ascertain.

[7] See Margret Boveri: *Der Verrat im 20. Jahrhundert*, 4 vols. (Hamburg; 1956–60).

Now obviously in great states we find many instances of irrational political behavior resulting from the psychological instability of persons in positions of power, and at times whole social groups can behave in a demented fashion. One may suggest, however, that in the Balkans these tendencies have sometimes been reinforced by the fact of national weakness. It is in this setting that political assassination, which as we have noted is not a regional peculiarity, may most fruitfully be analyzed. In what measure have assassinations in the Balkans shown, or failed to show, a traceable connection between political ends and political means? To take the most fateful of modern assassinations, the shooting of Archduke Francis Ferdinand at Sarajevo, can we find a real political purpose behind that act? If not, is it explainable in terms of the idiosyncrasies of a few plotters, or does it reflect a somewhat more deeply rooted political impulse?[8]

These examples are here offered only as suggestive, not as a conclusive demonstration, but we may at least put

[8] In commenting on an earlier draft of this essay, Rothschild remarked: "When one compares the size of Serbia, for example, on a political map of Europe in 1914, with the territory indicated as inhabited by South Slavs on ethnographic maps of the same year, one becomes aware of a dimension in which the assassination of Franz Ferdinand was neither more nor less of an *acte gratuit*—if I understand this term correctly—than, say, Bismarck's distortion of the Ems telegram in 1870. In each case something was to be gained by war and the consequent restructuring of the European power system. That the First World War was so much more destructive of human life than the Franco-Prussian one is hardly the responsibility of Gavrilo Princip." I would agree that the term *acte gratuit* is not really applicable; both were politically motivated acts. Nor can one fairly judge by the ultimate consequences of such acts. I would argue, however, that it is easier to follow Bismarck's line of reasoning, to discern just what he *planned* to have happen as the result of his act, than it is in the case of Princip, or his co-conspirators.

forward the proposition that the principal effect upon domestic Balkan politics of being a small power has been to create, especially in times of crisis, a polarization between a retreat to politics of impotence and a rage at the impotence of politics.

But even if this double typology—of "cynical" *vs.* "utopian" foreign policy and "prudent" *vs.* "reckless" domestic politics—has some validity, it does not explain why political behavior moves toward one rather than the other pole. It is certainly plausible to argue that a nation's status as an irredentist or a satisfied power, its stake in preserving or upsetting the status quo, would be influential in this regard.[9] And yet when we come down to cases the picture is not simple. While it is true that the three men mentioned earlier—Beneš, Titulescu, and Politis—represented states that were beneficiaries and supporters of the Versailles settlement of 1919, it is also true that Colonel Beck of Poland, another such beneficiary, was definitely "cynical" and antiutopian in his approach to foreign policy. Nor does there appear to be any simple correlation between external status and ambitions and internal political behavior. Certainly the differing styles of Serbian and Rumanian politics, for example, are to be sought in their domestic history and culture rather than in their external successes and failures, which on the whole corresponded fairly closely in the nineteenth and first third of the twentieth centuries. Perhaps the most we can say is that while the political behaviors of the Balkan states are the product of a vast complex of factors—as are those of any nation—the tendency toward polarization which has been discussed here does determine a certain field, a frame of alternatives for both foreign and domestic politics, which is characteristic of the Balkans as small powers.

[9] Again I am most grateful to Joseph Rothschild for his observations on this important point.

VIII ❧ Eastern Europe and the Balance of Power

[1956]

IN INTRODUCING A SYMPOSIUM OF REPORTS ON THE STATE OF the satellite, or captive, nations of Eastern Europe, Adolph Berle made the following observation: "Europe's balance of power—and with it the basis of world peace—depends upon a tier of states between the Soviet Union and the Western world. This is 'Mid-Europe,' extending from the Baltic Sea to the Black Sea and the Adriatic. Both 20th century world wars started in this area."[1] I should like to use this remark as my point of departure: namely, that the European balance of power depends upon the tier of states between the Soviet Union and the Western world.

This remark, of course, carries echoes of previous statements; for example, MacKinder's well-known phrase, "Who rules East Europe commands the heartland, who rules the heartland commands the world." But even earlier than this expression of the critical importance of Eastern Europe to the balance of power we find the concept of the balance of power as such. In a book appearing anony-

1 *The New Leader*, April 9, 1956.

mously in London in 1741, entitled *Europe's Catechism*, there appears this dialogue:

> Catechist : Hold, my pretty child, one word more. You have been asked concerning the balance of power. Tell me what it is.
>
> Europa : It is such an equal distribution of power among the princes of Europe as makes it impracticable for the one to disturb the repose of the other.
>
> Catechist : Tell me wherein consists the safety of Europe.
>
> Europa : In this same balance of power.
>
> Catechist : What is it that generally causes war in her bowels?
>
> Europa : It is occasioned by the balance of power being destroyed.
>
> Catechist : And how may that balance be destroyed?
>
> Europa : That balance may be destroyed by force or fraud, by the pusillanimity of some and the corruption of all.[2]

We may start, then, with two premises: First, that there is a balance of power which may be maintained or destroyed by the actions of states, and, second, that Eastern and East Central Europe have played and continue to play a decisive role in the maintenance or destruction of this balance.

I cannot attempt here to make a historical appraisal of the concept of balance of power or of its general adequacy in describing the past course of international relations, beyond noting that in actual fact diplomatic historians have had a good deal of trouble with the idea, and not least in agreeing on the meaning of "balance" and on the point of equilibrium. You will find one historian contending, for example, that the victory of the Entente

---

[2] *Europe's Catechism*, quoted in Edward Vose Gulick: *Europe's Classical Balance of Power* (Ithaca; 1955) , p. 2.

powers in 1918 was necessary to restore the European balance of power. You will find others arguing that this victory, as expressed in the Versailles Treaty, destroyed the balance. One man's teeter is another's totter.

But overlooking for the moment these historical difficulties, what do we mean by the idea of balance as it applies to Eastern Europe? It appears to rest on the reasonably plausible assumption that this satellite area, divided and not very powerful in itself, is so located and is of such importance that, if it is brought under the effective domination of one or another of the great powers on its flanks, Germany or the Soviet Union, these powers thereby gain such a preponderance of strength in Europe that the balance is to be redressed, if at all, only by calling in extra-European powers. There is no question that Eastern Europe has assumed this importance in the eyes of many diplomats and diplomatic historians, and indeed the critical importance of the area is displayed in past wars and in the variety of solutions to the problem of its position which have been tried at different times in the past. There was the partitioning of the area between the great powers on its flanks, as during the years of the Polish partitions in the eighteenth century, and again during the years of the Nazi-Soviet Pact, 1939–41. There was the effort, between the two world wars, to create an independent area, stretching from the Baltic to the Aegean, dependent neither upon Germany nor upon the Soviet Union. There have been arguments urging the necessity of resuscitating the Habsburg Monarchy or some equivalent supranational organization which could coordinate this region between the German and the Russian spheres. More recently, in the debates on containment and liberation carried on in the United States, one of the arguments for liberation was that the freedom of this area, its removal from Soviet domination, was indispensable to the security of Western Europe, and hence to the security of the United States.

Historically the significance of Eastern Europe in power politics has been largely locational. It includes many areas which have been of the greatest importance in military campaigns: Bohemia, the Moravian Gap, the Pripet marshes, the North German plain, the Carpathian approaches to the Hungarian plain, the Galați Gap between the Carpathians and the Black Sea, the mouths of the Danube, and the approaches to Constantinople and the Straits. Any state which controlled these strategic points was obviously in a very strong position to advance farther either to the east or to the west.

Lately, and particularly since the end of the Second World War, the importance of Eastern Europe has also been seen as one of capabilities. For example, the economic resources of the area, while not yet of the first magnitude, are considerable. Its rate of steel output is approximately one third that of the Soviet Union; its coal and lignite production is about equal to that of the Soviet Union; electric power nearly one-half; crude and synthetic oil production about one fourth. In general, as far as we can tell, the gross national product of the East European satellites is somewhere between one third and one half that of the Soviet Union. The population of the East European satellites is roughly one half that of the Soviet Union. Broadly speaking, then, one might say that the material measurements of the Soviet Union are increased by about one third to one half by the addition of the East European satellites.

But what does all this mean today? What does it add up to? In the classical formulations of balance of power we find the assumption that the power of states was made up of a number of well-defined components—population, industry, finance, balance of trade—and that these sinews of war, if properly applied to the creation of armies and navies, could, when combined with control or occupation of strategic locations, determine the strength of a nation. Moreover, it was assumed that these components were subject to measurement, comparison, and transfer from one scale in the balance to the other.

To be sure, in the nineteenth century Richard Cobden contended that the theory of balance of power "could be discarded as fallacious, since it gives no definition—whether by breadth or territory, number of inhabitants, or extent of wealth—according to which, in balancing the respective powers, each state shall be estimated."[3] Still, even though the estimates might in some cases be rough, there remained the confidence that a balance did exist, that it was made up of these material items and did, in the last analysis, serve to determine the outcome of a trial by arms, if it should come to that (though the idea of the balance was often used to avert the actual test of physical violence).

But what are we to say today in the presence of thermonuclear power and ballistic weapons: What do these innovations do to our notions of capability and location and to our idea of a balance? An algebraic equation can become very unmanageable when one begins introducing infinite quantities. $A + B > C$ may not mean a great deal when these terms approach infinity. Or, to put it more concretely, what is the significance of Rumanian oil production, or control of the Moravian Gap, in the presence of an abundance of thermonuclear bombs possessed by both sides and deliverable by ballistic missiles?

Admittedly, even on the premise of thermonuclear war these traditional factors that made up the power balance are not wholly without significance in contributing to

[3] Gulick: op. cit., p. 27.

defensive space and to certain differentials in the rate of production of fissionable materials and their means of delivery. But, on the whole, they appear to me to be of diminishing importance as we approach—and rapidly—so-called "atomic plenty": a sufficiency of stockpiles and means of delivery to achieve virtual—and mutual—obliteration of the opponents.

The chief difficulty which concerns me here is not the fantastic problems confronting the military planner, or even the meaning of economic potential if it is subject to destruction in a few hours's time but, rather, the effect upon all our traditional and habitual thinking about "balance of power" when "power" itself has so got out of hand. In such a situation the power a nation can command is not the sum or product of all the familiar components taken together in a general aggregate but something suddenly far greater. How does this affect our thinking, not at the level of military operations alone, but all the way down the chain of material capabilities?

These disconcerting developments have led a number of people to the conclusion that we have reached the end of the line as far as power politics is concerned, that since the graph of power has gone right off the end of the chart, we can no longer make a useful comparison of power or try to balance it.

There is a real danger here of dumping out the baby with the bath water. We cannot safely pay attention exclusively to the upper reaches of power and disregard or dismiss either other forms of power or the idea of a power balance, though I am sure we must do a great deal of reinterpreting our customary views. The state of affairs of Eastern Europe—its development or its political orientation—cannot become a matter of indifference to the United States.

In the first place, it is not to be excluded that there may be military engagements below the thermonuclear ceiling. Battles have been fought recently in Korea and in Indochina in which the ultimate powers of destruction were not employed. It is not impossible, though it may not be likely, that fighting of this sort could occur in Europe. And in such a case Eastern Europe, its location and the physical power it would add to that of the Soviet Union, could play a very important role and might indeed be of decisive significance.

The task, however, of trying to determine the balance of power with respect to what is called "conventional" warfare I am glad to leave to the military specialists. I will say only that because of the increasing integration of tactical atomic weapons into the armories of the various powers it is going to be increasingly difficult to give the term "conventional" any meaning. Moreover, aside from developments in the nuclear field, the striking power and speed of armed forces has multiplied enormously since the end of the Second World War. In other words, quite apart from the tremendous destructive power of thermonuclear energy, the general trend of our modern technology is for all features of power to tend, in respect to capabilities, to reach the upper levels of violence.

In the second place, it is not difficult to envisage a game of power politics played under the thermonuclear ceiling, not involving actual force, conventional or atomic, but having it in the background, as a form of threat or blackmail: the game of pressing to the brink of the abyss, in order to induce the other side to retreat, to give up points, to renounce territory. In such a game, Eastern Europe could play an important role. A number of East European areas have been considered as possible pawns in this type of play and counterplay: the possibility, for example, of pressure on Albania or on the Soviet zone of Germany. I definitely do not favor this kind of Russian roulette, but we may have to face it if it is forced upon us.

In the third place, there is the possibility of what one might call inverted power politics—a type of contest which may become increasingly common. In this case, instead of a move toward increasing violence, the capabilities of the nations are used in the effort to force the locus of conflict away from explicit power into the somewhat safer but still bitterly contested area of political warfare. Instead of an arms race, a disarmament-talk race; instead of economic warfare, welfare warfare; instead of turning plowshares into swords, using plowshares as swords. Here the elements of material power are clearly present, especially those of economic strength and industrial resources.

In this field of what I call inverted power politics, where the contest may move away from, rather than toward, the ultraviolent end of the spectrum, there may be a kind of balance of power, though of a rather unusual sort, of which we have yet to learn the principles.

In discussing inverted power politics, however, I do not mean to suggest any necessary diminution of the conflict of wills between the Soviet bloc and the West. The antagonisms and the stakes may remain as great as before, though the means are less immediately perilous.

Nor do I refer to what is usually called economic warfare. There is a tendency to regard economic warfare as equivalent to military warfare and, if conducted properly, productive of the same results. I am skeptical of this line of approach, especially when it is taken out of military context. Admittedly, during a war, economic measures can be an important adjunct to military operations in depriving the opponent of supplies, inhibiting his production, and so on—though these effects may be of marginal significance against an opponent of continental size. As for measures of economic warfare taken in advance of a military conflict, while they may reduce somewhat a potential opponent's capabilities, I am quite skeptical of their really sapping an opponent's strength until he is rendered helpless.

I am referring, rather, to what is already going on in the world: such things as the effort on both sides to create "show-windows," the appearance of Hungarian agricultural machinery in South African markets, the competitive efforts to extend technical assistance to underdeveloped areas, proposed American attempts to induce the satellites régime to improve the living conditions of their subjects, attempts to put the other side at a disadvantage by outpacing him on disarmament proposals—in brief, what might be called a desperate play of international gamesmanship, the effort to do in the other fellow by outmatching him in virtue and virtuosity.

There is no doubt that many of the customary components of the balance of power are important in this game. That Hungary is capable of manufacturing and exporting salable machinery, that Czech merchants and traders can be sent to Southeast Asia, or that the rapid expansion of the gross national product in the satellites can be waved before the eyes of other nations eager to industrialize—these are clearly assets to the Soviet orbit.

Perhaps even more important is the fact that the Soviet orbit *exists*, that a revolutionary *state* has become a revolutionary system, a camp, a way of economic life that shows great vitality, however this has been achieved.

But even if we grant that Eastern Europe is an asset to the Soviet Union, where does the notion of balance come in, how do we *weigh* the various items in this setting? As I have suggested earlier, our traditional idea of a balance meant a direct linkage between economic strength and war-making capacity. But in this discussion we have eliminated from our consideration one end of the linkage—war-making capacity.

I would not agree with those who feel that somehow the skillful employment of this type of gamesmanship, or inverted power politics, leads to such a softening up of the opponent—perhaps through making him economically dependent—that the military question can be bypassed. For example, there has been a tendency to overrate the significance of Germany's economic penetration of Eastern Europe between 1933 and 1939—the aspirin and camera campaign—as a means of gaining domination over these states. By and large these states did rather well in preserving their political independence until the diplomatic and military situation collapsed after the *Anschluss* and Munich.

In other words, I do not believe we can answer our problem of "balance of power" merely by assuming that the various items of resources, industry, and manpower somehow add up to an equivalent of a military potential which is never employed.

We must face one further difficulty in our attempt to determine the meaning of Eastern Europe to the balance of power, a difficulty which may, however, point the way to an answer of some importance.

When we refer to the classical idea of the balance of power we find that it rests not only on the assumption of measurement and comparison but even more basically upon the notion of *homogeneity* as a necessary feature of any operative balance of power. That is, the states in the balance are relatively similar in their makeup, the various items comprising "power"—manpower, industry, commerce—play roughly the same role from one society to another. Without this, of course, it is very hard to make valid comparisons. If, to take an extreme example, the copper production of a primitive tribe is used to make earrings and necklaces rather than electrical and industrial equipment, then clearly a comparison, or balance, based on measurement of copper output does not mean much.

In other words, when we are matching different *kinds* of societies, the problem of balance of power is much more difficult to handle—except, again on the level of an explicit showdown by means of force, when the various factors are assembled and put to the test, something we are excluding from our present consideration. It may be that one reason the European nations in the past were reluctant to consider the Ottoman Turks as part of the European balance of power—though they did in fact enter in from time to time—was this sense, based partly on religious differences, that here was an alien and strange society of different composition and purpose.

In dealing with the Soviet orbit we face a similar problem that greatly increases the difficulties of getting any precise notion of balance of power when it is not reducible to terms of physical striking power. These differences derive from the Communist ideology, from the way in which the Soviet Union was created and developed, from the manner in which the Soviet bloc was built up and is held together. The result is that the interrelationship of the various components may be quite different from what they are in the West or the United States. As a consequence we may run into serious trouble when we try to get a notion of balance—even an approximation—by "horizontal" comparisons between the Soviet bloc and the West.

To take one example, standard of living. Even if we are able to work out a rough comparison between the physical and material well-being of, say, the Polish worker and the

French worker, in terms of labor required for so many units of various commodities, what does this comparison mean? In a free Western society this standard is doubtless an important way of judging the success and effectiveness of the society. We may even derive conclusions concerning the society's capacity to enjoy the loyalty and support of its citizens. But it seems clear that we cannot simply transfer these criteria to the Soviet bloc, where "standard of living" has come to have a quite different significance, conceptually and in practice.

This difference more or less holds for nearly all the factors in the physical makeup of the Soviet bloc. They are combined in different ways and for different purposes. Hence the importance of Eastern Europe is not to be measured by any horizontal comparison of, say, United States and NATO coal as against U.S.S.R. and satellite coal or United States and NATO manpower as against U.S.S.R. and satellite manpower.

More than that, the role of the individual states in the Soviet orbit is not the same as in the West. A Czechoslovakia transferred to NATO would not be performing the same function as a Czechoslovakia in the Soviet orbit. A different percentage of her energies would be devoted to the "bloc," and the organization and control would be altogether different.

In brief, when we deal with a system having the peculiar and alien qualities of the Soviet bloc, the classic model of balance of power, with its ideas of relatively simple addition, multiplication, and transferability, breaks down.

If this is so, it seems to follow that our notion of balance becomes much more complex and subtle. Instead of "horizontal" comparisons we must first create "vertical" comparisons, comparisons that may indeed cover the whole of the societies and take into account these profound functional differences. But this in turn implies that a meaningful balance cannot consider just physical or material items but must place them in their social setting and in reference to the goals and purposes of the respective systems.

I would conclude, then, that when we speak of the meaning of Eastern Europe in the balance of power, we must, if we are to make much sense, think less of its contribution of so many tons of steel, so much grain, or so many barrels of oil than of the impact of the fact that whole societies are being geared to the purposes and ends of the Soviet system. This fact, while perhaps not amenable to precise measurement, is subject to some manner of weighting and comparison. The success or failure of the Soviet Union in harnessing the nations, resources, and peoples of Eastern Europe to its purposes is something that can and will be compared to the capacity of the peoples of the Free World to develop their resources and manpower for their quite different purposes; and the outcome of this comparison may well be decisive in the world's balance. It is the awareness of this deeper comparison—and not any narrow matching of physical capabilities, not even the sense of moral outrage over the involuntary Sovietization of Eastern Europe—that lies behind our malaise over the Iron Curtain and our national unwillingness to accept its implications. For it is precisely the accretion of Eastern Europe to the U.S.S.R., the expansion of a revolutionary state to a continental system, which gives apparent substance to the Communist claim of being the way of the future.

In the last analysis, it has always been this sense of confidence or despair, of loyalty or disaffection, that weighs the balance of nations, not in defiance of physical factors perhaps, but certainly not in any mechanical dependence upon them. We have only to recall Churchill's Britain of

1940 to realize the supreme importance in history's scales of this confidence that molds all the physical factors to the goal of survival and freedom.

I have no idea whether the movement of the balance in this sense will ever be decisive, whether we can keep physical violence from throwing its weight in the scales. If not, the future is not pleasant to contemplate. And yet it is possible that, having achieved the capacity for ultimate violence, we may for that reason be spared its actual use. If so, it will only be because we have grasped and marked the meaning of this new type of balance, a balance in which Eastern Europe does play an important role—as a recent tragedy, a present challenge, but a future hope.

PART THREE

Power and Stability in Soviet Russia

IX ❦ Causality and Contingency in March and November 1917

[1969]

FOR HALF A CENTURY PARTICIPANTS, OBSERVERS, AND HIS-
torians have speculated on the "might-have-beens" of the
Russian Revolution: Did what occur have to occur, or
were there reasonable chances for other outcomes? In contrast to E. H. Carr, who refers rather acidly to such speculation as a "parlour game" having nothing to do with
history,[1] my predisposition has been on the side of the
problematical: that many other things might well have
happened and that musing about them is a proper activity
for a historian. I have been inclined, consequently, to stress
the element of uncertainty. Thus, in speaking of Russia on
the eve of the First World War, I have argued: "Whether
these implied short-term crises that might have been met
by in-system solutions (whether, for example, the mounting wave of strikes would have slackened and the new
working class have been harnessed to urbanization), or
whether they were indicators of deep-rooted maladies,

[1] Edward Hallett Carr: *What Is History?* (New York; 1962), p.
127.

bound to get worse until a general explosion occurred, is difficult to say. Indeed, I think it is impossible to say, because of the vast number of contingent influences that could have affected the scene with each day of history."[2]

Recently, however, I encountered a problem that made me doubt my inclination, though without leading me to acceptance of Carr's position. In contemplating the courses of the March and November Revolutions in 1917, I found to my surprise and discomfort that my impressions of these two sets of events were tending markedly in opposite directions. The more I looked at the fall of the monarchy the less plausible seemed the various "might-have-beens" of timing, place, decision, and personality that have been advanced as being possibly able to avert it. Conversely, the more I looked at the Bolshevik seizure of power the more accident, chance, and happenstance seemed to dominate the picture. This was very untidy. The present essay is an effort to look into this problem.

It might be said, and probably would be said by a Soviet commentator, that these impressions are what one would expect of a bourgeois historian: pleased by the fall of autocracy, I see it as the consequence of substantial and necessary causes, an outcome proper to the nature of things and the course of history; dismayed by the advent of the Bolsheviks, I am led to see it as a fluke, an untoward occurrence not geared to any real political or historical necessity. This could be—it is very difficult to be fully aware of such impulses in oneself—yet I believe the problem is not simply the by-product of wishful, or wistful, thinking on my part.

This sense of a difference in the causal quality of the March and November Revolutions is not original or

---

2 See below, p. 247.

unique with me. George Lichtheim, for example, has made a somewhat similar observation. In dealing with the question, "With so many giant creatures floundering about in the political jungle, why did victory go to the Bolsheviks?" he remarks: "To treat the Bolshevik seizure of power in October 1917 as an event of the same order as the fall of the Monarchy eight months earlier, i.e., as the *necessary* consequence of Russia's internal development, is not only nonsense, but the reverse of 'historical materialism.' "[3] Lichtheim here is arguing that while the fall of the Tsarist régime was more or less in the cards, given Russia's history, Lenin's victory "was no more than an opportunity."

The objection may be raised at once that I am posing a pseudo-problem, inadmissibly mixing oranges and apples. In equating the March Revolution with the *fall* of the Tsar, and the November Revolution with the *advent* of the Bolsheviks, I obviously am not comparing two identical historical processes. If we were to compare, on the one hand, the fall of the Tsar with the fall of Kerensky's Provisional Government, and, on the other, the advent of the Provisional Government (plus the appearance of the Soviets) with the victory of the Bolsheviks, would we not find similarities in these two sets of pairings? A certain sense of necessity in the two collapses, a certain sense of the contingent and accidental in the two accesses to power?

This objection has weight, and indicates the main track for inquiry. But it leads at once to a difficult and abstract question. Why should we have, if we do, this sense of different kinds of causality, necessity, or likelihood for the gaining as against the losing of political power? This difference, if it proves to have any substance, takes us away both

[3] George Lichtheim: *Marxism: An Historical and Critical Study* (New York; 1961), p. 332.

from the "Cleopatra's nose" view of history, in which all manner of major outcomes can hinge upon trivial or irrelevant accidents, and from the view that would discern a structure or pattern in the entire course of a revolutionary upheaval, from beginning to end. Rather, it would suggest that events of a different order may require different types of analysis for comprehending them. With this possibility in mind let us look at March and November more closely.

The March Revolution has led to at least two hotly debated issues that concern us here: (1) The question of the "spontaneity" of the revolutionary outbreak in Petrograd, and (2) the question of "missed opportunities" on the part of the régime in averting total disaster once the outbreak had taken place.

In his history of the Russian Revolution, William Henry Chamberlin remarks: "The collapse of the Romanov autocracy in March 1917 was one of the most leaderless, spontaneous, anonymous revolutions of all time."[4] In E. H. Carr's judgment, "The February Revolution of 1917 which overthrew the Romanov dynasty was the spontaneous outbreak of a multitude exasperated by the privations of war and by manifest inequality in the distribution of burdens."[5] Against this George Katkov argues, "The theory of a spontaneous, elemental (*stikhiinoe*) movement of the Petrograd proletariat is only an admission of our inability to explain the course of events. Why should such movements have occurred then, and only then, in Petrograd? Neither before nor since have the Russian masses shown any such capacity for concerted

[4] William Henry Chamberlin: *The Russian Revolution, 1917–1921*, 2 vols., 2d ed. (New York; 1952), I, 73.

[5] Edward Hallett Carr: *The Bolshevik Revolution, 1917–1923*, 3 vols., (New York; 1951–3), I, 70.

'spontaneous' action."[6] Without becoming involved in the peculiarly Russian debates associated with *stikhiinost'*,[7] we may say that the point at issue here is whether general conditions suffice to explain the time, place, and intensity of the outbreak. In Katkov's view they do not. Not accepting the claims of the revolutionary parties to have set off the Revolution, he clearly feels a gap in the historical equation. This he fills by giving "unreserved support" to the thesis that German agents and German funds were behind it. Whatever the merits of this particular line of explanation, which has not gained general acceptance among historians of 1917, we can see the nature of the problem: whether some such specific instigative cause ("prime movers," in Katkov's words) is required to satisfy us in our search for an adequate explanation of the outbreak of mass disturbances.

In my own view such an agency is not required, and I am willing to accept the revolutionary outbreak as spontaneous, obviously not in the sense of being a causeless effect but in the sense we usually understand by the phrase "spontaneous combustion."[8] Still, I do share Katkov's dissatisfaction with such very general explanations as mass frustration, privation, or resentment. A more highly structured, concrete *mise en scène* is required. But this, I believe,

[6] George Katkov: *Russia 1917: The February Revolution* (New York; 1967), p. 419.

[7] For a discussion of this see Leopold H. Haimson: *The Russian Marxists and the Origins of Bolshevism* (Cambridge, Mass.; 1955).

[8] The metaphor of the spark and the powder keg is often employed in this way, though giving rather more weight to the precipitating act or agent. Thus the assassination of the Archduke Franz Ferdinand at Sarajevo is a historical event of considerable importance; things might have turned out quite differently if it had not taken place.

can be presented. If we accept, say, Leopold Haimson's picture of Russia on the eve of 1914 as suffering a double polarization of alienated urban workers and of a rift between privileged society and the régime, add to it the strains and problems of the war, take note of the evident frondeur mood of the elite in 1916, and reflect on the classic symptoms of a revolutionary situation that have been presented by Crane Brinton and others, we arrive at a picture of a structural crisis which leads one to conclude that an explosion in the capital city, with its concentration of political life, its large, ill-disciplined garrisons, and its war-inflated industries, does not require any instigative agent.

While we may be dealing with some statistical probabilities, deriving from the mood and behavior of large masses of people, the historical question is considerably more complex than simply one of activating latent resentments or igniting mob action. It is the *structure* of the situation in March 1917 that contains this high degree of likelihood of an outbreak, a structure some elements of which reach far into the Russian past, many of which are recognizable from 1904–5 or 1912–14.

When we turn to the days immediately following the outbreak of disturbances we encounter the same problem in a different guise. Once the crowds were in the streets, once the troops had mutinied rather than continue to fire upon them, could anything have been done to avert the collapse of the monarchy? When one reads the exchanges between Petrograd and GHQ (where the Tsar was), and especially those between the President of the Duma, Rodzianko, and Tsar Nicholas, one initially has the impression of missed opportunities, of a possibly fortuitous time-lag in which responses were too late and hence too little, of a delay in realizing the state of affairs in the capital, with the result that steps taken fell behind the course of events and hence were irrelevant, abortive, or disastrous.[9] One feels that somehow the Tsar, the government, the high command, and the Duma leaders could have reached in time an agreement on actions to be taken to prevent the catastrophe that all feared.

And yet I find that this impression of missed opportunities, of real contingency in the fall of the dynasty, tends to evaporate upon closer inspection.

In the first place, the fact that Tsar and Duma leaders should have been at cross-purposes in this moment of crisis was no casual accident of personalities or of misunderstanding. It was deeply rooted in the whole unhappy history of relations between Tsar and Russian "society." One might think that in the face of a looming menace all dreaded—the convulsive shrug of the Russian masses—they should have been able to resolve their differences. But it is a familiar feature of such situations that even evident and explicitly recognized common interests may not prevent the onset of a pattern of mutually ruinous actions that lead right to the brink of the abyss and beyond.[1] In the Russian setting each of the successive steps that Rodzianko urged upon the Tsar—a government of "confidence," the Tsar's withdrawal in favor of another member of the dynasty, the need to pull all Romanovs off the stage and to convoke a Constituent Assembly—was a mortal challenge to autocracy, even an autocracy modified by 1905. I cannot bring to life any formula that could have overcome this antagonism; each side to be true to itself had to

[9] Katkov (op. cit., p. 243) conveys this sense in writing of the Tsar's "ghostly journey through the snow-bound wastes of Russia, lasting close on forty hours, of which every minute saw a new turn of events in the capital."

[1] Some recent models in games theory are most persuasive in demonstrating how two parties can walk into a foreseeable mutual disaster despite the presence of better alternatives for both.

play out the antagonism. In the circumstances of the time this playing out may give the impression of a tragic mishap.

Moreover, even if an agreed upon course of action had been reached, if Tsar and Duma leaders had found common ground, what kind of workable solution might have been advanced? Neither repression nor accommodation seemed feasible (and a tactical combination of the two required a type of single-minded leadership that simply was not on the scene at the time). The limits of repression were well demonstrated by the mutiny of the troops of the Petrograd garrison *after* they had successfully dispersed the crowds: they were not going to do it a second time. It might be argued that more reliable troops, not infected by the political atmosphere of the capital, could have been brought in to restore order. This possibility cannot be dismissed out of hand, but I should think that a similar revulsion—against firing on fellow troops as well as on fellow Russians—would have been the most likely consequence.

As for an accommodation between insurrectionary Petrograd and the old order, I cannot find any satisfactory prescription. There was talk about a government enjoying public confidence. But who were the persons commanding such confidence, and could they have maintained it if they were associated with the imperial régime? A classic, if wholly indeterminate, formula for meeting such crises is: "If you can't lick 'em, join 'em." But in this instance I am reminded of the mournful cartoon character: "What do I do now? I can't lick 'em, and they won't let me join 'em."

My reference to the "structure" of the crisis of March 1917 and to comparisons with other revolutions suggests one tentative conclusion at this point. On the whole, comparative studies of revolutions, the search for similarities or an anatomy, have been most successful in dealing with the background and advent of a revolutionary crisis, the

breakdown of an established order. In this area many illuminating parallels are to be found. It is the Thermidors,
the Bonapartes, the Restorations that cause the difficulties.
I have the impression that there are discernible patterns,
even sequential stages, to a mounting revolutionary crisis.
This pattern is probably not one of "causes"—causes are
necessarily tied to the particular circumstance of each
historical case—but, rather, of symptoms or manifestations.
This pattern relates intimately to the destruction of an
existing structure; it is precisely the absence of structure
in the later stages of a revolution that causes difficulty for
any general theory of revolution; by that point we are in
the realm of contingency.

To look at this other side let us now turn to the November Revolution. Most accounts of the Bolshevik access
to power stress one of two apparently opposing interpretations. At the one extreme there is a picture of November
as a second welling of popular revolt which carried the
Bolsheviks to power. At the other is a picture of a pure
coup d'état executed by a small group of professional revolutionaries in disregard of, or in blatant opposition to,
the popular will. Insofar as these two interpretations reflect moral or partisan judgments they may appear mutually incompatible. Yet in fact a variety of combinations
is possible. One may give the Bolsheviks relatively little
credit for the event. Thus, Ulam writes: "The Bolsheviks
did not seize power in this year of revolution. They picked
it up. . . . Any group of determined men could have
done what the Bolsheviks did in Petrograd in October
1917: seize the few key points of the city and proclaim
themselves the government."[2] Others would grant the

---

[2] Adam Ulam: *The Bolsheviks: The Intellectual and Political
History of the Triumph of Communism in Russia* (New York;
1965), p. 314.

Bolsheviks a more positive role, as skillful surfers riding the turbulent crest of the breakers, or even as controlling and manipulating the upheaval. At the other extreme one could make it a pure plot, laced perhaps with German funds, or one could give it a modicum of popular backing, the support of the military forces in the capital, or the growing Bolshevik majorities in various workers' and soldiers' soviets. Debates over the respective role of the Petrograd garrisons as against the Red Guard indicate variants at this end of the spectrum.[3]

For present purposes, however, the most interesting feature of this whole range of interpretations is something that they share in common, namely a felt need to find, either through mass action or skillful planning or a combination of the two, an "adequate" explanation for this momentous event. Either the momentum of the masses *or* a high degree of organization seems to be required. (Do we find in this echoes of the familiar Russian polarity of "spontaneity" and "consciousness"?)

What is troublesome about November, however, is that the empirical evidence for either interpretation seems to break down upon examination. I simply cannot find this great surge of popular revolt but, rather, an eerie social vacuum. (Lenin himself, in October, spoke of the "absenteeism and indifference of the masses," which, however, he attributed to their being tired of words and resolutions.[4]) Nor do I find the skillful Bolshevik planning and organization. Robert V. Daniels's admirable *Red October* strikes me as most persuasive on this point: "The stark

[3] On this debate, see Raphael R. Abramovitch: *The Soviet Revolution, 1917–1939* (New York; 1962), pp. 83–4.

[4] In *The Russian Provisional Government 1917*, 3 vols., eds. Robert Paul Browder and Alexander F. Kerensky (Stanford; 1961), III, 1763.

truth about the Bolshevik Revolution is that it succeeded against incredible odds in defiance of any rational calculation that could have been made in the fall of 1917. . . . Lenin's revolution, as Zinoviev and Kamenev pointed out, was a weird gamble with little chance that the Bolsheviks' ill-prepared followers could prevail against all the military force that the government seemed to have and even less chance that they could keep power even if they managed to seize it temporarily."[5] Actually, this perception of accident and confusion in the Bolshevik access to power is nothing new. The reports of such eyewitnesses as N. Sukhanov and John Reed are full of it.

In meeting this difficulty some have sought to resolve it along the lines of the adage "In the kingdom of the blind the one-eyed man is king." Merle Fainsod, for example, observes: "Why then did the Bolsheviks triumph? The Bolsheviks, unlike most of their opponents, were willing to take the initiative and, for all their own disorganization, they represented a relatively disciplined force."[6] For all the dissension, foot-dragging, and confusion in the Bolshevik Central Committee in the weeks and days preceding the November Revolution, for all the uncertainties surrounding the planning and purposes of the "armed insurrection," the Bolsheviks were in less disarray than the Provisional Government, the Socialist-Revolutionaries, or the Mensheviks. In other words, by stressing *relative* assets (whether in terms of effective mass support or of planning and organization) our sense of an "adequate" explanation may be preserved.

This could be. It is an interpretation difficult to refute

[5] Robert V. Daniels: *Red October: The Bolshevik Revolution of 1917* (New York; 1967), pp. 215–16.

[6] In *Revolutionary Russia,* ed. Richard Pipes (Cambridge, Mass.; 1968), p. 219.

by the evidence, since it is able to adapt itself to the obvious facts of the case. Yet this line of analysis may carry us down the wrong track. My own reading of the story does not reveal the presence of islands of popular insurgency or the Bolsheviks' relatively better organization as really accounting for the November Revolution. I am increasingly struck by the decisive role of accidents, pure flukes, in these days, and they do jolt one's feeling of historical fitness.

This uncomfortable situation has led me to conclude that one must seek a different underlying causal structure to deal with this phase of the Revolution. Perhaps we should here re-examine a collapse of authority, this time the fall of the Provisional Government. It could be argued that the success of the Bolsheviks was in direct correspondence to the fall of the Provisional Government. Crane Brinton, speaking in more general terms about this stage of the revolutionary process, offers as a proposition: "The reasons why the extremists succeeded are but the other side of the reasons why the moderates failed."[7] There undoubtedly is a connection, but I doubt that it is so precise.

I would agree that the "moderates," the Provisional Government, faced an extremely difficult situation even from the outset, and that the cards were heavily stacked against them following the polarization of political positions in July and especially after the Kornilov affair. And yet, for all the fragility and uncertainty of the Provisional Government's position—perhaps, paradoxically, because of it—the Provisional Government was perhaps less bound to any "iron law" of disaster than was the Tsarist régime in its last days. The whole setting of its activities was the

[7] Crane Brinton: *The Anatomy of Revolution,* rev. and expanded ed. (New York; 1965), p. 148.

highly contingent and problematic one that followed from the disappearance of the *ancien régime*.

It is extremely difficult to construct for the imperial régime in its last days an alternate scenario that might, without an extensive rewriting of Russian history, have rescued it. In the case of the Provisional Government, the very contingency of the circumstances connected with its coming into being (the persons who happened to emerge, the disappearance of the Duma, the odd relationship, *dvoevlastie*, it had with the Petrograd Soviet) make its situation much more "open," though definitely not in any positive sense of increasing its chances for success. The problems of war, social reform, relations with the nationalities, that forced themselves onto the agenda, offered no easy answers, perhaps no answers at all. Still, it is the very chaotic quality of the time that makes it difficult, in the early months of 1917 at least, to lay down a precise pattern for defeat. While I am inclined to regard the wild mélange of hopes and fears that expressed themselves following the abdication of the Tsar as a somewhat morbid symptom in itself, it does reflect, on the subjective plane, this feature of openness.

But for all the basic contingency in the very existence of the Provisional Government, within six months or so it had in fact proceeded, not steadily but in ups and downs, to a deteriorated situation. Its actions, in whatever direction, promised to exacerbate rather than to diminish its difficulties, either by heightening opposition or apathy, or by setting forces in motion that might overshadow or overthrow it. In this sense I find the contingency of the disappearance of the Provisional Government declining with the passage of time from March to November, though even at the end its likely collapse rested on the prevailing uncertainties of the post-March period.

If this be the case, we might propose that the same circumstances which both rendered the Provisional Government fragile and increased the element of contingency in its fate were also conducive to making the advent of the Bolsheviks fraught with accident. We might offer as a hypothesis, that a well-planned, well-executed *coup* can be carried out only on the premise of a structured setting. (Do palace revolts occur in general chaos?) In times of widespread confusion and disarray there may be no such thing as elegant planning. A plan, to be sure, may be in someone's mind, but as soon as it moves out into the world to gain instrumentalities for its realization it is subject to the general atmosphere. The human agents share in the prevailing uncertainties (it is very rare that a group of people is so utterly alienated or so completely disciplined as to avoid this) ; channels of information, communication, and command are equally part of the broader environment. It is surely this sense that informs Tolstoy's historical observations in *War and Peace*.

Given the extent of disorganization in Russia as the months went by in 1917, I find it quite reasonable to interpret the "ten days that shook the world" as filled with flukes, lucky and unlucky breaks.[8]

I would suggest that in certain historical processes we find something possibly analogous to the second law of thermodynamics, of increasing entropy: that the movement from a structured to an unstructured situation, from co-

[8] To avoid confusion, I should add that we seem here to be dealing with two types of contingency, as contrasted with a statistical probability. A highly planned action, say, a perfectly executed *coup*, is in a way a highly contingent event. It is not a "likely" event, and its working out depends upon the absence of intrusive accidents. Hence it is a highly structured event; its chances of occurring depend in good part upon a structured setting. This type of contingent event is obviously quite different from something that happens through a series of accidents.

herence to chaos or randomness, operates in one mode of causality, whereas the creation of a structure involves a different mode. I have been tempted to press this analogy into the area of statistics and probabilities, but have withdrawn from that venture: it seemed to raise more problems than it solved, and to produce very little output for a lot of input. Thus, it is tempting to regard the revolutionary collapse of an established régime as a statistical matter: the action of large numbers, mobs perhaps, of the discontented and frustrated. There may be something to this, but it seems sounder to define the randomness, or disorder, of a system's breakdown as less a matter of disorderly crowds—more likely a manifestation—than as a disintegration of the complex of social, political, and psychological patterns.

To try a formula: in a highly structured situation not too many things are possible, but those that are possible are highly likely; whereas in a chaotic situation many things are possible, but all are unlikely. To apply this to the Russian Revolution: in the classic crisis of March 1917 the possibility of various scenarios respecting the fate of the monarchy is very limited, but the ones we can envisage seem to have a quite high degree of likelihood of leading to the fall of the Tsar. I would here include the planned *coup* by members of the Duma opposition, which apparently failed to come about simply because the March Revolution happened to strike first (it is doubtful that the consequences, however, would have been those hoped for by such men as Guchkov) .[9]

[9] Guchkov, however, was fully aware of the uncertain and problematic nature of his efforts: "Our methods of struggle are double-edged and can—owing to the excitable state of the popular masses and in particular of the working class—become the first spark of a conflagration, the dimensions of which no one can foresee or localize" (quoted in Katkov: op. cit., p. 183) .

Once the Tsar had fallen and the structure of the *ancien régime* began to fall by the way, there was a curious combination of structure and nonstructure, which may explain my sense of the Provisional Government: always in peril, but initially less locked into "increasing entropy" than it became later in the year. The odds were against its being able to bring about a restructuring, perhaps because all such possibilities became increasingly uncertain as things dissolved.

Finally, by the time the Bolsheviks came to power the scene was very chaotic indeed. The particular path by which they gained victory was a devious one, and quite unplanned at several decisive points. A wide variety of other outcomes succeeding the Provisional Government was entirely possible, the chances for any one of them extremely problematic. As for the Bolsheviks' prospects for reversing the drift to randomness, of creating a new structure, this, almost by definition, must be regarded as highly contingent at the moment of their access to power. The sense of contemporaries, including many Bolsheviks, that the November Revolution was going to be a very temporary affair, that the Bolsheviks could not retain power, was not an unreasonable one, though it was belied by subsequent history. Perhaps one reason why this may seem surprising to us is that suggested by John Keep: "Western historians, influenced by the later Bolshevik obsession with efficient organization and by Soviet historical studies, tended to assume that the Bolshevik party apparatus functioned much more efficiently than it ever could have in a revolutionary situation."[1]

I am uncomfortably aware of two nasty problems implicit in my approach, one general and one specific to 1917.

[1] In Pipes: op. cit., p. 223.

First, by having introduced, even by analogy, the dangerous idea of increasing entropy—a notorious troublemaker always—I am in peril of seeing the odds favoring the breakdown of structure as formidably, even overwhelmingly, greater than those for maintaining or increasing structure. If this were a historical force or law, things would always be unwinding and chaos would be the norm. Subjectively, this may represent our mood from time to time.[2] Yet obviously this has not been the course of history, though it could conceivably be the end of history. One might be tempted here to borrow from the sciences the idea of islands or eddies of reduced entropy, such as photosynthesis, though these, I gather, are at the cost of even greater entropy in the larger system. I am doubtful that such an excursion would help us very much. The patterns and structures I have been speaking of are only a part, even a superficial part, of the whole human situation, and many things lie largely below these tides of history: continuing biological needs and urges, social habits, family and other intimate group relations, and the like. These may provide enormous reservoirs for restructuring and rearticulation.

The second problem has to do with the role of Lenin. Somehow, making the Bolshevik victory such an unlikely and accidental event runs counter to one's picture of the decisive part he played in the Russian Revolution. One does not have to subscribe to the Soviet hagiography of an infallible, all-comprehending leader to feel the impact of the man; a reading of his flood of writings in 1917 will suffice. He just does not seem to be merely one of many leaves whirling in the revolutionary wind.

Nor does reference to his "will to revolution," though

[2] One thinks of Pope's "Dunciad," Byron's "Darkness," and Yeats's "Second Coming."

he certainly had that, resolve the matter. The will somehow had to make itself felt. If my preceding argument
has validity, Lenin's "genius for organization" is not the
main clue, at least not for 1917 (though very possibly for
the following years) . What, then, is the answer?

George Lichtheim indicates one answer which, I believe,
points in the right direction, though I am doubtful of his
particular solution. In dealing with much the same problem I have been discussing, Lichtheim remarks: "An analysis of Leninism which stops at this point is in danger of
underrating the originality of Lenin's achievement," and
goes on to say: "The uniqueness of Lenin—and of the
Bolshevik organization which he founded and held together—lay in the decision to make the agrarian upheaval
do the work of the proletarian revolution to which all
Social Democrats were in principle committed."[3]

The clear advantage of relating Lenin's victory to the
agrarian upheaval is that it would link his fortunes to a
powerful impulse involving a large majority of the Russian
people; this would seem to provide comfortable ballast
against the mounting uncertainties and contingencies of
the time: Lenin was banking on a good probability. The
difficulty, for me, is a purely factual one. Despite all that
has been said on the subject, it is simply not clear just
how the peasant upheaval brought Lenin to power in
Petrograd in November 1917, except in the negative sense
that it prevented certain other possibilities (such as a

[3] Lichtheim: op. cit., p. 333. I should note, however, that Lichtheim's view of the prospects of a planned *coup* in times of chaos
may appear to be diametrically opposed to the one I have proposed. He remarks: "In a fluid situation it was possible to bring
off a successful *coup d'état* of the sort Blanqui had planned, but
for which mid-nineteenth-century France was already too highly
organized—and too conservative!"

conservative counter-revolutionary movement of village against city). It is true that Lenin did not permit himself, for reasons of ideological purity, to be tripped up by the peasant question in 1917; that is important but also negative.

While not neglecting Lenin's willingness to make use of an agrarian upheaval, we must also consider other possible instruments for gaining power. When one looks at Lenin's communications to his party comrades in the weeks following the Kornilov affair, weeks when he was desperately urging them to make a decision for revolution, one can only be staggered by the variety of plans and schemes he hurls forth, of which making use of the agrarian disturbances is only one: a workers' insurrection, a military *coup,* bringing in troops from outside, transferring the uprising to Moscow, scanning the horizon for a revolution in Germany, and even, though he dropped this quickly, cooperating for a spell with the Mensheviks and Socialist-Revolutionaries. He was pressing frantically in all directions. Some have concluded that this was just blind thrashing; some have even found signs of mental imbalance.[4] I would suggest that Lenin's genius at this critical juncture lay in his accurate sense of the chaos that was mounting in Russia (Bertram Wolfe refers felicitously to Lenin's ability to "speculate on *stikhiia*"[5]) and that he was feeling about for any and all clusters, or partial structures, that might enable him to become master of it. In this light some of the points that have been made against Lenin —charges of expediency, inconsistency, manipulation, baffling zigzags—appear not as incorrect (the charges are

[4] See, for example, Katkov's remark on the "need for psychiatric analysis in explaining Lenin's behavior in 1917," in Pipes: op. cit., p. 222.

[5] In Pipes: op. cit., p. 133.

largely true) but as irrelevant to what in fact he was doing.

Lenin's use of Napoleon's phrase, "On s'engage et puis on voit," has frequently been cited as evidence of impulsive activism, the gambler's plunge. But this simply does not correspond to Lenin's personality. It is a manner of expressing, though not very effectively, Lenin's insight as to the way of meeting a situation of increasing chaos and disorder (which he, to be sure, had a share in promoting) : no set formulas—these would be engulfed—but a search for all possible instrumentalities to overcome, in some measure at least, the high degree of contingency implicit in any course of action at such a time.

Lenin does occupy the central position in 1917 that has been attributed to him, though perhaps his role should be cast in a somewhat different light, not as the master organizer, not as the drawer of blueprints for revolutions, but as a man with an instinct for the quality and depths of the Russian chaos and for the means by which, after it had served as the great solvent, it might be harnessed. His success in November hung on a multitude of accidents and he arrived at "his" revolution by ways not of his own devising, but of all the figures on the scene he was much the best endowed to swim upstream against contingency.

X ✖ Lenin and Power

[1967]

THE IMAGE OF LENIN, AT LEAST IN THE NON-COMMUNIST world, is that of the revolutionary genius, the uncompromising opponent and destroyer of the old order. Indeed, the hyphenate term Marxism-Leninism largely connotes the revolutionary elements in Marx together with Lenin's own additions, chiefly out of the Russian revolutionary tradition: a tightly disciplined body of professional revolutionaries, a stress upon underground and illegal activity, and a resolute refusal to compromise with "revisionists" or those who would seek an evolutionary path to the reform of the existing order.

And yet there is a respectable body of opinion that sees Lenin's genius not as that of the destroyer and uprooter but, rather, as the organizer, the creator, or at least as the man who achieved mastery over the elemental chaos of revolutionary Russia. Three writers, of rather different views, may be cited to indicate this picture.

Thus, E. H. Carr, in his *Studies in Revolution*, has a chapter on "Lenin: The Master Builder":

Lenin, for all his fame as a revolutionary leader, was a creator rather than a destroyer. He played no personal part in the events of 1905 or in the February revolution of 1917; nor were Bolshevik ideas an important contributory factor. What Lenin achieved in October 1917 was not the overthrow of the provisional government—that followed logically from all that had gone before, and was bound to happen— but the construction of something to take its place. The decisive moment of the revolution came when, at the first congress of Soviets in June 1917, an orator remarked from the platform that there was no revolutionary party willing to take over the responsibilities of government, and Lenin, amid mocking laughter, retorted from his place in the hall, "There is such a party." Only when the new regime had taken over did Lenin rise to his full stature as administrator, head of government, organizer and supreme political tactician.[1]

Adam Ulam, in his study of the Bolsheviks, offers an interpretation that is somewhat similar:

The Bolsheviks did not seize power in this year of revolutions. They picked it up. First autocracy, then democracy capitulated to the forces of anarchy. Any group of determined men could have done what the Bolsheviks did in Petrograd in October 1917: seize the few key points of the city and proclaim themselves the government. . . . Thus the Bolsheviks' achievement in 1917, great though it was, pales in comparison with the enormous task they accomplished in the next five years in conquering the very anarchy they had helped to create and in building out of the most anarchistic of the revolutions the most authoritarian state in the world. It is not in the maker of the revolution that we can see Lenin's genius in its fullest; far greater is his achievement as its conqueror.[2]

[1] E. H. Carr: *Studies in Revolution* (New York; 1964: first published, 1950), pp. 134–5.
[2] Adam B. Ulam: *The Bolsheviks* (New York; 1965), p. 314.

In speaking of Lenin in power Louis Fischer, in his biography, suggests, too, that the years of authority were the period of Lenin's real greatness, up to the moment when he was smitten by the illness that was to kill him. Speaking of 1922 Fischer remarks:

Yet during the year that preceded the mental collapse which ended Lenin's career, his intellectual grasp remained supreme and he dominated Soviet Russia as never before. His prestige grew and so did his command of persons and situations. Nobody could have suspected in those twelve months from March, 1922, to March, 1923, that they were seeing the flaming tail of a comet and not the rising sun. . . . In fact, Lenin's last year was his greatest. It was probably also his saddest for it is impossible to suppose, judging by what he said, that he failed to realize where he had failed.[3]

These observations, by serious and well-informed students of Lenin and the Revolution, that Lenin is most appropriately to be regarded as a creator or a ruler rather than as a destroyer, and that his last years, when power had been achieved and in considerable measure consolidated, represented the "highest phase" of his life, lead to some extremely intricate problems relating to the theme of this book, "power and responsibility."[4] In the case of a great revolutionary figure, as Lenin undoubtedly was, both the terms "power" and "responsibility" take on an ambiguous flavor. By "power" are we thinking of the seizure of power or its application in running a political order? By "responsibility" do we mean responsibility for the course of events, responsibility to some sector of society, responsibility to a set of ideas, or responsibility in the sense of rational political behavior?

[3] Louis Fischer: *The Life of Lenin* (New York; 1964), p. 566.
[4] This essay was originally written for a volume of studies entitled *The Responsibility of Power*.

This essay, which does not pretend to resolve these ambiguities—the evaluation of Lenin and his inheritance remains one of the great questions of our times—will try to offer some reflections on three themes: (a) the contradictions and dilemmas confronting the revolutionary before and after he has come to power; (b) the nature of his sense of responsibility, to whom or to what; and (c) the criteria of "responsible" behavior of an explicitly, indeed blatantly, revolutionary régime.

I

First, a minimum of historical stage-setting is required. The picture of Lenin as the person who chanced to come to power in November 1917—in the way an alert person happens to pick up a penny in the street—while having a certain element of truth, does justice neither to Lenin's revolutionary achievement nor to the complexity of the peculiar historical situation that led to Russian power being, in a way, something to pick up.

Admittedly, Russia, between the collapse of the monarchy in March and the Bolshevik victory in November, does increasingly give one the sense—though with ups and downs and moments of apparent recovery—of a situation in which "power" was there for the taking, whatever this "power" might turn out to be. In the last couple of months, particularly, and notably after the Kornilov affair, one has, in reading the records of the time, a curious feeling of emptiness, as though political structure and political meaning had evaporated. There is a marked falling off in local voting, no longer a rush to the polls as there had been in many areas in the earlier months of the revolutionary period. One has the impression that the Provisional Government is operating in a void, and a strange question comes to mind: Where is everybody? One explanation, of course, is that the masses of the discontented, disillusioned with a fumbling régime, were preparing themselves for the final assault. Such certainty is the common picture of the cities and of the diminution of delegated authority in the countryside.

Yet I have the impression that such was not the process, at least not for the bulk of the population, but, rather, that a great vacuum was setting in—anarchy if you choose, though perhaps that is too active a term—that a general societal disintegration was in train, that the Great Russian society, except in its smaller and more intimate units, was ceasing to exist. One feels this in the army, in the factories with the rise of shop committees as against trade unions, in the unorganized peasant activities which were rapidly mounting at this time, and in the movement toward autonomy or separation among the nationalities on the fringe of the empire.

In other words, the assertion that power *was* there, to be picked up like a penny, is itself open to question. As efforts to define "power" in the political setting have demonstrated, it is a most elusive entity: at one moment present, awesome, and commanding vast instrumentalities for its realization, at the next it evaporates or seems to be an epiphenomenon derived from a complex of social and political circumstances. This very uncertainty about the reality of power leads us to the question *how* this situation could have come to pass in Russia. How does a comumnity become this strange emptiness in such short order? It clearly operates against our sense of social processes and the usual pattern of history that such disintegration should proceed so far so fast.

For this we must consider, very briefly, the much-disputed issue of the state of health of prerevolutionary, or prewar, Russia. The "viability" of imperial Russia, had the First World War not slashed across the scene, has long been the subject of intense and passionate dispute. Here we can only summarize certain propositions: (1) The dynasty as such seems to have been beyond recovery as an autocratic force; whatever the course of events the Romanovs seemed slated to disappear from the scene or, at most, to become *rois fainéants*. (2) Russia, even in peacetime, and noticeably in the years after 1911, was facing a major domestic crisis, not of stagnation or lethargy, but of disequilibrating growth and change. One can pick from the wild mélange of evidence "proofs" of imminent crisis, of potential crisis, or of likely convalescence from the upheavals of 1905—but my own reading is that this was indeed a highly problematic situation in which an enormous variety of outcomes might have occurred. It does seem clear, however, that some sort of crisis in the old order was taking shape and not just because of dynastic ineptitude. (3) One has the sense, as in fact one has also for the Dual Monarchy and for Wilhelmian Germany, that a set of contradictory impulses was becoming increasingly dynamic, with which the existing constitutional order, even had it been run by abler men, was not in a position to cope. The introduction of universal suffrage in the Austrian half of the Monarchy in 1907 had not eased the national problem, but exacerbated it. It was evident that the German Social Democratic victories in the elections of 1912 were not something to be absorbed into the Bismarckian Constitution—something was going to have to give way. So, too, in Russia, though the form of the problem was different, one feels a structural crisis of the political system darkening the horizon, a crisis that "progressive" evidence, such as renewed and very rapid industrial expansion, the growth of private as against state entrepreneurial initiative, the likelihood of greater vigor and life in the Fourth Duma, would sharpen rather than dampen. (4) Whether these implied short-term crises that might have been met by in-systems solutions (whether, for example, the mounting wave of strikes would have slackened and the new working class have been harnessed to urbanization), or whether they were indicators of deep-rooted maladies, bound to get worse until a general explosion occurred, is difficult to say. Indeed, I think it is impossible to say, because of the vast number of contingent influences that could have affected the scene with each day of history.

II

It is into this dynamic, crisis-ridden, but highly prob-lematic situation of late imperial Russia that we must try to fit Lenin—Lenin the revolutionary before his access to power. It should not be forgotten that Lenin's great hour in 1917 was when he was forty-seven, and it would be reasonable to assume that the essential man and political outlook, whatever adaptations, changes, or reversals the acquisition of power might occasion, had been formed. Here again, only some very general and perhaps dogmatic characterizations can be made:

First, from a very early date—and the ultimate psycho-logical and social roots can be argued endlessly—Lenin was aiming at a "revolutionary" rather than an "evolutionary" resolution to the evils, as he saw them, in the existing Russian order. This was a basic, personal impulse, opera-tive in his analysis of Russian society, in his evaluation of the explosive potentialities of its various sectors and classes, and in his views on the organization of the requisite poli-tical party.

Second, between Lenin, who was a serious and, to his

mind, orthodox Marxist, with a belief in a pattern of historical progression, and this revolutionary impulse existed a basic tension that he never really resolved on the level of articulated political theory. Some of Lenin's most difficult and elusive political concepts—the democratic dictatorship of the proletariat and peasantry, his insistence upon "stages," his formula of democratic centralism for his party, his doctrine concerning nationalities, his pronouncements on the relation of war and revolution—can all be related to an effort to put into coherent political formulation this underlying tension.

Third, despite this problem of finding an appropriate "ideological" formulation and the often observed anomaly between, say, *What Is to Be Done?* with its stress on the Party, and *State and Revolution,* in which the Party is scarcely mentioned, Lenin's writings cannot be dismissed as manipulative *pièces d'occasion,* though certainly some of his writings bear that mark, but can be regarded as serious pieces in the sense that he *was striving* for a coherent and explicit theory of revolutionary action. It is more likely that the reason for the peculiar difficulties one encounters in analyzing his writings lies in the inadequacy of the particular intellectual categories within which Lenin was obliged, or had elected, to work. But—and this is of decisive importance—below this "literary" level, Lenin had, even during his long absences from the Russian scene, some basic and essentially consistent views and intentions that were not fantasies of cloud-cuckoo land but very much in touch with "reality," however distorted and ambiguous their overt expression may appear to have been.

Fourth, among these basically realistic insights and aims one might include the following: (*a*) Lenin never had any intention of permitting a real period of "bourgeois" power to follow the fall or overthrow of "feudal" tsarism. He may, as Haimson pointed out some years ago,[5] have been obliged to give a rather peculiar definition, at least in Marxist terms, to the bourgeoisie; but surely his instinct was not far from the mark in feeling that the Russian bourgeoisie had neither the strength nor the will to assume power (indeed, Joseph Schumpeter doubted whether they ever had anywhere) , and hence that if social eruption occurred, he was going to be in on it and see that it moved toward his goals. Much of his confusing and shifting policy with respect to the peasantry—the vast majority of the Russian population—is intimately related to this consideration. (b) Lenin had a real sense both of the "blind" forces of spontaneous combustion that were present in Russian society and were profoundly difficult if not impossible to compose by in-system reforms, and of the obstacles presented by inertial drift and habit and by the advantages that are enjoyed, partly for that reason, on the part of the "powers that be." It is from this double realization—both facets of which strike me as sound insights into the structure and behavior of societies—that we find through much of Lenin's writing and action a fear both of being outflanked by anarchy and spontaneous *buntarstvo* and of being involved in "adventures," premature actions. It is Lenin's quite reasonable appreciation—given his aims —of this twofold danger that accounts for some of his disconcerting swings to the Left as well as for his periodic hesitancies to take decisive action. The problem, however one chooses to formulate it, was a real one, and a man with a strong sense of reality had to be looking in both directions at once. If you permit your party and your goals to be swept along by the unmeasured force of spontaneous

[5] Leopold H. Haimson: *The Russian Marxists and the Origins of Bolshevism* (Cambridge, Mass.; 1955) .

Russian resentment, you may well be engulfed and lose any control over a wild tide sweeping across the land. On the other hand, if you are obsessed by the concern for this danger and disregard the *vis inertiae,* you may become equally isolated, dispersed, undermined if not destroyed by the habitual and residual strength of the existing order. For a rational revolutionary there is no pat solution to this most difficult of quandaries. It is so bound up with the "balance of forces" of the moment that an abstract revolutionary theory will not do; one must have a feel for the particular configuration at any given moment of time. And this talent Lenin possessed, though it was often cloaked in the vocabulary and jargon the Russian Left required.

Finally, there is the question of Russia and the outside world. I would submit that Lenin had his basic impulse—a revolution in Russia—tempered with a perfectly rational recognition of the dangers involved in a relatively backward country making the sudden leap into socialism. Here, as in so many of his writings, one encounters contradictions: the formal analysis of *Imperialism* in conjunction with his 1917 writings on the matter of a separate peace and defeatism, and the harsh reality of Brest-Litovsk. But again, it would seem that for all the historical and analytical holes one can punch in Lenin's characterization of imperialism and for the far more important question whether it was luck or insight that enabled him to survive Brest-Litovsk without Russia's falling under permanent German hegemony, Lenin was, in his Zimmerwald formulas and in his general position on the war, trying to meet, with an acute sense of reality, an almost insoluble problem (I think that in this particular area Lenin was luckier than insightful). Without doubt, the outbreak of the First World War *did* represent a mortal crisis for the old European order—we still live in the shadow of its consequences—and also the Second International, to use Schumpeter's adaptation from Dante, did commit *lo gran rifiuto*. Lenin was probably right in his sense that the war presented a fundamental crisis—as is illustrated by the increasing inability of the European governments, at least from 1916 on, to make sense of the war for their citizenry. The outburst of radicalism, in both hemispheres, suggests the failure of the effort to make this hideous bloodletting intelligible to the people, whatever the perfectly "rational" diplomatic or strategic reasons for the various abortive campaigns may have been.

It is not surprising, then, that Lenin, with his instinct for the jugular, should have felt that this was *the crisis*—which Russia alone might or might not have produced through its own internal difficulties—and hence that from the outset he generalized and combined war and revolution. I think that this was a point where his analysis went astray, but the point here is simply that, however inadequate Lenin's theory of imperialism may have been, he was working against a real possibility in which, as it turned out, a number of contingencies—the timing and outcome of military actions, the entry of the United States, and the like—pushed events in a direction different from what he had not unreasonably anticipated.

Whatever the external opportunities or accidents, it seems clear that Lenin, from the onset of the Revolution, was driving for a seizure of power, an overturn that would bring his party and his views into the saddle. Admittedly, there are moments of hesitation, as in the confusion during the June and the July days, the anomalies in *State and Revolution* written while he was in hiding, and even very late in the day, after the Kornilov affair, in his interesting article "On Compromises," suggesting still the possibility of cooperation with other sections of the Russian Left in a nonviolent solution. Still, in general, his temper in these months of 1917 is unmistakable, and upon hearing of the Kornilov affair his instinct that *now* was the time burst forth like an erupting volcano. Despite his being in hiding, despite Trotsky's success in working through the Soviet and the Military Revolutionary Committee, one can probably accept the latter's verdict that without the driving power of Lenin the Bolsheviks would not have made their own revolution. It is quite possible that they would have assumed office, conceivably along the lines variously envisaged by Trotsky, or even by Zinoviev and Kamenev, but that would have been a quite different situation and very likely with a quite different outcome.

This leads in turn to a consideration of Lenin's situation as the wielder of power, the ruler of a state. It can and has been argued that Lenin, in authority, "inherited" a very difficult situation and that much of the brutality of the years of civil war and War Communism, which presumably shaped many of the lasting features of the Soviet régime, should be seen as the necessary acts of a head of state fighting both domestic and foreign enemies. This argument is not wholly without foundation; certainly we cannot hold Lenin responsible for all the problems the new régime faced: the war, imperial mismanagement, the economic crisis, plus the whole background of an outdated autocracy would have assured a terribly tough job for any ruler of Russia. And yet, I do not think that Lenin can be let off this hook so easily. While the problems he faced were not by any means all of his own making, it can hardly be denied that he was, in fact, now obliged to face the consequences of much that he had desired and willed to happen, whether or not his intentions and will had been the major causal factors in bringing about the actual course of events. For example, the disintegration of the Russian army was, despite the claims of friends and foes, probably something that would have occurred in any case at that stage of the war. But certainly Lenin's efforts, so far as his effectiveness went, were in the direction of increasing and promoting this disintegration. The same can be said with respect to the peasant problem, the upsurge of the nationalities, and so on. In other words, Lenin's chickens were coming home to roost, whether Lenin had set them loose or not. In that fact lies, I believe, an essential element of irresponsibility—in the meaning of nonrationality—that was to plague Lenin throughout his years of power and that has been built into much of the subsequent history of the Soviet system.

III

The fact, then, is that Lenin is centrally responsible for the willingness, under admittedly difficult circumstances, to assume a Bolshevik monopoly of power, seized by violence, and purposely so. Lenin did not want to be bound by constitutional fictions or hampered by questions of "legitimacy." Still, this was no free-booting power-grab of a robber baron or a competent warlord. To repeat, Lenin was serious. And at the time he was at odds with Zinoviev and Kamenev as to whether the situation was ripe for revolution, he hotly denied their contention that the Bolsheviks were in the minority. He insisted that the Bolsheviks did represent the majority of the Russian people. This, of course, raises an interesting question. That the Bolsheviks were, by nose-counting, a distinct minority is evident, as was subsequently demonstrated arithmetically by the vote for the Constituent Assembly shortly after the Bolsheviks seized power and in which they received approximately one quarter of the vote.

Trotsky in his history of the Revolution argues, while

admitting the fact of the voting, that Lenin was correct as against Zinoviev and Kamenev. His argument, on Lenin's behalf, was that one had to take a dynamic view of public support, that the Bolsheviks had won over the "advanced" sectors—the capital city in particular—that the drift of support was clearly in their direction, and hence that it was only a matter of time for the rear to catch up with the vanguard. While his argument is a bit questionable, it cannot be dismissed entirely. The analysis that Oliver Radkey has given to the elections suggests that this argument was not wholly spurious.[6] An examination of the election returns indicates that Bolshevik influence was clearly radiating outward from the capital and other industrial centers and progressively affecting the surrounding areas, including even some predominantly agrarian regions in western Russia. Admittedly, it would be hard to imagine just how one could develop a coherent set of political standards from Trotsky's kind of argument: it is perilous to give the mandate to what is, at the time, only a possible "wave of the future."

But a more interesting feature is that this rather convenient if dubious line of argument is *not* the defense that Lenin himself used. On the contrary, in refuting Zinoviev and Kamenev, he pursued a quite different pattern of reasoning: the Bolsheviks represented the majority because that majority, including now the aroused peasantry, was behaving "objectively" in a manner that made the Bolsheviks the majority party. In other words, in respect to the question of the relationship between the taking of power and responsibility to the population—"constituency" is too precise a term in these chaotic circumstances—Lenin followed

[6] Oliver Henry Radkey: *The Election to the Russian Constituent Assembly of 1917* (Cambridge, Mass.; 1950).

neither the classical democratic legitimation of power through the ballot nor even Trotsky's notion of justification by the future (and Trotsky clearly felt this need—that sooner or later the people would swing around in *conscious* support), but his own and, so far as I know unique, belief in the "objective" identity of interests—necessarily as he conceived of them.

This view, while ultimately destructive of any true democracy or responsibility, has a central bearing on the question of Lenin *in* power; it helps to explain, indeed it may be the central clue to, his capacity to make the transition from the destroyer of a political order to the creator of a new one, a pair of tasks rarely carried out by the same person in the course of a major revolution.

IV

What, then, are the criteria of "responsible" behavior in a totally confused situation, to some measure of one's making or desire, but to a large degree a consequence of the brutal and disastrous course of events, the full causes of which are of infinite complexity? I should say that, despite Lenin's sense of reality and of the contradictoriness of reality, and despite the fact that a Russian upheaval, by 1917 at any rate, of a deeply chaotic character was in the cards (with or without Lenin), his behavior was irresponsible or nonresponsible. He was uncompromising in his determination to recognize no responsibility to an entity, be it a party or a person, outside the frame of his own will and thought—cloaked perhaps as loyalty to a revolutionary ideal (and this can be combined with personal modesty and the absence of overt egotism—it was all disconcertingly impersonal, this feature of his personality). Conversely, or correspondingly, in seeking instrumentalities for the achievement of his will and his revolution he exploited—again with an uncanny feel for "reality"—impulses, rages, frustrations, social flaws—which it is precisely the act of true responsibility to correct, repair, or alleviate. This is not meant in any Metternichean sense or even in the formulae of classical political liberalism. It is, rather, a matter that lies at the very heart of social, human, or humane organization. It is charged that throughout 1917 Lenin played the demagogue in advancing crude slogans—peace, bread, and land—incapable of real achievement, to poison, paralyze, and disrupt the uncertain and increasingly chaotic "dark masses." I am not particularly impressed by the criticism put thus—there was, or could have been, a positive and creative content in all these slogans even if they represented massive oversimplifications of the complex problems Russia faced. Rather, I have the impression of an almost demonic ability, often expressed overtly in his drumming on slogans, to play upon an even deeper layer of disruptiveness—the profound resentment of people, and more particularly the Russian masses, against (and this may seem a trivial symptom) the "rudeness" of their "betters." This plaint, in the demands that seem to recur as a *leitmotiv* in prewar strike slogans, in the flavor and actual content of the famous Soviet Order No. 1, in the evident popular mistrust not only of the Duma and the Provisional Government, but even of the Petrograd Soviet (as in the July days), has struck me as a singularly malignant symptom, since it cannot be satisfied by fiat. One cannot legislate a man out of his "rudeness"; he can merely make its manifestations more subtle—but both sides will understand what is going on. In other words, the necessary element of brotherhood, *fraternité*—that indispensable third part of the French revolutionary triad as a link between the other two—was in 1917 lacking, and Lenin, for all his rhetoric about the common interests of the masses, was plucking away at that raw spot. In so doing—and I suspect that his effectiveness in 1917 may lie here rather than in the supposed superior qualities of Bolshevik organization—he was in touch with reality, but a destructive and ugly and ultimately insatiable one.

In this respect, Lenin's drive to power was a historical act of the profoundest irresponsibility in its willingness to unchain, with all their unknown, unknowable, but surely and predictably cataclysmic consequences, the truly dark forces—not those of Satan but, rather, those of a tortured Caliban. The genius of Lenin lay perhaps in his capacity to behave "responsibly," and not in panic or in frenzy, within this tumultuous universe he was helping to bring into being. This gets us, admittedly, into some deep and uncertain waters, but some such appraisal seems necessary for a comprehension of the quality of "responsible" behavior in the next and final stage of his career—as the man in power.

One of the salient features of Lenin's actions after the seizure of power is the number of reversals of policy that quickly followed and that seemed in such blatant contrast to his 1917 writings and actions. *State and Revolution* did not come to serve as a blueprint for the new order; indeed, Lenin cheerfully granted that many of the ideas advanced in 1917 concerning the economic and fiscal management of a society had been simplistic or plainly erroneous. Workers' control of industry was soon dropped as unworkable. The peasantry did not join in the anticipated alliance but, rather, a form of tension re-emerged between town and country that has persisted to this day. The doctrine of national self-determination, including the right of separation, while never formally abandoned, rapidly became emptied of content as conflict flared up between the

Bolsheviks and the various national groups, above all the Ukrainians, that sought full independence. Above all, despite Lenin's pledges not to make a separate peace with the imperialist German enemy, he was obliged, amid perhaps the severest crisis within the Party, to force through acceptance of the terms of Brest-Litovsk. With the draconic measures of War Communism, to be followed by the admitted retreat to the New Economic Policy—and all this in a world that, while hostile, had failed to provide the hoped-for revolutionary backdrop—one might argue that Lenin, once in power, had betrayed, or failed in his responsibility to, the revolutionary ideal that had sustained him for so many decades.

It is true that the Party remained intact, indeed became an even more tightly organized body with the provision against factionalism at the Tenth Party Congress in 1921. It is true, too, that such potentially disruptive challenges as those provided by the Workers' Opposition, the Democratic Centralists, the rebellious peasants of Tambov, the sailors of Kronstadt, and the nationalist movements in the Ukraine and the Caucasus had been put down, defeated, or driven into the wilderness, but these, unlike the successes in the conflict against the "Whites," the interventionists, and the Poles, were bitter victories. Meanwhile the "state" was re-emerging in full panoply, the old Russian demon of "bureaucracy" was coming back into its own. And Great Russian chauvinism, as displayed by Stalin in his activities in his native Georgia, was clearly reappearing, to Lenin's dismay and anger.

And yet, if our view of Lenin is correct, these marked changes that occurred, once the Bolsheviks were in power and had to fight for the preservation, consolidation, and re-extension of their writ, should not be regarded ultimately as either betrayals or a belated recognition of harsh fact. For if, as we have suggested, the key to Lenin as a political figure lies below the level of articulated political theory but encompasses a sense of reality, of politics as the art of the possible, then these palpable shifts in the years 1918–22, while representing "betrayal" to left Communists and auguries of a "return of normalcy" to hopeful outside observers, were in fact neither, but simply a continuation in a period of power and authority of essentially the same perceptions and insights that we find in Lenin during the pre-revolutionary period. For *if* the régime he had managed to bring into power were to survive, most if not all of these changes were unavoidable.

If one examines the various alternative plans and schemes against which Lenin fought, from the crisis of Brest-Litovsk through to the tensions of the critical year 1921, one can only conclude, unless one is bound by ideological preconceptions or a dedication to *fiat justitia,* that they would all have failed, in the sense of destroying what they were supposed to support and strengthen—the Bolshevik régime.

This is not to posit, of course, a justification of Lenin's positions while in power, except in the Hobbesian sense that if such and such a goal is premised, then certain acts follow; otherwise a self-destroying contradiction sets in. It might well be maintained that there was no manifest reason *why* the Leninist system should survive to become the core of the Soviet state (which it was, whatever happened later under Stalin). Indeed, one could argue—though it would be risky because it would be difficult indeed to trace the infinitude of domestic and foreign consequences—that it would have been for the best if this *tour de force* had explicitly failed and if Russia had undergone in due course a Restoration of sorts (doubtless without Romanovs). One need not be put in the position of asserting the necessity of the Soviet system. Possibly a breakup of Russia into a variety of national entities might have led to a more stable international situation—though it is not hard to advance arguments to the contrary (for example, the implications of an independent Ukraine and its vast resources, vis-à-vis a revived Germany in the 1930's; the scenario becomes too complex for useful reconstruction).

The only point to be stressed is that Lenin in power behaved "responsibly" as a practical political being—but within the frame of the basic irresponsibility I have sketched in the preceding pages. I have tried to bring out above what seems to have lain in the very creation of the Soviet system—the decision to wrest and maintain power, in the service of a revolutionary ideal of which Lenin felt himself to be the sole custodian. And it is this particular feature of the Soviet system, though its survival even in Lenin's day involved doing violence to aspects of that ideal, that seems to have become part of its very fiber as it has evolved over the last half-century, and from which full emergence, or emancipation, still appears to be a major problem for Russia's future. *Tempora mutantur et nos mutamur in illis*, perhaps, but against this comforting notion that time changes all—with new generations, new problems, perhaps even a new culture—there seems still to reside in the Soviet Union of today a certain quality embedded by Lenin before, during, and after the actual Revolution itself, derived in part from earlier Russian history, or portions thereof, but crystallized or precipitated by Lenin's own genius. It is not just a question of authoritarianism—this is but symptomatic—but, rather, something deeper, more than purely habitual or historical: the juxtaposition within one person—perhaps more than a juxtaposition; a powerful and lasting amalgam—of the hater of external, autocratic power being at the same time profoundly unwilling to accept *vox populi,* fighting the former in the name of the latter, but with himself (and his extension, the Party) sole mediator to bridge the abyss.

V

This leads, in turn, to a final question, that of Lenin's sense of failure at the end of his life. As I have said above, I am somewhat skeptical, at least on the superficial level, of the verdict that things had not turned out as utopian as some of Lenin's writings might, in our reading, have led him to anticipate. In this respect he was a realist throughout. More may be said of the view of the impact of sheer physical impairment, the ebbing of the tremendous will to make the moribund body perform while the mind still perceived. Here one can well imagine Lenin's anguish and the poignancy of the communications, long-suppressed, relating to his mounting concern and anger about the figure of Stalin. Lenin surely sensed his physical, and perhaps organizational, impotence against this looming figure.

But perhaps there is more to be said than simply the familiar story of the "old bull," the day past when "Not another dared him then, Dared him and again defied." For along with Stalin, death, too, was stalking Lenin, and I would suggest that it was not merely death in its universal role as the oncoming destroyer of the physical being of the Bolshevik leader, but the fact of death itself (human mortality is still 100 per cent sooner or later) that suggests the ultimate irreconcilability between power and responsibility in Lenin, whether he was aware of this or not, and in subsequent Leninism. For human mortality—whatever one's beliefs about immortality or an afterlife may be—is *the* one sure, common possession, or fate, of us all. Unlike taxes, there is no reprieve or evasion. Hence any responsible position toward the question of political power, in cluding that of state-building, must take this universal fate into consideration—in this plight, or release, is the one indubitably common quality of all members of mankind.

From this, certain consequences follow. It does not necessarily mean the creation of a heaven—though some would argue so; it does not even mean, necessarily, the refusal to take life—though others have argued so and with some cogency; one may still have a well-reasoned doctrine of the "just war." But at the very least it does entail that, unless the human being is to become pure "object," in which case power ultimately operates in a meaningless waste, one must come to terms, as best one can in this world, with a recognition of the common rights arising from a common fate. One's fellow, even if one's enemy, is a "subject." And here, it would seem to me, lies the ultimate irresponsibility of Leninism in power. Not that Lenin was inhuman personally in this regard, as is evidenced by his sadness over Martov who was dying at the same time, but in the hideous—the word is strong but intended—disjunction between those human sentiments Lenin certainly felt and his political ruthlessness. If a person is beyond the pale politically, sentiment cannot interfere, and then the use of the "instrument," be it the Cheka or whatever, moves in as a matter of logical consequence. What in Lenin's psyche ultimately created or permitted this disjunction I am unable to say. But as a central constituent of a power apparatus it is more than drumhead justice or revolutionary *élan*; it is something much colder and more inhuman. It is a commonplace that the Bolsheviks have always had trouble coming to terms with death: it makes the New Soviet Man slightly, but decisively, less than an ideal model. But the failure to absorb and grant this, among other unavoidable human foibles, was productive, under Stalin, of the dreadful and reverse meaning that was to be given to Engels' hopeful statement that in the new order the "government of persons is replaced by the administration of things."

XI ❧ The Crisis in the Soviet Empire

[1957]

IF WE ARE MUCH TOO NEAR THE TUMULTUOUS AND TRAGIC events in Poland and Hungary to write their history or to venture any predictions for the future in Eastern Europe, we can at least make a serious, if tentative, appraisal of what we feel we know and do not know about the nature of this crisis which has shaken the satellite empire. What is the significance of the changes and disturbances in the Soviet orbit since Stalin's death, and more especially since the monolithic apparatus of party and state control which he perfected has come under criticism by Communists themselves?

When we consider four of the more illuminating developments in 1956—the Twentieth Party Congress of the C.P.S.U. and the secret Khrushchev report; the stormy advent of the Gomulka régime in Poland; the Hungarian Revolution and its suppression by Soviet troops; and the reactions of Tito's Yugoslavia to these happenings—we see that the trend away from Stalin's rigid pattern of organization and control has proceeded along three different, and conflicting, lines: (1) toward *modified centralized control*; (2) toward a *"polycentric system,"* to use a phrase adopted, though not invented, by Palmiro

Togliatti; and (3) toward the ascendancy of *centrifugal forces*. Within the Communist world the play of these divergent trends is framed, on the one hand, by the almost universally felt need to reduce some of the rigors and excesses of the Stalin era, and, on the other, by the need to prevent the return to a non-Communist political and social order. There is no reason to question the reality, from the Communist point of view, of either of these needs. Some party members may feel that things were simple in the old days, but there is ample evidence, for example in Khrushchev's secret report, that even the most powerful Communist figures felt the pistol pressing at the base of their skulls.

Within the Soviet Union itself, where both the state and the individual have long been under the control of the Party, the problem is largely one of managing this "decompression" so as to arrive at what is rather cloudily termed "a new stage in the creative development of Marxism-Leninism." From the perspective of the non-Communist observer, this is no easy task and may call for a nice sense of balance and timing—rather like a fakir shifting position on his bed of spikes. Still, we have a good deal of evidence that over the last forty years the Russian people have been rather thoroughly conditioned to the Soviet system, and on the whole the Soviet leaders have shown a reasonably accurate sense of what the Russian people will or will not accede to.

It is another matter when we turn to the Soviet Union's relations with the satellites. Here, too, despite statements about the fraternity of Communist parties and admissions of domineering behavior in the past, it seems clear, and natural, that the Soviet leaders should prefer a pattern of modified centralized control, stressing the notion of *primus inter pares*. It is quite likely that there may be some difference of opinion among the Soviet leaders as to the actual application of this principle in dealing with the satellite parties, but it appears almost inevitable that the Soviet Union, having been the creator of these régimes, should continue to demand acknowledgment of its parental status. Nevertheless, the Soviet effort to maintain a modified form of centralized control does encounter both the highly important fact of national pride and the relatively short span of Communist control in the satellites.

National pride and the absence of a generation's conditioning have obviously had a decisive part in the events leading to Gomulka's "national Communist" régime in Poland. Indeed, it is hard to see just how the Russian Communists, for all their ideological blinders, could have failed so profoundly to take adequate account of the fierce pride of the Poles and their still vivid memories of 1944–5. Yet one cannot but have the impression that the Russians somehow made a serious miscalculation in estimating the effect of de-Stalinization in Poland. As it turned out, there was formed a working alliance between a leading faction of the Polish Communist Party and Polish nationalism against Soviet interference and control. The new régime, however, has not moved toward withdrawal from the Warsaw Pact—perhaps because of a continuing and generally held concern about the security of Poland's western frontier—nor has it gone beyond the limits of a single-party system. In other words, Polish Communism for the moment enjoys a coordinate rather than subordinate relationship to the C.P.S.U.—the pattern of "polycentricity."

This appears to be an inherently precarious, though possibly durable, situation: it could easily be impelled further in either direction. Except for Gomulka's personal tribulations under Stalinism and the fact that the new régime has stood up against Khrushchev and Bulganin, there are few *positive* bonds uniting the Polish people and the present leadership. It is quite conceivable that further domestic demands, political and economic, may well up and sweep beyond the limits of even national Communist tolerance. The Hungarian tragedy and the preoccupation with Germany may moderate their expression. But we certainly do not know enough to predict or even to guess how the Gomulka régime, or the Russian, would respond (and perhaps respond in anticipation) to such demands.

Notwithstanding its tragic outcome, the Hungarian case resembles the Polish in several respects: an intense pride, a tradition of national battles against Russians, a schism in the local Communist Party, and rising popular demand for a change.

At this point we probably lack the information we need to explain fully why the repercussions of de-Stalinization led to such catastrophically different consequences. The absence of a frontier dispute with Germany; the rather different, and apparently less well organized, development of the opposition within the Hungarian Communist Party; the uncertainty and delay in dealing with Rákosi and Gerö; and, of course, the preceding events in Poland— these doubtless contributed to the explosion. But it may have been simply accidents of timing and of individual behavior that set it off: inept handling of troops and unnecessary provocation. At any rate by the time that Imre Nagy (who seemed slated to be the Hungarian Gomulka) was called in, the panicked Communist leadership had already called for military aid against the people. In consequence, the revolution, under the pressure of conflict, quickly moved beyond the "national Communist" position to one that was increasingly anti-Communist and anti-Soviet. The Soviet decision to crush the revolution by force seems to follow directly from this movement beyond the confines of Communism and the Warsaw Pact. In addition, of course, the Russians had good reason to fear the spread of the recalcitrant Polish and Hungarian temper to the rest of Eastern Europe; the sudden and, for the Russians, fortunate eruption of fighting in the Near East may have led them to conclude that the time was favorable for a crackdown. Whatever the particular reasons—and this is a subject for historical inquiry—the Hungarian revolution clearly demonstrates the momentary ascendancy of centrifugal forces which were rapidly bearing Hungary out of the Communist orbit until the Russians moved in with Stalinist severity.

The reaction of Titoist Yugoslavia to all these events is of particular interest, since Tito for some years has been the explicit advocate of a "polycentric" system of national Communist régimes, independent in their relations with Moscow and with one another, but also proceeding along the road, or roads, to "socialism," as the Communists use the term. In the Yugoslav case, the working alliance between party and national interest goes back to the origins of Tito's real power, his leadership of the Partisans in the Second World War, and was greatly strengthened during the years he successfully defied Stalin and the Cominform. In this respect the positions of Tito and Gomulka are in no way similar. It is to be observed, however, that this working alliance has not meant any great advance in political liberty; indeed, when Djilas urged in 1953 that "to weaken the monopoly of political movements . . . is the demand of the times," he was slapped down. Kardelj defended the need for "certain elements of coercion in order to get away from old and backward ways as soon as possible," and Tito declared that extending democracy to the bourgeoisie would lead "to anarchy, to a terrible uncertainty." Here, then, in a régime that was relatively stable and not under immediate pressure either from the Soviet Union or from an aroused populace, the limits of Communist tolerance were clearly and frankly demonstrated.

The Yugoslav régime's reaction to events abroad, in Poland and Hungary, is in full accord with their reaction to the Djilas challenge domestically. On November 4, 1956, the Foreign Affairs Editor of *Tanjug* made the following comments:

> The justified revolt of the people against the policy of Rákosi, Gerö and others began to follow the course which obviously was not desired by the forces which were in the majority and whose purpose was to eliminate all the negative consequences of the past, which hindered a normal and healthy development of the consolidation of Socialism and Socialist Democracy in Hungary. . . .
>
> An objective and coldblooded analysis of events forces us to approach the present-day happenings and the most recent situation from a realistic position. This means that a return to the old regimes either in Hungary or in other Eastern European countries is, under the present circumstances, impossible to imagine or suppose. . . .
>
> As far as we in Yugoslavia are concerned, as fighters for Socialism, for active peaceful coexistence and for consolidation of peace and progress, it is clear, as we have many times reiterated, that there is neither peace nor progress, nor independence in the countries of Eastern Europe except on the basis of Socialism. Every attempt to change the state of affairs in these countries contrary to the objectives of Socialism, as was tried in Hungary, can lead to consequences which are not in the interest either of these peoples or of the preservation of peace in the world. However, a normal development is possible which would enable the strengthening of real democratic relations on the basis of true Socialist growth which is in the interest of the people, peace, international cooperation and a relaxation of tension in the world. Poland is proof of this where the development leads to the consolidation of Socialism, Socialist Democracy, in-

dependence and equal relations among Socialist and other countries. . . .

Of course, we consider to be a negative fact that the new government had to appeal for the help of the Soviet Army. The use of foreign troops to deal with domestic affairs is in contradiction to the principles on which Yugoslavia bases her foreign policy and which should rule in international relations. However, we cannot overlook the fact that the use of these troops is precisely the result of such a negative development which we refer to above. . . .

For the Yugoslav Communist there is thus a definite similarity in the Polish and Yugoslav positions (with the important exception that Yugoslavia is not in the Warsaw Pact) ; the Hungarian revolution is regarded as an understandable but impermissible retrogression which had to be checked, regrettably by force. That an open Soviet attack on the Titoist critique should have occurred, however, on the same day, November 19, that the Yugoslav Government was reported to have arrested Djilas for attacking national and Soviet Communism alike is a most striking illustration of the double tension generated by the Titoist line.

In some respects we seem to be witnessing one of the classical problems in politics: how to retreat from a full dictatorship without losing control over the course of events or opening the way to a "restoration." That this is a delicate problem is illustrated by the troubles Cromwell found in seeking an alternative to the Protectorate or Napoleon III in creating his "Liberal Empire." Still, it might be argued, such a task, while difficult, is not necessarily impossible; a proper balance of popular forces and party controls might create a new pattern of political and social organization in Eastern Europe along the lines the Yugoslav Communists anticipate.

It is not necessarily impossible. Nevertheless, Thomas

Hammond correctly points to "the difficulties which the Yugoslav leaders are having in finding a new kind of 'Socialist democracy' which is supposed to be different from both Soviet Communism and Western democracy. With no other models to go by, there is always a temptation for them either to continue to imitate Soviet methods or to move in the direction of Western democracy, although actually they want to copy neither."[1] In addition to the lack of models to go by, there are two further difficulties, one of which relates to the nature of Leninism itself (to which Tito as well as Khrushchev subscribes) and the other to the international repercussions of de-Stalinization.

When we seek for parallels and analogies to the Communist Revolution and its consolidation in the Soviet system, we should perhaps think less in terms of the swing of a pendulum than of a *tour de force*, and see Lenin less in the company of a Cromwell or a Napoleon III than of a Napoleon I or a Bismarck: that is, as the creator, through his own will, insight, and aims, of a quite new "solution" to a political and social issue, a solution which is in no sense a "natural" outcome proceeding from the interaction of political and social forces, but a *tour de force* which would have been very difficult to anticipate before its achievement.

In Lenin's case this element is particularly dominant. As early as the turn of the century, he was attacking "worship of the spontaneity of the labor movement" and stressing the decisive role of theory, of consciousness, and of the "distinction between the vanguard and the whole of the masses." This intense, disciplined will to revolution in turn involved a reforging of Marxism to make it apply, by main force if need be, to conditions in Russia. Certainly

---

[1] Thomas Taylor Hammond: "The Djilas Affair and Jugoslav Communism," *Foreign Affairs* (Vol. XXXIII, January 1955), 314.

there was nothing inevitable about the Bolshevik capture of the Russian Revolution; rather, it stands out, much mythology to the contrary, as one of the great demonstrations of the role of contingency, accident, and personality in history. Nevertheless, the capture took place and was maintained; and the whole subsequent history of Communism has been deeply influenced by this *tour de force*. Indeed one might say that it is precisely the heart of the theory and practice of Leninism. This mistrust of "spontaneity"—i.e. of the free popular will—is not just a passing mood or even a personal feeling of scorn or misanthropy (though these attitudes are certainly fostered in the system) but integral to Leninism.

As a result, the search for a popular or national Communism as a real system of government may be a search for a chimera, not because a "mixed" economic or political system is impossible to achieve but because Leninism is an explicit denial of control by the people, or even by a class. The question arises, for example, whether the Polish Communists can possibly hold free national elections, not necessarily because they would lose them—very likely they would, but it is certainly possible that some day a Communist Party might win a free election somewhere—but because they may be unable to admit the premise of having elections as the determinant.

It is for this reason that the concept of "two stages" in the liberalization of a satellite,[2] while logical enough from

2 See, for example, Walter Lippmann in the *New York Herald-Tribune*, November 6, 1956: "There are, we have every reason to believe, two stages in the liberation of a satellite. The first stage is Titoism or national liberty, which is not anti-Communist and which remains within the Soviet sphere of military and political influence. The second stage is complete liberty at home and abroad. No country which has once been within the Soviet orbit—not even Yugoslavia—has ever reached the second stage."

the non-Communist point of view, may—in suggesting that the tragedy of the Hungarian rebellion was the effort to bypass the first stage—miss the mark as far as the play of forces in Eastern Europe is concerned. The prospect of passing to full liberation via national Communism is, up to now at least, purely a mental projection. The actual road, it is granted, has nowhere been constructed, and the mere possibility of this second stage can serve, in the first instance, to inhibit liberalization in the national Communist stage and, in the second instance, to intensify Soviet suspicion that national Communism may indeed be the first step toward the reintroduction of capitalism. The very hope which non-Communists may entertain of a gradual, natural process of moving by stages toward liberation is well calculated to ring the alarm bell of "spontaneity" in Leninist ears.

We have not, then, been able to gain any clear picture from recent events in the satellites of what a more "normal" and stable situation in a still Communist Eastern Europe might be. It is not that democracy is necessarily the only answer; in our view it is the preferable one, though historically it has not been the prevailing form of government in that region. Rather, it is that the essential traits of Leninism have survived not only the passing of Stalin but even the creation of independent centers of Communist power, and that these traits, deeply rooted now in underlying premises, habits of thought and practice, and institutions, may operate to some extent independently of the persons involved and indeed profoundly condition their behavior.

The difficulty of envisaging the course of an evolutionary path out of the present situation in Eastern Europe, or even a stabilized grouping of national Communist régimes, is heightened by the existence of tension between

Soviet Russia and the Western powers. This tension, of course, in no small part arises from the situation in Eastern Europe. Indeed, the two are so intimately and mutually related that one cannot be understood without reference to the other.

The obvious Soviet fear, which is certainly comprehensible, is that a satellite which threatens to become non-Communist and withdraw from the Warsaw Pact, will soon be anti-Communist and seek Western protection. The vigor and brutality with which the Hungarian revolution was suppressed, in urgent disregard of damaging reactions elsewhere in the world, testifies to Soviet sensitivity on this point. It seems evident that in this case military and ideological considerations, which may not always be in harmony, found common ground in destroying the Hungarian revolt.

From this it is tempting to conclude (especially in view of our failure to make any effort at intervention in support of the revolution) that the better part of American policy is to accept the "national Communist" solution and drop the idea of democracy and independence. This, however, requires some consideration. Admittedly, half a loaf is better than none. Most of us would agree that Titoism or national Communism is preferable to the solid Stalinist bloc. But there is no need to make necessity, if it is that, virtuous, as we are frequently inclined to do. National Communism may be a lesser evil; it is not a positive good. This is so partly because we do not know what it may become (nor do the national Communists), but chiefly because the element of autonomy, of free choice, is still absent.

Many people in the United States and abroad feel that Americans are too formal and moralistic on this question of free choice. It may be that we do place too much emphasis on the particular touchstone of "free elections" in situations where problems are both delicate and complex and the chances of such elections remote. It may be that elections must be the final product, the ultimate symbol of autonomy rather than its first condition. But all this really misses the point. Americans, I believe, would be satisfied with other real evidence of autonomy, if it were forthcoming, such as, for example, an uninhibited communication with all elements of the population and a sense that the people felt able to speak their own minds freely to approve or disapprove of the régime which governed them. But such evidence is lacking.

Nor should our making do with "national Communism" promote the illusion that this will necessarily promote international understanding. It might, but we should not forget that we and the Soviet Union look at this phenomenon in diametrically opposed ways. We see it as a moderate increase in national independence, with the hope of an eventual further reduction of Communist power and influence. The Soviet leaders, insofar as they are willing to accept it, probably see it as a necessary concession to maintain a Communist camp, and perhaps some of them entertain the hope that it may prove a more flexible device for the eventual victory of Communism. The situation might resemble the Stresemann-Briand cooperation of the 1920's—Stresemann welcoming cooperation as a step to the revision of the Versailles settlement, Briand welcoming it as a reinforcement of the settlement; both sides were subsequently disillusioned.

If Soviet-Western tension influences the crisis in Eastern Europe, the converse is no less true. Even in the brief interval since the Soviet intervention in Hungary a number of very important consequences have emerged. The first is that even in a case where an anti-Soviet uprising managed to achieve a territorial base, the United States took no steps to give effective support for "liberation." This is not the place to pursue the question whether the United States could have done more under the circumstances or whether it had raised false hopes among the insurgents; these are matters requiring closer study and further knowledge of pertinent facts. It is clear that the incredible bare-handed heroism of the Hungarians caught everyone by surprise and that in the somewhat different setting of the Polish crisis the United States had already indicated that it would not intervene militarily. But whatever the final judgment of our role may be, there is little doubt that the Soviet Union, at no little cost to the "thaw," demonstrated that it was the only Great Power that counted on its side of the Iron Curtain.

Not only that, the Soviet threat to intervene, through "volunteers," in the Suez conflict has had a very marked effect on that crisis. When we look at the two crises together—as all the world is doing—the unpleasant fact emerges that the Russians have been much more successful in exerting pressure in the non-Communist world than we have been in the Communist orbit. The conclusions that may be drawn from this, especially by the uncommitted nations, can obviously be very damaging. Moreover, in the game of "walking to the brink" the Russians have, in this case, outmatched us, and the exploitation of this advantage could lead to most dangerous blackmail against our allies and ourselves.

The question arises whether the best way to check this development is to exert corresponding and equivalent pressure on the satellite area or to take all steps necessary to block Soviet actions on this side of the Iron Curtain. Apart from the obvious and perhaps unavoidable risk of war in both cases, each approach has its disadvantages.

Limiting our actions to the curbing of Soviet activities in the Near East leaves us entirely on the defensive, and in an area which, while non-Communist, is certainly not pro-Western. On the other hand, exerting counterpressure via the satellites may not have the effect of diminishing Soviet pressure in the Near East but might only produce a revolving-door effect, with the intensification of both crises.

In the light of its international repercussions, then, the crisis in Eastern Europe, while not without serious costs to the Soviet Union, does appear, when taken in conjunction with the Suez conflict, to have had unfavorable consequences for us. Still, beneath the more spectacular and violent events of these days we catch intimations of certain other developments that may eventually prove to be of the greatest importance: the fact that even after being struck down militarily the Hungarians persevered in passive resistance, sufficiently effective, it appears at this moment of writing, to baffle efforts to re-establish a working régime; the stories of Russian soldiers who refused to fire on the crowds and who were horrified to discover they were not wanted; the continuing ferment created by the admission of "errors" committed under the "cult of personality"; and finally the overwhelming desire of the Russian people themselves for a "thaw," for a respite from their forty-year forced march. In all this we see signs of real "spontaneity" which could become so pervasive as radically to alter the world situation.

XII ❧ The Succession to Khrushchev in Perspective

[1965]

KHRUSHCHEV'S ABRUPT REMOVAL FROM OFFICE AND POWER in October 1964 was, for me, but another in a sequence of unanticipated events in Soviet affairs, a sequence that has made the subject both fascinating and perplexing. It is not the failure to foretell the occurrence itself that causes chagrin—the contingencies surrounding any particular event are so great that I am content to await the fact— but, rather, that such an event has a way of negating, or at least badly muddying, one's general picture of what is going on in the Soviet Union. The victory of one American presidential candidate over another, or even the shocking interruption of our political process, as the assassination of President John F. Kennedy, does not, it seems to me, produce quite this disconcerting sense of derailment that I feel in the Soviet case, this rueful "back to the drawing board" mood, as though one's general notion of the Soviet political process were badly awry.

Now this may merely reflect a professional warping on my part—too much squinting at, and brooding about, the

Soviet Union. The answer may be, as Yeats advised regarding another "bitter mystery":

> Young man, lift up your russet brow . . .
> And brood on hopes and fear no more. . . .

We are inclined to ask of our study of the U.S.S.R., the craft of Sovietology, more than can reasonably be expected of it. Precisely because the subject is so important, the stakes so great, we have a strong compulsion to ask of our appraisals of the Soviet scene more perhaps than we would expect to gain in connection with our own society—given our still limited though advancing knowledge of political processes. Indeed, at times I have felt that this might be *the* central explanation for my malaise: that we were simply placing our expectations too high, that we should be more modest in what we felt our studies could achieve.

There is also, however, a problem in the subject itself, and not merely in our level of expectations as observers. Hence, when I comment now on the Khrushchev succession "in perspective," my intention is not to tie up the loose ends and produce a coherent pattern "in the long light of history," but, rather, to look back on the Soviet and Russian past, to point up, emphasize, perhaps even to caricature, certain features of perversity in Russian affairs that are troublesome. In broadest terms they have to do with the gaining, maintenance, concentration, and transfer of political power and authority.

I

Let us start with the most recent case in point: Khrushchev's ouster and the succession of Brezhnev and Kosygin. For a number of years now, with the evident actuarial likelihood that Nikita Sergeevich would not be on the premises indefinitely, the Khrushchev succession question had been much discussed: both the most likely immediate heirs—and Brezhnev was favored successor—and the general turmoil that was expected to follow. This latter expectation remains a lively one, and not unreasonably so. The extent to which we are cued to it was evidenced recently when a report that *Izvestiia* was late in appearing sent a flurry of speculation through the Sovietological dovecots.

But of course the singular feature of the Khrushchev case is that he *was* ousted. However we may rate the extent of his control after 1957, however "first" he may have been among his "equals," the fact remains that this is the first time in the span of Soviet history that the man apparently in the saddle was unseated by other than natural causes—death or disablement. I am not at all sure that there will not be a struggle for power among Khrushchev's successors, but the simple fact that his career was terminated in a fashion different from Lenin's or Stalin's suggests prudence in devising models based on the earlier cases. And it is right at this point that we start running into what strike me as rather serious analytical difficulties.

It is, of course, from the post-Lenin and post-Stalin experiences that we have come in recent years to develop a sense of a succession crisis as a hardy perennial in the Soviet way of politics. In these two "classic" cases, the death or disability of a by-then unchallenged leader led to bitter struggle among his chief lieutenants, a struggle productive of much infighting, wobbling of policies, and general uncertainty, until a new leader seemed to emerge from the contenders: Stalin with his victory over the Right opposition in 1928, and Khrushchev with his victory over the "Anti-Party group" and Marshal Zhukov in 1957.

As a problem for political analysis this pattern of struggle has been seen as the result of two major sets of factors:

(1) The enormous concentration of political power in the Soviet Union gave the whole issue a much sharper focus than in the case of a pluralistic or decentralized form of régime; power, both economic and political, lay in a very restricted arena.

(2) At the same time there was no clearly defined way to make the orderly transfer of this enormous concentration of power; there was not even an adequate constitutional statement of the locus of power: both the Soviet constitution and the Communist Party statutes are obviously deficient in this regard. In other words, there has been the question of the legitimation of authority and of its transfer.

As to why this should be so, it is evident that there is an intimate connection with the revolutionary origins of the régime, which were the antithesis of a "legitimate" assumption of power. There is a connection, too, with the determination of the Bolsheviks to maintain their revolution and not succumb to a Thermidor or a Restoration. Deeply ingrained in the Communist outlook is a will not to be trapped by constitutionalism or established ways. Underlying this temper there is doubtless the ideological imperative. It has been argued that an ideology with absolute pretensions to correctness—to being the unique vessel of truth—must ultimately rest upon a single source and symbol of the doctrine, else there is a danger of pluralism and relativism. From this it is concluded that any shift in authority will be impelled, so long as the ideology is active, away from collegial efforts toward one-man control. This need not mean a succession crisis, as is clear from the election of the popes. But it does suggest that in the absence of an orderly sequence of rulers—whether by inheritance and the divine right of kings, or election by a college of cardinals, or through more secular forms of election in polities where power is centered in a president—the succession crisis will take the form of this compulsion toward a re-establishment of one-man supremacy.

Myron Rush, who has devoted much thought to this problem, has recently summarized his views, especially with respect to the likelihood of future crises, as follows:

> A succession crisis *is* to be expected. This conclusion is not simply grounded in history; the nature of the Soviet political system appears to make such crises inevitable. There are two reasons why this is so. First, in the Soviet system, there is no established decision-making center whose authority is recognized at all times. Second, for this reason, and for others to be cited, no orderly method of succession has been or is likely to be devised. . . .
>
> There is a paradox here. The Soviet system has been most stable until now when it has had a dictator, yet dictatorial authority inheres in no office or title. It is unprovided for in the fundamental laws of Party and state, which establish collective organs of leadership without exception. As a result there is no rule for establishing the legitimacy of the dictator. . . .
>
> In the USSR, then, the new ruler evidently comes to his office not by an orderly transfer of authority but by arrogating power to himself. As a result, for a time, at least, the functions normally performed by the ruler go undone. Moreover, the process by which this state of affairs can be rectified, namely, the concentration of great power in the person of the successor, is disruptive. It is these two consequences of the failure to provide for succession that produce political crisis in the Soviet system. . . .[1]

I have no objection to this analysis, and I, too, have a feeling that the post-Khrushchev leadership in the U.S.S.R.

[1] Myron Rush: *Political Succession in the USSR* (New York and London; 1965), pp. 72–8.

may not prove to be particularly stable. But two questions trouble me, or, rather, two considerations which may not fit into this picture. One is analytical, the other historical.

II

As I have said, one feature that distinguishes the Khrushchev succession question from those following Lenin and Stalin is that Khrushchev was ousted while apparently holding power. Rush observes:

> Khrushchev, to my surprise, failed to preserve the power he had concentrated, perhaps because his overconfidence enabled his intended successors to acquire too much power. Fundamentally, however, his overthrow illustrates the double dilemma . . . of a ruler in the Soviet Union who attempts to govern without terror and to arrange for his own succession. . . . The effect of the Khrushchev succession on the regime will, if anything, be increased by the way it was initiated.[2]

The analytical problem, as I see it, is that the introduction of such terms as "overconfidence" or "govern without terror"—perhaps needed to explain the ouster—at once puts some exceedingly problematic, human elements into the equation. While they quite properly belong there—surely Khrushchev's human foibles, and the fact that the amount of terror to use may be a human decision, must be granted as relevant—the more significant their role is seen to be, the more one undercuts an analysis based on more abstract considerations of power, authority, and sovereignty. If a man enjoying, after his successful scramble to the top in a succession struggle, such a great concentration of power is then capable of being toppled,

2 Ibid., p. xii.

not through an act of God but just through blunders, then suddenly our whole picture of power becomes a bit shaky and insubstantial.

To put it another way, insofar as we see the succession problem in the U.S.S.R. as a systematic oscillation between the stability under an established dictator and the uncertainties during periods of contending aspirants—the stability of the former deriving from the lack of effective challengers—Khrushchev should not have been ousted. On the other hand, once we grant that the dictator at the height of his sole power is sufficiently subject to human error to lead to his downfall, perhaps in preparation for his own succession but presumably at any time, then the pattern is so much the more uncertain.

Nor, from the analytical point of view, do we gain much by reference to the undoubted facts that Khrushchev lacked the "moral authority" or charisma of a Lenin, or the ability to use terror of a Stalin. Indeed, I am increasingly troubled by our tendency to believe that such terms as "charismatic leadership" or "rule by terror" advance us very far analytically. These are descriptive terms for uncustomary but observable phenomena, but when we inquire just *how* a leader succeeds in exerting his charismatic or terroristic influence, and why the followers, or the people at large, respond appropriately (rather than shrugging their shoulders to the charisma or putting a knife in the back of the would-be terrorist), we must obviously in each instance seek the answer in a very particular set of circumstances. "Charisma" or "moral authority," to be effective, must evoke a response; otherwise one is simply a voice crying in the wilderness. The application of terror requires both a populace that can be cowed by it—not too many "village Hampdens with dauntless breasts"—and executors to exercise the terror and not turn and fall upon the leader. To me these are not simple or easy circumstances to create.

III

All of which reinforces a suspicion I have long nourished, but which I must leave to my political science colleagues to confirm or refute: that any rigorously systematic model of the political process, and most obviously one employing mechanical or physical analogies—power, balance of forces, and so forth—ultimately breaks down in its own terms, becomes involved in self-contradiction. This strikes me as a fatal flaw in all such efforts from Machiavelli and Hobbes on down.

In the Soviet case it is precisely because the régime and ideology are themselves so power-conscious and power-motivated, that we are more than usually inclined to seek a systematic explanation in power terms.

Based on the Lenin and Stalin successions, I am not sure we can build up a self-sufficient argument for an internal necessity for further succession crises; the Khrushchev ouster, *by its prematurity,* can be used as an argument against as well as for such a necessity.

Yet, this being said, my own feeling is that power and its transfer somehow constitute a rather special problem in the Soviet case, but it may be that part of the reason is *historical* rather than *systemic.* To examine this possibility, I should like to make a few random excursions into earlier Russian history, to see what we may come up with. My examples are from earlier rather than immediately pre-Soviet history, and this of course raises the question whether we are in fact dealing at all with the same problem. Still, let us look at the examples and see what they suggest.

IV

If we go back to the dim Kievan past, we are told that among the rulers of the Rurik dynasty, the pattern of inheritance and succession was a rather unusual one, not from father to son, but through a series of lateral transfers in the various holdings by seniority among the members of the ruling dynasty. In time this system broke down, not surprisingly. Between 1054 and 1224 no less than sixty-four principalities had a more or less ephemeral existence, 293 princes put forward succession claims, and their disputes led to eighty-three civil wars. I shall leave this merely as a suggestive backdrop.

With the emergence of Muscovy, however, we get a reversal of the pattern, a move—whatever the causes and occasion—toward autocracy, combined with the "in-gathering" of lands previously lost or distributed through civil conflict and foreign invasion.

Not only did autocrats emerge, but they managed to pass on the succession of autocracy. For example, Ivan IV, known as the Terrible, came to the throne at the age of three. How did this infant, surrounded by older relatives and boyars, come to re-establish the autocracy and indeed to strengthen it? Not a medievalist, I remain perplexed by this phenomenon, which seems incapable of explanation by mechanical means.

Following the death of Ivan's weak heir, Muscovy was convulsed—by the Time of Troubles—but again an autocracy emerged with the Romanov dynasty. Why this, and not an oligarchy of chieftains? In this respect the contemporary Polish experience of the whittling away of the crown's power whenever there were breaks in the regular succession seems the more natural. Admittedly, we have instances in Western Europe where, after weak or infant kings, or civil wars, autocracy was able to re-form: Louis XIV after the Fronde, the House of Tudor after the War of the Roses. But the cases seem somewhat less extreme.

The reign of Peter the Great somewhat repeats the pattern of Ivan the Terrible—a youngster without power somehow contrives to retrieve and extend absolute individual authority.

In the eighteenth century, in the absence of a clear line of inheritance, the succession question was fearfully confused. And it is worth noting that at one point in the period, at the accession of Anne in 1730, the lady was obliged to sign a document limiting autocratic power and accepting control by a grand council. This proved to be very unpopular and she, too, was able to restore the principle of unlimited autocracy. According to a contemporary source, one of the nobles who helped reverse the action said "That he was deputed by the whole nobility of the empire to represent to her, that she had been, by the deputies of the council of state, surprised into the concessions she had made; that Russia having for so many ages been governed by sovereign monarchs, and not by council, all the nobility entreated her to take into her own hands the reins of government; that all the nation was of the same opinion, and wished that the family of her Majesty might reign over them to the end of time."[3]

From the beginning of the nineteenth century this "succession" question seems less a feature of the Russian landscape, partly because of regulated inheritance. The confusion at the death of Alexander I, with which the Decembrist uprising was connected, seems to have been

[3] Quoted in *Readings in Russian History*, ed. Warren B. Walsh (Syracuse; 1963), I, 198.

rather a problem of communication than a real question of succession. Rush suggests that the "succession" crisis "played a role, though not a great one, in the fall of the tsarist regime in 1917, which was somewhat hastened by the refusal of Archduke Michael to assume the throne left vacant by the forced abdication of Nicholas II."[4] But it is doubtful whether that belated episode played any significant part in the onset of the Revolution or the course of Russian history. By the time of Nicholas II, a weak man with a hemophilic son and a brother whose chief recommendation for the throne apparently was that he was stupid, the pattern of monarchical succession in the Romanovs had pretty well played itself out.

I am not certain what conclusions, if any, may be legitimately drawn from these scattered episodes from Muscovite and early imperial history. They do, however, bear a certain resemblance to succession issues in the Soviet case: (1) a political system with an enormous concentration of political authority; (2) a not always satisfactory method of transmitting this authority in an orderly fashion; and (3) a tendency to reconcentrate power.

V

In considering these parallels I do not wish to suggest the persistence of a "national character"—that Russians by nature love despots—nor that Bolshevism has been a reincarnation of Muscovy; such leaps are persuasive only if some plausible means of transmittal from one age to another can be advanced.

There is, however, one possible line of explanation that may have some bearing on our contemporary concerns.

---

4 Rush: op. cit., p. 3.

As we have noted, the periodic crisis of succession and re-establishment of autocracy tended to fade out in the nineteenth century. At the same time, despite the fact that the Tsar remained an autocrat, at least up to 1905, in the course of that century Russian society was becoming far more articulated; between the sovereign power and the populace there was interposed a growing complex of intermediate strands—middle-class elements, intelligentsia, new formations in the bureaucracy. And while this was not adequately reflected in any corresponding constitutional or political change, even so vigorous a reactionary figure as Alexander III was not, in reality, the autocrat that his seventeenth- and eighteenth-century predecessors had been. One hears more about the bureaucracy and ministers, even though they are still responsible only to the Tsar. While some revolutionaries hoped that getting rid of the individual monarch might topple the system, there was growing disposition to believe that this was insufficient, that the system was held together by many other forces.

In other words, whatever the reasons for the peculiar concentration of authority and the correspondingly peculiar features of its transmittal in earlier Russian history, the nineteenth and early twentieth centuries witnessed a significant growth of elements making for pluralism, recognized or not.

The 1914 War, the Revolution, and the Civil War—vast upheavals demographically and socially as well as politically—had the effect of *scraping away*, through deposition, death, confiscation, and emigration, a very considerable part (it might be worthwhile to attempt a quantitative measurement) of these intermediary elements, in addition to the autocracy itself.

From this I would venture the conclusion that when

Russia entered its Soviet period there had, in fact, been in certain respects a historical retrogression. It was not merely that through the overturn of revolution more primitive elements of society had been flung to the top, but also that in the relationship of sovereign power to society a great many of the cushioning or modulating elements had been removed. The *objects* of governmental policy—the Soviet citizenry—were in very large measure premodern peasantry.

Under these circumstances the ideological impulses of Marxism-Leninism (already carrying influences from the Russian past) could easily lead, in their concrete application to society, to that curiously atavistic despotism we know as Stalinism. For all of Stalin's undoubted if ferocious talents, the fact that he was able to *impose* his will the way he did with the results that ensued, tells us as much about Russian society of his time as it does about his aims and abilities.

VI

If this suggestion has any merit, we might then see if it has application to more recent developments. There is no question that Russia, whatever our judgment of the human costs, has gone far since the 1920's in terms of modernization and industrialization. Against the wreckage of those early years a highly articulated society has again been erected, even though there has not as yet been an adequate political or constitutional reflection of this change. Within the Soviet cosmos important new groups have again emerged—managers, intellectuals, bureaucrats—an increasing percentage of whom, as time passes, have been spared the scarifying impact of the Stalin era. In this "rearticulation" of Russian society we may, then, be witnessing a healing, after half a century, of the great social rift or amputation resulting from the Revolution. If that be so, then it may follow that the dictator-succession crisis-dictator sequence could fade away, not because of ideological erosion (though that, too, is not to be excluded) , but because of changes in Soviet society. The lord may pull the bell-rope, but the servants may not come.

Do these suggestions find either support or refutation in the post-Khrushchev period? I am afraid not. These processes, even if they have substance, are clearly of a long-range nature; the passage of time, the rise of new generations, the slow growth of self-conscious interests of groups are all involved. I have no idea whether Khrushchev's replacement by Brezhnev and Kosygin is a step in this direction or merely another turn in the cycle of Communist infighting atop an inert society. I am acutely aware of this perennial conflict which seems to prevail as a way of life in Communist parties, in the U.S.S.R. and elsewhere. I am also impressed by the persistence of the Stalinist heritage, especially among the *apparatchiki* now at the top, whose school of advance was the late 1930's. Moreover, for any appraisal of the immediate situation and the future we must take account of things I have not even touched on here: economic concerns, inter-Communist issues, and, of course, East-West relations.

Still, the Khrushchev ouster, for all the obscurity and dubious legality (if the terms have meaning here) of the procedure, may be considered, from our perspective, as more positive than negative. Admittedly, this can be challenged. Leonard Schapiro, for example, has argued that Brezhnev and Kosygin "seem to lack even the kind of legitimacy that Lenin, Stalin, and Khrushchev all had." And of course within the framework of the revolutionary tradition this is quite true; Lenin made the Revolution, Stalin played a part in the Revolution and laid claim to being the legitimate heir of Lenin; even Khrushchev, in his anti-Stalinism, had some claim to maintaining the Leninist tradition. The element of continuity is far less apparent in the case of Brezhnev and Kosygin, men of a younger generation, who reached the top under Khrushchev.

This marked diminution of ties with the sources and symbols of Communist authority may prove to be problems for Khrushchev's successors, and could well lead to instability in working out the succession.

On the other hand, the very fact that such men were willing and able to take power from Khrushchev—plus the incomplete and not altogether satisfactory reasons for this that have been provided thus far—may at least intimate the beginning of Soviet politics in a new key. There may be instability; the consequences in terms of United States–Soviet relations may not be favorable. But at the very least the fact that a not unimpressive First Secretary of the Party could be deposed suggests that, even now, the political ground rules may be changing—to something hectic, perhaps, but perhaps also more familiar.

XIII ❧ Soviet-American Relations: Problems of Choice and Decision

[1958]

"IT IS ONLY AGAINST A BACKGROUND OF HARD REALITY THAT choices count." This observation by Ben Shahn in *The Shape of Content* applies to much more than the world of the artist. Indeed, in the realm of international affairs I am increasingly impressed with the difficulties of discussing choices of policy without close and continuing touch with reality and without the burden of responsibility. This is not to suggest that discussion should be confined to governmental circles—any such limitation would be both impossible and undesirable. But just as it is hard for a person to understand the game of poker (unlike chess) unless he plays for real money, so the effort to discuss policy-formation away from the point of decision where choice must be turned into action can lead to serious and possibly dangerous misconceptions.

At least three fallacies may be involved in making international policy decisions: the failure to think in context, the oversimplification of the problem, and the demand for omniscience and omnipotence. All three errors occur commonly in the area of Soviet-American relations, where the issues are incredibly complex and difficult, the stakes fearful, and self-evident answers not at hand.

There is nothing mysterious or unusual about the need to think in context. We do it all the time in making personal or family decisions. Any parent who has had to take an action concerning his child's health or education is aware of the distinction between a decision accompanied by the burden of responsibility and the advice or recommendation of an outsider, whatever the latter's qualifications or competence. It seems difficult, however, to transfer this distinction to the larger, more remote, and less personal spheres of national and international politics. The result is a characteristic type of policy proposal, often containing a fruitful or suggestive idea, which is presented as a matter for choice or decision but which in fact is nothing of the sort. These proposals may originate in the press, in academic circles, or even in branches of the government itself; what they lack is not necessarily sobriety or insight but the sense of context.

For example, the proposal that the United Nations be given a monopoly of arms, or that the United States double its aid to underdeveloped countries, or that Germany be reunited by a mutual disengagement of NATO and Warsaw treaty forces, or that the United States support colonial peoples against the metropolitan powers (or vice versa) — while each concerns real problems and could conceivably be part of a program of action, it is not amenable to simple acceptance or rejection. It is not that the responsible policy-maker must be a cautious trimmer—at times neither caution nor hedging is possible—but that he must operate within a setting in which timing, the form in which particular issues emerge, the general state of domestic as well as foreign politics, and indeed his own personality and style of performance are an integral part of the act of decision. Neglect of this obvious fact only creates unwarranted hopes in panaceas, and a necessarily frustrated demand for "bold new programs."

The second fallacy represents an effort to reduce the "hard reality" with which we are confronted to more manageable terms. Certainly it is useful to develop concepts and techniques that may bring at least partial order out of the chaos of international politics. The fallacy appears when we begin to play games with ourselves at the expense of our grasp of reality. Several examples come to mind. One is the attempt to proceed deductively from some such concept as "the national interest": the term is defined and then national objectives and policies are expected to flow from it like Euclidean corollaries. Usually the "national interest" turns out either to be a tautological or circular definition or to represent special pleading for a particular line of policy which was in mind at the beginning of the exercise.

A second device for simplifying a particularly ambiguous and intricate problem is that of setting up "alternatives," as though forming policies were like selecting one French pastry from a number on a tray. There is a deceptive modesty about this device: all sides are presented and the choice is left open. But even when the presentation is not stacked in favor of one alternative there is a serious difficulty: How is one supposed to make the final choice? If there are additional and decisive considerations they must be introduced, in which case one alternative may clearly be called for; if it is just a matter of flipping a coin, we are no longer in the area of serious political decision. Moreover, the pattern of alternatives, while perhaps attractive architecturally, frequently does not represent real choices open to the policy-maker. In retrospect, "containment *vs.* liberation" appears to have been an untenable set of alternatives; the actual problems confronting the United States in Germany and Eastern Europe were such that we could not make a choice in these terms.

A third device for stating a complicated problem in manageable terms is the method of "abstraction," an effective tool of analysis in some situations, but liable to dispose of the baby along with the bath water in others. For example, to abstract Soviet political motivations while studying the economic objectives of Russia's foreign trade and aid activities would probably cause more confusion than clarity. Related to this procedure is the "tentative hypothesis." A year or so ago I encountered the suggestion that it would be good to study the requirements of American policy over the next decade under two differing assumptions: (*a*) that the Soviet régime remained strong and cohesive, (*b*) that the Soviet régime suffered internal strains and disintegration. Unfortunately, most of the problem lies precisely in these assumptions and it is evident that the answers resulting from such a study would be of little use.

Finally, in attempts to simplify a highly complex situation there is the tendency to speak in terms of a "calculated risk": in the event of an uprising in Eastern Europe the United States should supply aid, as a "calculated risk." Whatever the merits of such an action, it is surely anything but a "calculated risk." (Unless we mean simply, it is risky and we know it.) The likelihood of the various possible outcomes is demonstrably incalculable, as is the relationship between the odds and the size of the stakes. Risks may have to be taken in our dealings with the Soviet Union, but it adds nothing to introduce a spurious if comforting sense of mathematical precision. A statistician could demonstrate, quite rigorously, that such major political decisions simply do not lend themselves to treatment in terms of probabilities.

The third type of fallacy also arises from the complexity of Soviet-American relations. Those whose thinking is clouded by this fallacy, instead of oversimplifying the picture, fall into the opposite fault of demanding of those responsible for policy, usually by implication, omiscience and omnipotence.

Perhaps the most significant form of this fallacy is the capabilities-intentions analysis, which is useful in dealing with a limited and definable situation but which can get out of hand when applied to the Soviet Union. By this procedure we undertake to discover *what* our opponent wants to do and whether he has the wherewithal to do it; the combined estimate which emerges then provides the basis for our requirements. Unfortunately, the distinction between capabilities and intentions is not as clear-cut as it might appear to be. The meaning and significance of capabilities may depend upon the intentions behind them and may not even be usefully measurable without reference to those intentions. Conversely, certain intentions may not be directly ascertainable but must be inferred from the nature and growth of the capabilities. Beyond that, of course, Soviet capabilities and intentions are not independent variables; both are in constant interaction with American capabilities and intentions, and any estimate for the future must take account of the additional influence of this interaction.

But the real trouble with this line of analysis, in dealing with the Soviet Union, is that the types of requirements it assigns to the United States are, in the end, both limitless and without criteria for priorities. It is not hard to show that if we try to devise a pattern of complete insurance against an opponent of equal present and future military, economic, and political capabilities, whose intentions may be to work against us with any available means—except perhaps those which are self-destructive—we have set ourselves an insoluble problem. The debate on the kinds of warfare we should be prepared to fight—general thermonuclear, conventional, tactic-atomic, brushfires, etc.—has been plagued with this difficulty. Reliance on any one form of defense fails to take account of the potentialities inherent in Soviet capabilities and possible intentions; the attempt to develop military capabilities to meet all contingencies appears to involve an impossibly heavy burden. And, of course, the Soviet Union may prefer to stick to the "peace" line and economic penetration.

In other words, we are in danger of being in the situation of an individual who tries to buy insurance policies against all eventualities, including insurance against bankruptcy from paying his premiums. If the second fallacy, that of oversimplification, attempts to get around the "hard reality" of Soviet-American relations by avoiding some of the awkward features of that reality, the third, of which the capabilities-intentions analysis is only one example, suffers from the attempt to impose a total solution, a task which is probably not within the realm of possibility.

There is little doubt that these difficulties and frustrations have contributed to the periodic attempt to break through the uncomfortable and exasperating terms of the problem, either by demanding a "forcible showdown"— though these demands have been less in evidence with the arrival of the ballistic missile—or by deciding that the Soviet régime is evolving into a more amiable and cooperative form of government, a pleasant thought but one for which there is no convincing evidence.

The answer, however, cannot lie in denying the question. We would do better to recognize that it is a "hard reality" we face. It is not a "game" to be played: the rules are not given and we cannot pull out and go home. It is not even a problem, properly speaking, since there is no given solution.

This does not mean, however, that rational decisions are impossible. Nor are we caught in an inexorable historical process against which our actions are in vain—though the Soviet leaders may think so. But as in all human situations the task is one of coping with, rather than solving, a series of concrete challenges which are never quite the same and never entirely different.

Probably the best approach to decisions under these circumstances is that of a continuing dialogue, or debate. Actually there are two debates going on simultaneously, one between us and the Communist leaders, an antagonistic debate, and one among ourselves, domestically and with our allies, a consultative debate. These debates, which include actions as well as words, both influence and are influenced by the development of Soviet-American relations, and at the same time provide the material for policy decisions.

It is important to realize that the relations between the Soviet Union and the United States are not fully reciprocal; the absence of symmetry in the motivations, goals, and organization of these two great states makes it quite inappropriate to regard their controversy as simply a "great-power conflict." Nevertheless, they constantly interact upon one another, to the extent that by now the political and diplomatic position of each is unintelligible without reference to the other. Both, in other words, are in part a product of their continuing encounter. This being so, it is to be expected that the policy decisions will be in the setting of this antagonistic debate, the terms of which will shift as the debate continues. The end of the debate is not in sight.

The domestic debate is in good part a response to the external debate: a constantly recurring effort to work out patterns of action that can meet the shifting requirements. The debate may follow party lines, or it may cross them. It is rarely conclusive, partly because the terms of the debate change, or appear to change, partly because neither line of recommended action may be feasible. Still, for all the uncertainty and lack of precision, choices are made, actions are taken.

If we review the course of the years since the end of the Second World War we find that the pattern of debate— both domestic and foreign—has passed through several distinct stages, each raising different questions and each producing a different set of responses. The first of these, which lasted roughly from 1945 through 1947, was dominated by the confusion resulting from Russia's role as a wartime ally against Germany and its subsequent promotion of active Communist expansion. While the terms of our postwar relationship were being debated internationally in a series of increasingly hostile and sterile conferences, the domestic debate was expressed in the terms, "toughness *vs.* cooperation." For a time our national policy tried to combine the two, in Secretary of State Byrnes' phrase, "patience with firmness," but the hope for cooperation proved vain.

In the second period, from 1948 to 1953 or 1954, the terms of the problem were quite different: internationally the lines were drawn, the Iron Curtain was down, the Cold War was in progress, accompanied by a shooting war in Korea. Domestically the pattern of debate was expressed in terms, "containment *vs.* liberation." While the debate was exaggerated by polemical fireworks and while the choices were considerably more complex than is suggested by these two words, there was an important problem to be explored through this debate, a problem set by the existing international conflict. By this time there was general agreement that the Soviet Union was an opponent with hostile intentions, not just a suspicious war-ravaged power. The difference lay in the definition of our response. Put in simple terms the position of "containment" held that our national strategy should be to hold the existing line between the Communist and non-Communist spheres, to work hard to strengthen and unite the Free World, but not to press for a roll-back of Soviet control and influence from areas of postwar expansion. While there were hopes that such containment might cause the Soviet system to fester internally, the principal argument was that our national security could be maintained by this means and without the threat to peace that a policy of "liberation" appeared to carry with it. The argument for liberation, which involved pressing Soviet power at least back to the Russian frontier, was that mere containment gave the advantage of initiative to the other side, would lead to an erosion of the Free World, and would ultimately imperil our own security. Hence even with a possibly greater chance of conflict, the areas of freedom had to be expanded when and where possible.

As it turned out, neither line of argument was able to produce very relevant answers to certain problems that our policy-makers had to contend with. Containment had little to offer with regard to a divided Germany; liberation faltered when it came to dealing with uprisings in the Soviet orbit. As a matter of fact, American policy, Democratic and Republican, contained elements of both positions, but not because any higher synthesis had been achieved.

The fact that neither containment nor liberation has much currency today would suggest that we have passed on to a new stage in our relations with the Soviet Union. One factor leading to this shift was that both earlier positions conceived of the division between the two systems as being a territorial line, at which you stood, or from which you retreated, or across which you advanced. But this linear concept, while corresponding to the existence of Communist and non-Communist states with frontiers between them, raised problems when it came to a divided state like Germany, and it didn't encompass such significant features of the international scene as the movement of ideas, broadcasts and propaganda, Communist and pro-Communist parties in the free world, and rifts within the Communist bloc. Perhaps even more significant was the advent of thermonuclear weapons and the ballistic missile: war and weapons could not be thought of in the same spatial terms with which they had been considered in the past. The terms "containment" and "liberation" seem increasingly inappropriate as we contemplate the fantastic revolution in the art of warfare that we, and the Soviet Union, are creating.

The death of Stalin and his successors' tentative experiments with some measure of "decompression" also contributed to this shift in perspectives. The domestic Soviet "debate"—in the peculiarly bitter and murderous setting of that political system—may have had a function analogous to those in our own. On the whole, however, recent events, and especially the renewed campaign against revisionism, would indicate more continuity with Stalinism than appeared in prospect in 1955 and 1956.

The combination of these various developments since

1953 seems to have set the division between the Communist and non-Communist worlds less in terms of lines or curtains than in terms of zones or areas, not necessarily to be defined geographically. Perhaps this can be best illustrated by reference to two terms that now appear frequently in discussions of Soviet-American relations, "disengagement" and "exchange." (It may be noted that neither is included in the theme either of containment or of liberation.)

Proponents of "disengagement" feel that the status quo with its unresolved tensions will be increasingly precarious as time passes. They also proceed from the premise that the Soviet régime, for the foreseeable future, will remain intact and largely invulnerable to external influences. From this it follows that any arrangement for altering the status quo must be through mutual agreement. Among the terms of such an agreement might be a withdrawal of armed forces from their more advanced position, usually in conjunction with a reunified but neutral Germany. Under such an agreement the Communist and Free worlds are to be separated, not by an Iron Curtain, but by a large, uncommitted area or zone, created by concessions on both sides. This line of argument derives in part from certain apparent lessons of the Hungarian revolt: that even such an explosion did not undermine the effective power of the Soviet Union; that the United States was unable to support the revolt without risks which it was unprepared to take; that such upheavals in the satellite area merely increase Soviet vigilance and could, if they threatened to get out of hand, lead to war; but that the Soviet Union may feel overextended in some regions and might consent to a partial withdrawal if the Western powers made some corresponding move.

Against this impulse toward disengagement there is a

contrary one toward greater engagement. This may take the form of "exchanges"—cultural, academic, technical, economic—or, if one prefers a grimmer term, of "infighting." As with the position of disengagement there is agreement that the Iron Curtain is increasingly porous and may not be the decisive point of contact in the future. But this position would have some confidence that the reasons for the changes that took place in Poland and Hungary may also, in time, be operative in the Soviet Union itself. Hence one accepts the challenge or risks of mutual interpenetration of the two systems, not with any simple hope of achieving neighborly relations, but in the expectation that this will foster, in some fashion and at some time, beneficial change within the U.S.S.R. itself.

It is obvious that both approaches have their difficulties, and neither is able to guarantee the achievement of its objective. On the one hand, the Soviet leaders have given no sign that they are prepared to witness the de-Communization of an area that has once been Communized; on the contrary they have stated explicitly that this is not to be permitted. Disengagement may be blocked by this formidable obstacle. On the other hand, the recently renewed emphasis on orthodoxy shows that the Soviet leaders are fully aware of the danger of ideological erosion or backsliding through contact with the "imperialists." This may effectively block the hoped-for consequences of exchange.

Whatever their prospects of success, these two approaches diverge in several respects from earlier policy and also emphasize some different and possibly incompatible lines of action. The diplomatic stance for a policy of disengagement, with its overtone of nonintervention and noninvolvement, may not fit easily with the more active scrambling of closer engagement. And yet it is doubtful that a clear-cut choice on either is feasible, for reasons indicated earlier. Decisions must be made in context, whether in connection with negotiations on exchange of persons, or in meeting a Soviet proposal for a summit conference, or in gauging the significance of a new crisis in the Soviet orbit. The issue is not one between theory and practice, or between principle and expediency, but between relevance and irrelevance. Our actions must be relevant to the threat, challenge, or opportunity of the given situation. The function of these approaches is not to serve as blueprints for policy but to indicate avenues of possible action, to suggest the implications of particular acts, and to warn against certain pitfalls.

The emphasis placed in these pages upon the importance of concrete decisions by officials with the burden of responsibility does not mean that public discussion of foreign policy and general analysis of the international scene is a waste of time. This is certainly not the case. The argument here is not for policy-making by an exclusive group of officials, nor for spur-of-the-moment decisions. While it may, in fact, be impossible for the United States to have a completely articulated foreign policy designed to cover all contingencies, and while many private citizens will continue to feel aggrieved at the failure of administrations in Washington to come out with electrifying new programs, constant debate on these matters and the continuing effort to relate general principles to specific requirements are at the heart of the democratic process. Indeed, it may prove to be that this circulation of ideas, the creation of at least partial solutions from the play of divergent views, is a significant source of strength in America's encounter with the Soviet Union. While the Soviet leaders, at times, display greater flexibility in their diplomatic tactics than the United States is able to do—a natural consequence of their governmental structure—it remains true that their great enemy is spontaneity, which, as events of 1956 and 1957 demonstrated, is always a danger to their political system. Their practice of alternating repression and relaxation may have some effect in stimulating and reviving, but, like artificial respiration, it is no real substitute for the natural breathing of a free society.

XIV ⚡ The Russian Revolution as History

[1967]

I SHOULD LIKE TO RAISE THE GENERAL QUESTION OF THE absorption or digestion of a cataclysmic set of events, the Russian Revolution, into the historical process, at least as we now can envisage it fifty years after 1917. The conversion of an event into something that is historic—perhaps in the sense of being noteworthy but in any case belonging to history—can be seen either as an objective occurrence, as something come to rest in the endless flow of time, as something definitely "past"; or, as a more subjective entity, as something to be classified by the historian, given its causes, course and consequences, and placed within whatever historical frame or pattern the historian holds or can devise.

There is an intimate and, in considerable measure, reciprocal relationship between the two, although it is by no means a symmetrical one. An event can be, or at least appear to be, safely "past," and still remain a live object of changing views and interpretations. Changing views, however, are less likely to bring the past to life like a

Lazarus *redivivus* (though this is not impossible). The relatively recent decipherment of Linear B script has certainly altered our historical picture of Mycenaean civilization, but when I last saw Nestor's palace in Pylos, it seemed safely dead despite the discoveries made on that site.

When we get closer to the present, however, the relationship between the subjective and the objective becomes more complex and intricate, precisely because we are not sure that the past *is* past and hence our reading of it may, like a correctly pronounced incantation, summon forth a new or revived reality.

But can we, in fact, speak of different kinds of past? What has happened has happened and in that sense is irreversible and unchangeable. A street riot yesterday is, chronologically speaking, just as much past as the July days in Petrograd in 1917. But if we take the past in this sense, then, correspondingly, the future is everything that will happen a split second from now and henceforward. The present, in consequence, as E. H. Carr seems willing to have it in a discussion of this question, has only "a notional existence as an imaginary dividing line between the past and future."[1] But I cannot help boggling at this and would suggest that there is utility, though a rigorous defense may be difficult, in the idea of what we might call the "cluster of the immediate"—that bundle of recent pasts, present awarenesses, and current anticipations that we, individually and collectively, carry with us. To take one example: the fall of France in 1940 became, as soon as it occurred, part of the past, but the "cluster of the immediate" that, say, Winston Churchill observed and felt,

[1] Edward Hallett Carr: *What Is History?* (New York; 1962), p. 142.

was obviously *qualitatively* different from the fall of Constantinople in 1453, and indeed the *pattern* of events was open and in a certain real sense reversible—in the destruction of Hitler—in a way that the fall of Constantinople had long since ceased to be. In other words, I would argue against the attempt to be prematurely historical about an event in the recent past, to tuck it into place and feel that there is little more to be done than to designate its appropriate niche in the catacombs of history.

For a student of recent Russian history a central question is whether, at fifty years' remove, the 1917 Revolution is part of the "dead" past—like the fall of Constantinople— or still part of the "living" past, part of this cluster of immediates. This question, of course, has over the years been hopelessly entangled with the conscious political wish and effort on the part of many people to undo the Revolution, to witness the overthrow of the Soviet régime. Such an impulse is, to be sure, one of the components of a live past —as was Churchill's will to victory over Nazi Germany— but it is not identical with it.

I have the impression, therefore, that those historians are being both unfair and lacking in a certain historical feeling who argue that all discussion over contingency *vs.* inevitability in the Russian Revolution, any exploration of the "might-have-beens," or concern with the defeated parties, is merely a cover for a conscious or unconscious desire to negate the Revolution, to have the story come out with a different ending. It is unfair because it frequently does injustice to the nature of the intellectual concerns, which may be quite disinterested, that lead to this type of inquiry; and it is lacking historical feeling because of a failure to sense this "cluster of the immediate"—though this clearly diminishes by the year. Finally, though this brings in the subjective side of 1917 as an object of historical scrutiny, I would submit that the examination of the might-have-beens, of the tracks that led nowhere or were covered by snow, is an important part of our quest for an understanding of the Revolution and its historical setting.

To what extent can we speak of the Russian Revolution as part of the truly *past* past? Our answer today would, and should, be different from one that might have been given in the 1920's or 1930's or even 1940's. For one thing, a living past does largely depend upon the life span of the generation involved in the original event; it is in their minds and purposes that much of the cluster of the immediate is preserved. Quite evidently with the passage of half a century, this element is diminishing rapidly. We have noticed this in recent years in connection with the rapidly shrinking body of Menshevik survivors who emigrated to the United States. Not only has death taken a very heavy toll, but I have felt that there was a marked change in temper within the last half-dozen years, a final unclenching of the fist, a reluctant but real letting go— the embattled stance that lasted so long, against such odds, that survived in hopes of a basic change, being converted into a sense that their experiences now belonged to the past, were more a matter of historical record than the basis for an active political position.

But more than the passage of a generation is involved in converting the Revolution into a past past. The appearance of new generations for whom the Revolution was a remote but glorious myth, even of a generation who knew not Joseph, has had a tendency to jell the Revolution and its aftermath. As the dissident, and now imprisoned, writer, Abram Tertz, remarked: "We will start with the Revolution." Just as the introduction of the metric system became increasingly irreversible the more it was applied and built into the system of things, so the appearance of new generations born within the Soviet system places the origins of that system in the past: it is no longer raw topsoil; layers of successive experience and practice have been deposited on it for fifty years.

When we look at the political system itself, the prospects of a "Restoration" have long since past. (I mean by this an explicit repudiation of the Revolution, its symbols and values, not the murder of revolutionaries and the hidden substitution of values which is observable in the period of High Stalinism and the Great Purges.) For one thing, Restoration in the classical sense depends on having someone or some system to restore; these have passed from the scene. Moreover, I doubt whether a monarchical, *ancien régime* restoration was really ever in the cards as the final movement of the cycle of the Russian Revolution. The experience of the Hohenzollern and Habsburg dynasties, which were toppled at approximately the same time, suggests that in the broader sweep of European history after 1917–18, the odds were very great against any such Bourbon or Stuart Restoration. Here the Russian experience is obviously linked with a much larger trend in world history: *anciens régimes* are *past* and so presumably are the movements that overthrew them.

When, however, we move from these particular features of the Russian Revolution that I would regard as definitely part of the *past* past, and turn to the question whether the Revolution, and in particular the November Revolution and its creations, are equally part of the past, we run into more troublesome problems. Thus, a recent book summing up the fifty years since the revolution, cites Alexis de Tocqueville's remark:

Experience suggests that the most dangerous moment for an evil government is usually when it begins to reform itself. . . . The sufferings that are endured patiently, as being inevitable, become intolerable the moment it appears that there might be an escape. . . .

and goes on to conclude:

The present stalemate is so tense on both sides that it is unlikely to endure indefinitely. At some point the Kremlin will be driven to act. Either it must carry reform far beyond the present half-measures, to the degree of diluting its political monopoly, or it must again resort to terror. In either case it will be putting its survival on the line in a life-or-death gamble.[2]

In this view the strains and tensions that were set up by the Bolshevik seizure of power in 1917 and heightened by the Stalin era are still very much alive history: the past has carried a time-bomb into the present.

I should certainly not dismiss this view out of hand. One is reminded of land-mines planted in the Libyan desert in the Second World War that lie there quietly until some donkey or farmer steps on them, and off they go. History has a number of such explosives planted here and there. The unexpected resurgence of certain nationalisms that we had thought were clearly of the past, even Scots or Welsh nationalism, suggests that things that seemed clearly of the bygone past can be triggered into action. I am increasingly impressed by the way in which aspirations, goals, and even political sentiments that appeared safely historical have somehow maintained an unnoticed subterranean existence to reappear in our troubled age.

The question, of course, is whether we are dealing with what in fact was live history, but concealed and transmitted

[2] Eugene Lyons: *Workers' Paradise Lost* (New York; 1967), pp. 377-8.

through the generations by means and channels that we really do not understand, or whether the use of old symbols and goals is an act purely responsive to current problems but making use of past symbols for their evocative power. I take it, for example, that the use of Magna Carta in seventeenth-century England was such a device, and that one would be hard put to it to find a continuous line of connection between Runnymede and the opponents of Charles I.

In the Russian case the lapse of time is far shorter. Moreover, the very dogmatic quality of the Soviet system, its rapid institutionalization and canonization of the guiding impulses and views of the Revolution (or selected parts thereof), make it much more difficult to tell just what kind of phenomenon we are witnessing: whether a running sore that had its origins in the Revolution and never really healed though often concealed, or, rather, a new set of discontents, reflective of an industrialized mid-twentieth-century Soviet Union, finding certain echoes in past controversies, on such matters as the peasant problem, the police, a command economy, and the like. Perhaps it is a mixture of the two.

If we take the example of Russian agriculture and the peasant problem, we seem to have just such a mixture. There can be, I believe, no doubt about the continuity of the peasantry as a problem from the Revolution (and before) to the present. Given the suspicion of the régime toward the countryside, its unwillingness, except in the initial seizure of power and to some extent in NEP, and after Stalin's death, really to meet the demands and interests of the peasantry, one could say that this is the live past, and potentially still an explosive one; that there is a living continuity in the peasant question, still unresolved from 1917 to the present. And yet, despite this appearance of continuity, I am not at all sure that this is the full picture or even the most important feature. After all, collectivization and the introduction of the kolkhoz-sovkhoz system did effect over time a tremendous transformation in organization and techniques. It is by no means certain that current complaints and desires are essentially the same as those of the land-hungry peasantry of 1917 (though I wish we knew more about the peasants in that year). After thirty years of collective agriculture it would be extremely difficult to go back to the smallholder ideal or to the commune. Well-informed Western observers have argued that the peasant wishes are quite other: some would prefer being straight hired labor on a well-run sovkhoz; others would be content to rent land, if the terms were clear and secure. Perhaps the old sense of land possession, whether individual or collective, has faded from the scene.

This possibility of a transmutation of the real terms and concerns of what might seem a continuing problem renders our question of the connection between a *past* past and a *live* past much more difficult: the obvious danger is that one mistakes appearance for reality and finds in an endemic problem evidence of continuity in its causes.

Here one must move, for further elucidation, from what I have called the objective to the more subjective side of the picture. For at this point the significance of the events and processes themselves and the tie between past and present become increasingly problematical. Facts do not speak for themselves, and we must call into service some sense of structure or pattern, which necessarily involves the observer and inquirer. Let us turn, then, to the second half of our theme: the historical quality of the Revolution, as viewed by the historian.

Among historians there is, of course, no consensus about defining the year 1917 as the focal point of recent Russian history. There is always the tendency of historians—who, I fancy, temperamentally prefer continuities to discontinuities—after some cataclysmic event, such as a major revolution, to find as many ties as they can with what went on before; to see the event as an eddy in a stream. This may be warranted as a corrective against crudely apocalyptic thinking; it is also a professional reflex. I happen to think it is fallacious in the case of 1917, which does represent a real break, interruption, discontinuity, whatever the later revenge of the infrastructure upon the superstructure, as Richard Lowenthal has put it.

Even if one grants that a major crisis was taking shape in Russian history in the last century or so, one can hold widely differing views as to the climactic period. The school of thought that emphasizes modernization and industrialization as the basic elements in the crisis might put the developments in the decades immediately after 1860 as crucial for Russia's historical development, with 1917 as something of a digression, not central to the story and perhaps not even disrupting the basic flow of events. Others, centrally concerned with such things as totalitarianism, a command economy, and the atomization of the population, would lay greatest stress on the Stalin era, arguing that Lenin's revolution was a kind of last act, with Russia belatedly following, idiosyncratically, a pattern familiar in the great changes in Western European society earlier on, and finding in Stalin, as in Hitler, the real turning point. From this perspective 1917 shrinks considerably, and the live problem stemming from the past is that of coping with the Stalinist heritage, the resolution of which does seem to be open-ended in a way that the 1917 Revolution no longer is.

These are vast questions. Here I can only record my impression, as a historian trying to make sense of the course of Russian history, that the modernization theme is too broad for my purposes; the screen is too coarse to catch the notable peculiarities of Russian-Soviet development. On the other hand, the Stalinist era is too immediately derivable from the Leninist, and hence from 1917, to serve as an adequate lever for prying meaning out of Soviet history. By this I do not mean that Stalinism was the necessary or inevitable outcome of Leninism; other possibilities were present in the 1920's and were hotly debated. But, given the combination of circumstances as they were and the available cast of characters, I find the Stalin régime, even including what Alec Nove has called its excessive excesses, as emerging not unnaturally out of the Leninist background.

If, then, for present purposes we accept 1917 as the crucial and climactic year in the recent history of Russia, where does it belong within the wider frame of modern history? Perhaps to the irritation of colleagues in the social sciences, I must say that it strikes me as unique: I do not think it is a "case study" or a model. It stands all by itself, as do most events of that colossal magnitude.

I would defend this judgment on two levels, the theoretical and the comparative.

In the first place, given the span of man's known history, virtually all great events are happenings unto themselves—like the complex involving the advent of Christendom and the decline of the classical world, or the complex of the Renaissance-Reformation. They are such central components of our view of "universal history" itself, that to ask where they fit *into* the pattern is equivalent to asking, *what* is the pattern. I doubt whether we can, without resorting to metahistory, "fit" such macrocosmic events of the magnitude of 1917 into a pattern. They themselves, and what we can extract in meaning from them, constitute, or, rather, through our minds come to create, the pattern; it—the pattern—is not an antecedent given.

As for comparison, I do not think that 1917 is amenable to an "anatomy" of comparative revolutions, though obviously a great deal is to be learned from such comparisons. On the whole, I have found comparative history to be at its most useful in exposing anomalies, things that didn't fit, generalizations that proved not to be valid when tried on for size in a different setting.

In the case of the Russian Revolution, despite the evident insights we gain by comparing, say, the pendulum swing toward ultra-radicalism and back, with the experience of the English Revolution of the seventeenth century and the French of the eighteenth, despite the poignant similarities one finds in the personalities and roles of Charles I, Louis XVI, and Nicholas II, despite the fact that revolutionaries envisaged themselves, or their opponents, in the role of historical predecessors—Cromwellian, Jacobin, Bonapartist—despite these parallels, which are surely not without some real significance, I do not find the comparisons complete in the sense of providing any guiding pattern. One reason is obvious: precisely because there had been a major preceding revolution that had gone through such and such stages, the participants in a later revolution, being conscious and self-conscious persons, would not permit the later revolution to duplicate the first. Surely the fear of Thermidor or of Bonapartism was not an inconsiderable element in the history of the Russian Revolution, and, say, the fate of Trotsky—unless one is to regard the human actors as more or less the pawns of "objective forces" regardless of their awareness.

Moreover, while one can regard the Russian Revolution as being structurally and in its pulses somehow akin to the English and especially the French Revolutions, one could also argue that it resembles the American Revolution (which Hannah Arendt and others see as a special case) in still being open-ended—not explicitly closed by a Restoration and a reaffirmation (though obviously modified) of traditional values, but being still the incarnation of a *Novus Ordo Seclorum.* In this light the continued dynamism of each, internally, and as influence and example, makes them appropriate objects of comparative study, and may indeed explain the strange cross-purposes of their encounters since each entered the world stage—adumbrated by Wilson and Lenin—but in reality since 1945: as the two great protagonists, not because of economic and military prowess alone but because of the open-endedness of their revolutionary traditions.

This feature of confrontation brings me to a last point of consideration regarding the Russian Revolution as history: namely, its meaning to us in the year 1967.

Despite my sense that from the point of view of the historian the events of 1917 constitute a break, not only in Russian but in general history, and in that sense are a major landmark both as a historical occurrence and in determining the way subsequent generations respond to the challenges of their time, 1917 does, from our perspective of 1967, begin to dwindle in significance as against vast and urgent problems, in which 1917 and its aftermath had only a marginal though not inconsequential role. These problems are more than obvious; they occupy the day's headlines: the fact that the gap between the have and the have-not nations seems to have widened rather than narrowed in the two decades since the Second World War. Overlapping that, the demographic explosion, which in actuarial terms poses a ferocious problem within the next quarter-century or so. Also overlapping, the clear shaping up, domestically and internationally, of a confrontation of peoples of different color. Beyond this cluster of problems the staggering task of absorbing the technological innovations and their rate of acceleration in recent years: the symbol may be the mushroom cloud, but the reality is increasingly penetrating all lives every minute. Overlapping, and perhaps in response to that, is the much discussed generations problem: something America, Western Europe, and Russia share in common.

These are the fateful issues for our time. And while it is common practice these days to speak in an apocalyptic vein, it does seem to me quite plain—insofar as one can make extrapolations—that unless we can get on top of these problems, the human race may well have run its course. This is being said all the time. It can be true.

Now where does this lead with respect to our more limited subject? Simply that while we do not underestimate the historical importance of the Russian Revolution and its consequences, both the United States and the Soviet Union, and all humanity, are involved in coping with these problems that have appeared or taken on extreme urgency in the years since 1917. It is important for us not to confuse 1917 and its aftermath with them, although there are certain obvious or superficial connections. The confrontation of the haves and the have-nots is explicit in Marxism and, on the international scale, in Lenin's theory of imperialism. Yet I would submit that it is, in its ultimate impulse, distinct and independent, though often finding its mode of expression in the rhetoric of the Russian Revolution. Similarly, we can relate the frightening technological race to the Soviet impulse to overtake and surpass—and this, too, can be traced back to Lenin. But it is an impulse transcending anything Lenin had in mind. Finally, the generations problem—the act of revolt against elders—can easily be given the coloration of the thoroughgoing revolutionism, refusal to compromise, that we find in 1917 Bolshevism. But this, too, in its present form and manifestation goes well beyond the fathers-and-son conflict in Russia or the generation malaise that preceded and accompanied the First World War. The forces producing it, and the corresponding responses, are larger by an order of magnitude, and equally affect both the U.S.S.R. and the West.

One of the dangers of our time is that, although a quite new array of problems is confronting mankind, unprecedented in nature and intensity, both the United States and the Soviet Union will link them to the fifty years of conflict between the two systems, each attributing to the other a poisonous agency that is infecting all domestic and international relations.

Hence, while I would as a historian argue strongly for the enormous historical role, and uniqueness, of 1917 in our sense of historical pattern in this century, it is far more important that we—in the United States and the Soviet Union alike—become sensitive to the novelty of the new challenges and not fall into the ghastly and mutually destructive role of fighting the Russian Revolution and Civil War all over again. To most of our *current* challenges these events are as relevant as Waterloo or Gettysburg.

EPILOGUE

A HALF-DOZEN YEARS AGO, IN SPEAKING ON "THE FRONTIERS of Slavic Studies," I remarked that, just as the course of world events after 1945 had undoubtedly been a major stimulus to Soviet and East European studies, so future developments "might lead us (or some contingents of us) out of the field of Slavic studies narrowly defined." I cannot now recall my own mood at the time, but it is true that in the last several years my attention has been drawn in several divergent directions. It is not a matter of retreating from an unanticipated side-track that I wandered into twenty-five years ago—such extended excursions become a part of one's life—but, rather, that a further working out of certain continuing concerns seems to require somewhat different settings. These can only be sketched here, as they really point to work yet to be done.

At the most evident level, international affairs, it is now a commonplace (and therefore to be regarded a bit warily) that sometime in the 1960's the Cold War became *passé*. A glance at my bookshelves reveals such recent titles as *The Cold War Years*, *The Age of Containment*, *The Rise and Decline of the Cold War*, *The Cold War as History*, and *Beyond the Cold War*. I also share this feeling of satiety; the cold warrior's mantle chafes. Still, I am bothered by any too-easy relegation to the ash-heap of this particular phrase. Soviet-American relations remain on the gelid and hostile side. To the Communists, United States Imperialism remains the principal enemy. The curious genetic strain Marxism-Leninism- (Stalinism) -Maoism→ continues to provide a central challenge to our society. Moreover, at this moment a Soviet-American antagonism, should it move from cold to hot, is still the only enmity capable of producing a universal holocaust. Recent events may seem to have put the two superpowers somewhat in the wings, but they could both move Stage Center with alarming ease.

Nevertheless, the premise of an exclusively bipolar world no longer seems appropriate. The Sino-Soviet rupture, the prospects of nuclear proliferation, the curious way in which the Antiballistic Missile controversy is posed on both sides as a tricky and dangerous exercise in games theory suggest that profitable inquiry simply must operate in broader and different frameworks. A central task here, both personal and national, is simultaneously to avoid being caught up by fads that disregard some very hard-earned insights and lessons, and yet not to be trapped in obsolescent or unserviceable categories merely because they were arrived at through much sweat and anguish.

Not long ago a colleague observed that I was having difficulties with my categories, that I was spending a lot of time fretting about hermeneutics. The preceding chapters will probably confirm that this has been persistently and increasingly a problem for me. In part at least it is a personal quirk; I have always cherished Paul Tillich's remark: "For Protestantism is something more than a weakened form of Catholicism only when the protest against every one of its own realizations remains alive within it." I sus-

pect that my inclination to seek out the inadequacies of
any formulation I have previously made is deeply ingrained. I am aware that it could get out of hand and lead
all too easily to complete paralysis of pen and mind. Still,
I have in fact found a pressing need to reconsider my conceptual resources and try to seek or devise new ones. I have
felt this particularly in my study of the Russian Revolution. At various points in my efforts to comprehend that
event I have discovered the available tools of the historian's
craft to be insufficient. Increasingly I have sought answers
from other disciplines, from psychology to statistics. Whatever my own aptitudes in this endeavor, I am persuaded
that it is a necessary one. I am certain that many decisive
truths lie in the interstices of our various academic disciplines. The job of ferreting them out demands much
more than exhortation or "inter-disciplinary" enthusiasm.
In a word, I would regard the task of fashioning the intellectual instruments for examining and characterizing the
crisis problems of our times as *the* most important item
on the agenda.

Somehow combining these two areas of malaise—the inadequacy of the Cold War, East-West framework, and the
insufficiency of our conceptual tools—is a very strong feeling
that, as I have put it, "Clarity begins at home." Undoubtedly in this I am simply participating in the widespread
and much noted turning-inward of American thought and
attention in the 1960's. To some degree this may be escap-
ism, a weariness of forever facing outward on the parapet.
But it is clearly more than that: the universal concern
about American society, its social and racial inequities,
the anguish of the cities, our imperiled surroundings, the
turbulent and troubled mood of our youth—these things
are central and real, defining both what we are and what
we may become and making it imperative that we under-

stand ourselves. Here, too, our categories for comprehending and valuing appear to be dissolving.

At the end of the Second World War a friend and I were discussing what we planned to do next. He said that in his view the United States faced two outstanding problem areas: our external relations, particularly with the Soviet Union, and our domestic life, particularly the racial question. He went south to wrestle with the latter. I, a European historian, turned, rather, to the former. I do not think that right or wrong choices were at stake here; both issues, the external and the internal, were vital. Nor are the two distinct and separate; the foreign and the domestic influence one another in hundreds of ways. But it may be that a certain fluctuation, or cycle, of emphasis upon the one or the other is in the nature of things, partly as a matter of momentary priority in urgency, but more fundamentally as being our mode of progress; we walk in alternate strides. In any case, I find that my twenty-odd years of preoccupation with Eastern Europe and the Soviet Union has had among other things the specific effect of enormously intensifying my need to understand my own environment and my place in it.

INDEX

A NOTE ON THE TYPE

The text of this book has been set on the Linotype in a type-face called "Baskerville." The face is a facsimile reproduction of types cast from molds made for John Baskerville (1706–75) from his designs. The punches for the revived Linotype Baskerville were cut under the supervision of the English printer George W. Jones. John Baskerville's original face was one of the forerunners of the type style known as "modern face" to printers—a "modern" of the period A.D. *1800.*

This book was composed, printed, and bound by H. Wolff Book Manufacturing Co., New York Typography and binding design by Bonnie Spiegel.